The New Introduction to Macroeconomics

by Brian de Uriarte

The interior of this book was designed and typeset by
Darren J. Averett of Anything & Everything Graphics.
The cover was designed by Elena Kayak-Von Ancken.
The text was printed and bound by Harwill Express Press
of Hightstown, NJ.

In memory of
SIDNEY WEINTRAUB
and
ALFRED EICHNER

AUTHOR'S PREFACE

An Invitation to the Student

Suppose a foreigner, not a native English speaker, approached you and asked, "What is economics?" You might say that it's about running a business. Or you might say it's about all matters financial—making money, saving money, spending money. Had someone else been asked, he or she could have offered other views of the field: it's about costs and benefits, prices and quantities; it studies markets.

Certainly, economics means different things to different people. But as you open this book, you take a journey through a field of study whose myriad facets have been discussed for over 2000 years. During Greece's Golden age, Aristotle, one of several prominent Athenian philosophers, composed writings on the distribution of income. St. Thomas Aquinas, a scholar of the Roman Catholic Church, penned opinions regarding just prices and usury, the charging of (excessive) interest. During these 2000 years, a history has developed, a history of human deliberation concerning material well being, production, and exchange.

This text partakes in that discussion. Its purpose, however, is not to offer original ideas; rather it seeks to introduce students to the economic way of thinking. The author hopes that you, the new economics student, can acquire sufficient command of economic vocabulary and principles so that you can partake in an intelligent conversation about any matter economic.

Some of the issues discussed in this text might not coincide with your present understanding of the subject and therefore cause you some consternation. If so, be patient; the struggle to master the subject is akin to learning a new language. In the practice of their science, economists lend more precise meaning to some highly familiar terms — like profit, costs, and saving — and in so doing create a gulf between scientific and everyday discourse. To succeed in the course that gulf must be bridged by the student's sheer willpower. Your time will be well-spent if in the long run you can explain why, for instance, many economists would consider divvying up study time for two upcoming finals to be a classic example of an economic problem; and why many of those same economists would contend that money has no overwhelming influence on the size nation's output of goods and services.

This text will be especially worthwhile if, upon completion, you can read the events of the day with more insight, account for the true cost of, say, a college education, and understand the claims of someone like Mr. Ross Perot as he rants about international trade. For the author has written this text to combat an ignorance. This ignorance does not merely entail the nuances of economic theory – actually, the most subtle aspects of theory should be secondary in an introductory course. The primary ignorance involves the lack of awareness of the role played b economic ideas in determining society's welfare. Where this ignorance exists, citizens in society forfeit control of their economic destiny to their political leaders.

The late British economist, John Maynard Keynes, write eloquently about this fate:

> ...the ideas of economists and political philosophers, both when they are right and when they are wrong, are more powerful than is commonly understood. Indeed the world is ruled by little else.

> Practical men, who believe themselves to be quite exempt from any intellectual influences, are usually the slaves of some defunct economist....so that the ideas which civil servants and politicians apply to current events are not likely to be the newest.[1]

So, the prominent theme of this text is that economic ideas affect the material quality of live. Consequently, economic decisions on faulty economic logic or theory diminish society's prosperity.

But that is not all.

If the ideas of economists are as potent and prevalent as Keynes describes here, then economists takes on genuine moral import. For its ideas, disseminated into the public realm, become — we suddenly realize — "dangerous for good or evil."[2]

---

[1] John Keynes. The General Theory of Employment, Interest, and Money. New York: Harcourt Brace Jovanovich, 1964. p. 383.

[2] Ibid., p. 384.

TO THE INSTRUCTOR

The book is written in protest and in hope.

More than a generation ago Paul Samuelson wrote what has been since the most influential introductory text in our discipline. He set the standard. He reaped economic profits.

As our theories would predict, entrepreneurs imitated his effort. Attracted by profits, they invaded the market. By now, the market for Intro texts is perhaps our best example of monopolistic competition. Each author would have you believe that his or her text features some quality, or serves some special niche, which justifies its purchase. Yet these authors know full well that the core theory remains the same and that presentations alone could never alter the substantive message of the discipline. How does the behavior of these authors square with economic truths, with our lessons on efficiency? Just another example of optimizing behavior, I guess.

I believe, however, that our students have been hurt in the process. And it is these people we must serve for ends greater than mere profit. Since Samuelson, students have been shortchanged (in real terms) of the richness of the economics discipline. They learn little economic history, little of the development of economic analysis; and for all that which replaces those neglected aspects, students at the end of a year's study still might be unable identity a cost at the margin, let alone understand why it might be helpful to do so.

This has occurred through an undue and misguided emphasis on the more technical aspects of the science. Traditionally, for instance, textbooks have opened with the Production Possibility Curve. But why is such a thing necessary to make the simple point that "you can't have your cake and eat it, too"? Why should an intelligent student be even inclined to think that this typed of analysis will be advantageous? Most are justifiably bemused. Many are rightly unenthused. For these lessons do not inspire students to believe that economics is a discipline with an improved method of analyzing problems, but convinces them that it is an abstraction with little resemblance to reality. (Once during a discussion on consumer decision making principles applied to the conditions of Newcomb's paradox [Chapter 19], a student challenged the efficacy of standard theory. Divorcing all previous learning, he raised his hand and said, "Yeah, but [Newcomb's paradox] is a real decision.")

It is this author's observation that students have a latent interest in things economic. But to tap that interest we must address the student at his or her peculiar level of sophistication. Otherwise our best and sincerest efforts are for naught. To nurture a student's interest into understanding, he must first be given concrete examples of economic processes. Yet, I have discovered, the standard economic examples (guns and butter) seldom fit the bill toward this end. My own experience indicates that it is more helpful to approach the concept indirectly, as it were, by citing things known familiarity to him, but not usually viewed economically.

Put another way, we teachers must first awaken economic intuition which evidence shows (and theory asserts) is part of the make-up of all individuals. This text tries expressly to arouse that intuition via its discussions of athletic contest (for principles concerning competition), of a car's historical gas mileage performance (for diminishing marginal returns), collections (for the principles associated with optimizing benefits from one's expenditures).

Meanwhile, the initial unit on the history of economic thought is a primer—an interesting one I hope—for many of the principles that students will learn at the introductory level. Beyond the intuition, the unit introduces vocabulary informally. More rigorous development of concepts gets postponed until a substantial familiarity and, we hope, some appreciation and command for the style of economic analysis can be safely assumed. I justify this tack with an appeal to a pedagogical principle that John Marshall applied: if the idea is not understood in plain

English first, no amount of graphs and mathematical analysis would actually advance a student's understanding.

It is my hope that this book's approach represents an improvement over past ones by directly addressing the pedagogical challenges of economics. I have spent many hours in and out of the classroom trying to systematize a more effective teaching technique. I have taken great care to organize and select the lessons so that they might reflect what I have learned—and I presume what you have learned as well—through trial and error. Of course the result is subject to the usual constraints.

But from the beginning I've been mindful that the most effective presentations are those that lead and force students to think economically on their own—as if they discovered the idea themselves. I've refrained from that type of presentation which suggests that the economist's word is final.

ACKNOWLEDGEMENTS

Many people helped in this project. I'd especially like to thank the faculty and students of Middlesex County College who have shown interest in my efforts. Professors Sanford Helman and Arthur Peterson have through conversations given me ideas and suggestions all along the way. Professors Patricia Graber and Nancy Bailey have been extremely supportive and enthusiastic of my efforts. Professor Doug Brown has been my mighty encourager and to him I am grateful for helping me realize some of the lofty ambitions I have for this project. And several former students have made contributions which have found their way on to the pages of this edition. To Donald Gray goes much thanks for his computerized rendition of the Tableau Economique and the "ultimate" macro-flow diagram. I also thank Darren Averett whose work on the design and layout of the text has been most professional. Finally, I am much indebted to my friend Elena Kayak-Von Ancken whose cover work, like herself, is original.

Thank you all.

Contents

PART SIX: MONEY AND BANKING

PART ONE

HISTORY OF
ECONOMIC THOUGHT

"...the first discovery of a science is the discovery of itself."

J.A. Schumpeter

CHAPTER 1

WHAT IS ECONOMICS?

DEFINITIONS

Definitions have a way of sorting out what's important. For example, suppose we want to learn about a thing called sports. What should be included in this study? Everybody will agree about football, baseball, and basketball. But what about log-rolling? What about car racing? Or yachting? These sports are more or less physical, but are they physical in the way baseball or basketball are? Are they really *athletic*? Maybe we should include hunting, so long as we're willing to include yachting. (Hunters have contests, too.) But if what matters is whether there's a contest or not, then we'll have to include chess. (Many a good chess player will tell you that a person needs to be physically fit to play his best.) So, what's a sport?

What is economics?

Economics is a science--a science, in some ways like physics, but in important ways, unlike it. All sciences represent a disciplined human effort to understand a certain group of phenomena. As a result, each science has its own purview for investigation, its own field of study: each claims a certain turf. Physics' turf concerns motion, energy, and substance. When Newton described the forces of gravity, he developed a theory which (in part) explained the forces between physical objects. He had nothing to say about, and his theory could not be applied to, the romantic attractions between human beings. Those forces are psychic. So, psychologists study them, because psychology is the study of the mind and mental experience.

What is the distinctive set of phenomena for study in economics? *The economic science focuses on that group of questions associated with material wealth: how it gets created, distributed, produced, and valued in society.*

Motivated by this broad concern, an economist undertakes a systematic observation of various economic activities. He or she might investigate the behavior of a firm as it tries to deliver goods to society at a profit. Others may study the economic institutions in society, such as the modern banking system, which facilitates exchange by acting as, among other things, a clearing house for payment activity. Some economists will devote their attention to consumers' buying patterns. There're dozens upon dozens of possibilities. Yet economists of divergent interests share an analytical style and language with which they conduct their work.

Thus far then, we can say that economics is that science, having its own specialized vocabulary and method, which studies matters pertinent to material wealth. From here, things get somewhat trickier. We've hit a point similar to the one we confronted when trying to define sports: sports is about athletic endeavors, and athletic endeavors are physical ones. But somehow *physical* has to be specified very clearly, or else we don't quite know what to include and exclude: chess or no chess?

Our immediate task, then, is to understand the basis of some alternative approaches to matters governing material wealth. Some economists consider the problem of material wealth to be essentially a problem about the *scarcity of goods*. This idea leads to an emphasis on the *choices individuals and society make as reflected both inside and outside of markets*. Markets become the major, though not exclusive, focus because production, distribution, and value becomes realized in market activity. Other economists consider the *creation of wealth* in society to be the more enlightening focus of economic study. This approach leads to wide-ranging investigations into the *historic changes in economic society, the role of entrepreneurship, the place of investment in producing wealth, even ethical concerns such as developing means by which society might alleviate poverty.* Let us learn a bit more about each.

The study of the allocation of scarce resources

One way to view the economic world begins with the very crafted notion of **scarcity**. Economists took many years to develop this idea precisely. But once properly conceived, it seemed to explain much about the world we live in.

The old saying, *"You can't have your cake and eat it too"* captures the essential point. On the one hand, mankind has tremendously great wants. On the other, the planet's resources for the provision of those wants are limited. By and large, mankind's wants far outstrip nature's ability to satisfy them. And in this case, what applies to men and women generally applies to them individually as well. If we asked someone whether she would want a second car, a second home, or an extra month's vacation--all free for the taking--the response would surely be an enthusiastic "Yes." If we pursued the point and asked why she doesn't go out and buy another car, house, or take a longer vacation, she'd probably reply that she can't afford them. To the economist, this simply implies that the person's available (financial) resources cannot meet her every desire. That's the predicament each economic person faces: nobody--no society, no individual--ever gets around it. It may not be a pleasant picture, but it seems nonetheless authentic.

So the old saw, "You can't have your cake and eat it too" conveys an important truth about economic life: human existence is fraught with sacrifices, with trade-offs. You can have your cake, but that choice implies accepting the fact that you can't "eat it" as well. And you can eat your cake; but then, having consumed it, you will have it no longer.

Thus, to many practitioners of the science, economics is the study of the scarcity problem, mankind's struggle to reconcile his unlimited wants in circumstances where resources are limited; it explores how individuals and society can best utilize their given resources for the optimal satisfaction of wants.

Scarcity, sacrifice, and opportunity costs

To pursue this point in a practical but non-market context, consider the situation faced by the typical college student--perhaps, you!--who's taking five classes. Come finals, the student must budget a certain amount of time for all five examinations from an available allotment of time to spend--say, 15 hours. Now, one obvious way to divide the time is to spend three hours of study time for each test. But to do that might not be the wisest choice. If in one class the student is teeter-tottering between passing and failing, he or she might be better off spending more than three hours in preparation for that course's final

exam. Inevitably, though, additional time devoted to one reduces the time available for others, and so there's some chance that some other grade may suffer as a result. But notice: *no matter which way the time is divided, an hour spent on one subject comes at the expense of an hour spent on another.* So choosing how to divvy up the time entails making a trade off. The formal term for this is **opportunity cost**; it is one of the most important concepts in all of economics.

Opportunity cost refers to the forfeiture of some desired item in order to acquire the object one finds even more desirable. Whenever and wherever human beings face a conflict between wants and availability, whenever the desire for goods outstrips nature's provisions for them -- in a word, where there is scarcity -- then people face choices and must incur an opportunity cost.

Scarcity, decision making, and the market

If you walk into a hamburger joint with only five dollars, you will find that you have a limited range of choices. You might like to have three burgers, two orders of french fries and a soda. But that choice is unfeasible. Your five dollars won't permit it. You can whittle down your choices to a single burger, fries, and soda; but you might find yourself having to choose between having cheese on the hamburger or a large soda; i.e., if you have the cheese, you'd have to settle for a medium size beverage; if you choose a large drink, the opportunity cost is the cheese on the burger. Thus, in a world of scarce goods and opportunity costs, persons are forced to select among various possibilities. There is, indeed, no free lunch.

So we might say that economics is, in part, a science about making decisions--making decisions about how to spend time and money as best we can when several possibilities face us.

Approached this way, the natural course of economic study leads to one of man's great institutions: **the market**. The market is modern man's primary means for producing and distributing scarce goods. There are many different types of markets just as there is a variety of goods which people desire. But all markets have a similar function: markets foster two-way **exchange**, and, via exchange, ration goods.

And who gets the goods? Those who are willing to labor in order to earn the necessary financial resources, and then willing to sacrifice appropriate amounts of money. Moreover, in a well functioning market, there will be a sufficient number of items to satisfy those willing to pay the market price. Thus, prices should, optimally, reflect the opportunity costs incurred in bringing the item to market. Thus, the market effectively *resolves*, though does not eliminate, the fundamental human economic condition called scarcity.

meaning of scarcity: a clarification

In everyday conversation the word "scarce" is synonymous with "rare". So it's tempting to assume that as far as economics is concerned the same connotation applies: scarce goods are the rare ones. Unfortunately, this association would be only half true. Rareness does indeed convey a sense of limited availability, and that's certainly relevant; but not all rare items are desirable. We do not, for instance, see our local department store making available vials of sand from the Australian outback. Why not? Clearly, there's no strong consumer desire for the item. Firms would not be likely to bring it to market profitably. So they choose not to sell it. Just as no one would pay for a car or television he doesn't want, businesses will not offer products which hold no prospect of sale. Hence, vials of sand from "down under" are not, *economically speaking*, scarce goods. (But if you happen to find one here in the States, it would be a rare find indeed.)

Thus, *a marketable commodity must be rare **and desired** in order to be scarce in the economic sense.* Since the aspect of desire is included, a simple equation of scarcity and rareness tends to confuse and mislead.[1]

An investigation into the economic process

For another group of economists, the truly interesting problems of economic life revolve around the *creation, and continual re-creation, of value* itself. What is the source of value? How does society make something of value? After something gets produced, does it automatically possess value? How much value? What encourages the production of value-bearing commodities beyond what's actually needed for man's survival? To address such matters, these economists prefer to view the economy *as a process in motion, almost like a machine, directed towards a final end.* The driving forces propelling the machine--to extend the metaphor--emanate from the activities of labor resources, together with the expenditures by firms for those workers; likewise, from the contributions of non-human resources such as land, raw material and machinery and the payments for those productive inputs. Such expenditures are designed to provide desirable goods to consumers and bring profits to the firm. These profits allow a business to amass wealth for itself, much of which will be utilized, i.e., reinvested, to reap still more profits and wealth. *Thus, the economy resembles, on a grand scale, a perpetual value-in-motion machine.*

When we speak of firms' committing expenditures for resources, it becomes worthwhile to highlight expenses made to acquire **capital**. Capital is the durable plant and equipment owned or operated by a business enterprise. It would include, for instance, the printing plant owned by a printer and binder; the oven operated by a restaurant, and the robotics hardware used by automobile manufacturers to build vehicles of all kinds. Any expenditure for such capital is properly termed **investment**. When firms invest they do so in the hope of sustaining, even increasing, **profit** in the future. The capacity and quality of a particular firm's capital equipment influences its ability to make profit, which can be preliminarily defined as a firm's normal or average return from the capital (and other resources) it owns and employs.

---

[1] In order to more fully appreciate this point, consider what a *free* good is. Free goods have no price! This implies that either people deem the item wholly undesirable or it exists in such abundance that there's no need to *ration* it. Just as there is no market for sand from the Australian outback, there never could be a viable market for air: we cannot expect companies to profit by selling air for human "consumption." While air is truly desirable, even necessary, it remains so plentiful with respect to that desire that it cannot be classified as an *economic* good. Hence, economic goods must be scarce goods, i.e., goods which require rationing because fewer exist than are desired. Scarce goods, consequently, will always carry a price.

Thus, in the view of this second group of economists, the economic discipline studies the continuous processes relating inputs and output, production and consumption, investment and capital, spending and profit making.

economic production, processes, and growth

The contemporary economic world relies greatly on various forms of capital, both heavy machinery as might be seen at an oil drilling station and sophisticated computer hardware used to store data necessary to provide modern services. But, centuries ago, society was primarily organized around agricultural production, using land, non-automated tools, and animals as the primary basis for producing a correspondingly limited range of goods. The Amish community of Pennsylvania and other states gives a glimpse into that simpler economic life. In these societies, economies can be said to replicate themselves as products get consumed and resources age and wear out. Working, productive living, is essentially a cycle as familiar as day and night.

As a society modernizes, it shifts to an increasing reliance on capital to create products and augment societal wealth. As capital resources come to predominate economic production, economies themselves change in several ways. First, *capital-intensive* production processes promote the integration of associated industries and places: thus, the development of the steel industry spawned advances in the transportation sector, for example, within the railroad industry. In turn, the ability of human beings to transport themselves with increased ease helped to establish economic ties between once-distant locales, hence creating still greater opportunities to build factories, to make and truck products, all requiring a greater production of steel. The developing web of economic relations promoted a positive sort of economic interdependence.

But the changes do not end there. Embedded in the capital equipment utilized by firms is the human know-how that went into building it, what we usually call **technology**. Capital-intensive production processes promote innovation, invention, and economic development because the activity itself advances our understanding of physical, logistical, and engineering processes associated with economic production. The expanding base of knowledge, coupled with the entrepreneurial motive to win profits, lead to infinite possibilities for advancement. Again using the transportation sector as an example, the desire for more efficient transit led to the development of the automobile. This required calling forth more labor resources, and more steel resources, for the direct production of cars; in addition it supported the development of the rubber and tire industry, each having its own requirements for labor and steel resources. The labor dedicated to these new industries earned income. Then, as consumers, these same workers proceeded to buy all sorts of final products, not the least of which were cars.

The obvious consequence of all the above is **economic growth** and its by-product **wealth**. Expanding wealth, then, turns out to be the final end of the modern economic process, and growth is the necessary condition to building society's wealth. In the final analysis, modern economies become growth machines, whose operation depends very critically on relationships involving investment, capital, profitability, and technology. It should not take much to convince anyone as to how the **Industrial Revolution** changed local and national economies in profound ways because of the interplay between these influences.

This, perhaps sweeping, view of economic study, though distinct from the scarcity approach, offers genuine insights. Recognizing them requires some appreciation of economic history and the development of economic theory.

historic economic development and theory

While economic concerns have always preoccupied man, economics did not appear as an independent science (*it did not discover itself*) until the 18th century. The subject grew out of social and political philosophy[2] and was originally called **political economy**. Adam Smith's <u>Inquiry into the</u>

---

2 Thomas Hobbes's <u>Leviathan</u> and John Locke's <u>Of Civil Government</u> are two of the more influential works leading to the eventual science of economics.

<u>Nature and Causes of the Wealth of Nations</u>, published in 1776, set the standard for analysis in the fledgling discipline.

Some interesting links exist between the historical growth in the employment of capital for production and the "founding" of the economic science. For one, political economy's birth came in the rush of the world's first industrial revolution. Second, Smith was from that nation, Great Britain, which saw these changes make their initial imprint. (Smith himself was Scottish.) In other words, economics became a formal study just at the time that capitalist production, with its emphasis on profit-making, began having an impact on economic life. Moreover, these changes were most pronounced in the native land of the father of the science. Coincidences? Not really: people living in the midst of social upheaval need an interpreter to articulate the changes they observe but don't fully understand.

VANTAGE POINTS

Let's think again of physics, and what it does.

A person can study the physical universe in two ways: with eyes turned outward toward the sky, or focused intently on the make-up of physical specimens here on earth. The first way leads to the science of astronomy; the latter leads to atomic physics (among others). Yet both areas of study are part of physics.

In economics, questions come in two kinds as well. These distinct types of questions help differentiate microeconomics from macroeconomics.

Microeconomics

Microeconomics examines questions pertaining to individual firms and consumers as they participate in the economy. For example, the factors which influence a firm's decision as to when to produce and how much output to deliver to the market would be amongst the many concerns of a microeconomist. In microeconomics, the foundations of the laws of supply and demand are rigorously developed. From these laws we can discover the underlying principles that govern markets.

Macroeconomics

Macroeconomics might be best considered as the modern equivalent of the older study called political economy. Macroeconomics focuses on what transpires on the national level. The phenomena of **inflation** and **unemployment**, for example, would be studied by a macroeconomic specialist. Specific questions he or she might investigate would include: What economic influences can cause a **recession**? How does foreign trade affect a nation's economic well being? By taking the big-picture approach, macroeconomics seeks insight into the large social and economic forces that propel all domestic commercial activity.

METHODS

Up to now we've been concerned with *what* economics studies and its basic subdivisions. But just *how* economists go about their work is another matter. A method of study needs to be outlined so that we have a consistent and reliable basis on which to accept information and observations about economic life. Then, too, economists need a way to organize and interpret the data which have been collected. It is not enough to have thousands of observations lying around. They must signify something, just as letters signify sounds. Without having a means to make the data understandable, unified, and coherent, all the observations are for naught. This is where science and theory meet.

The science of economics

Economics is a social science. As a science it must adhere to the conventions of modern scientific research. Specifically, it must employ **empirical** methods of investigation, i.e., collect and use data exclusively from the observable world.

Towards this end, science has developed an experimental method that delineates its investigative approach. Initially, the scientist develops a hypothesis. This may be based on a hunch or impression that was developed from casual observation. Then he or she designs the experiment. The experimental design should be able to validly test the hypothesis. But to do that, the scientist actually has to conduct two tests. One is called a **control**, the other a **variable**. The control test defines all special features of the experimental environment. The variable retains all those features but one. Finally, the experiment is run. (See Diagram 1-1.)

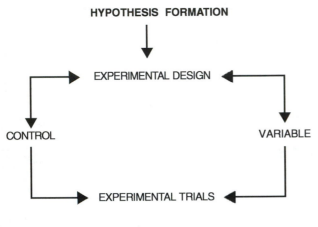

Diagram 1-1

It is critically important that while one thing is changed in the variable run, everything else remains the same. Only under such conditions can the experimenter associate changes in results to the single change in the experimental environment. If we want to test, for example, the effects of various amounts of fertilizer on plant growth, we'd have to ensure that the type of plant, soil conditions, lighting, etc. remained identical. Only then can the person running the experiment legitimately relate fertilizer amounts to plant growth results, i.e., that the altered variable induced some new result. If all other things were not equal, the experimental relation is dubious.

ceteris paribus and normal conditions

All the physical sciences (physics, chemistry) employ the scientific method for their experimental research. But social sciences such as psychology and economics confront unique difficulties as they conduct their investigations. Unlike the hard sciences, which can conduct experiments under controlled "laboratory conditions," the social sciences cannot, for the most part, ensure that *all* other variables remain constant. Human life simply does not permit such blanket control

over the factors which influence human behavior. Still, when economists make their inquiries, they need to approximate **ceteris paribus** conditions: the state where all variables are held constant except one.

How can this be accomplished? There are several techniques designed to accommodate the difficulties involved in developing meaningful observations of economic events. One method is best explained by example.

Consider the labor market and the occurrence of unemployment through the course of a year. Let's think about a very specific phenomenon. Take June. What happens in the labor market during June? Thousands of employable students finish school for the year and look for a job. Will they all get one? (Need we ask?) Since not all of them will likely find employment--even in the best of years--we can *expect* unemployment to rise. That would be **normal** for June.

Now let's look at November. During the last quarter of the year retail firms gear up for increased holiday shopping. Labor hiring *normally* rises as a result. Thus, we'd expect unemployment rates to drop a bit in November, assuming, of course, that it's a *normal* year.

Now assume that during 2002, say, economists took a gross measure of the nation's unemployment rate for both June and November. They found that the rate fell 1% in June (from 6% to 5%) and then likewise in November (from 5% to 4%). Are the two outcomes comparable? No. Why? Because all other things are *not* equal. As we just noted, in June the available pool of workers normally expands significantly, but in November hiring by firms strengthens. The differences in the normal labor market conditions between June and November suggest that a crude measure of the unemployment rate would conceal as much as it might reveal about labor market conditions. In other words, comparing June and November is like comparing apples and oranges.

On the other hand, we *want* to make a comparison between the unemployment rates from June and November in order to assess interim trends in the economy. How then can we make legitimate comparisons between June and November? How can we, with scientific accuracy, discern which part of a given change in the unemployment rate reflects a normal, expected change and which part is distinct or abnormal? If the rate in June 2002 fell to 5%, then to 4% in November, how much of this decrease would indicate genuine improvement in the economy and how much would indicate the fact that we can *anticipate* November's rate to be better? The answer to each of these questions is that we must statistically establish ceteris paribus conditions. That way we can compare apples to apples.

The first step entails accounting for *normal* fluctuations in labor market and employment patterns through the span of a year. Suppose that, on average, unemployment in June is 1.5% higher than in any other month. We could then subtract 1.5% from the June figure to get an *adjusted* unemployment statistic, to reflect what normally happens in June. The opposite might be done for November since it's normally a period of heavy hiring. When all the adjustments are made, *the statistic remaining for any given month will be comparable to any other*, and the remaining differences would be attributable to other macroeconomic factors--a change in the economy's rate of growth, perhaps, or a change in military spending.

If you've ever read an economics article in the newspaper, you will sometimes see notes to the effect that the statistics in the article are *seasonally* adjusted. Unemployment data includes many seasonal adjustments, the June and November examples representing two well-known modifications. Economists make the adjustments in order to more closely approximate the ceteris paribus condition necessary for rigorous scientific research. Thus, when we read economic statistics showing that June's unemployment rate was 5% and November's was 4%, we can be sure that the difference indicates an exceptional change in macroeconomic conditions.

Theories and models

Like children, economists play with **models**. Model building constitutes a fundamental human intellectual exercise. Modelling reduces a subject to its most essential elements. Coaches of athletic teams use models when they speak to their players. Artists effect emotive responses by rendering *partial* depictions of their subjects. Model trains omit some engine parts, yet can elicit as much enjoyment as the real thing.

An economic model depicts some economic reality. The subject of the model might be the market or, perhaps, the participants in the market (economic agents). Let's examine briefly how economists put together a model from a group of observations.

Suppose an economist wants to learn about the **stock market**. He knows already that in the stock market people buy and sell portions of ownership rights in corporations, called **shares**. He knows that on the trading floor thousands of transactions occur each day. How is this trading coordinated? How do the prices for these shares get determined? Are there unseen patterns in the activity which can be revealed through careful observation? To address these issues he sets out one day to collect some data. From the many things that he notices he writes down the following:

1. Many prospective buyers and sellers.
2. The price of any one share fluctuates a little some days, a lot on others.
3. Traders scream at the top of their lungs.
4. Traders can buy and resell at anytime; trading is continuous.
5. The men wear suits; there aren't many women on the trading floor.
6. Traders pursue the deals they think will give them the greatest gain.

At this point, the economist will try to put together what he's seen in bare-bones form. He whittles down his list of observations, throwing out the irrelevant (#3 and 5). He ponders: "Was there something I missed?" In order to divine some logic to the day's events, he rearranges the list several times.

Let's help him here. It seems that traders come in with a certain attitude. They want to make the most they can from the day. So that should be a given. And each day there are many traders at work doing this, so that is a constant of sorts. Plus, based on observation #4, the traders have tremendous freedom in their pursuits. Now the price of a particular share varies through the day, but usually not by too much. Perhaps there is some constraint on it. But, in fact, there are no rules as such to limit price movements.[3] So, while we can imagine a jittery price level, the reality exhibits some price stability. Given that these many individual participants have absolutely nothing to tie them down, what is the source of this stability?

Our comments here are an attempt to sort out the basic conditions of the market (the thing to be modeled) from the day's results. Observations 1, 4, and 6 we treat as fundamental to any particular market event and the general course of trading through the day. Observation #2 characterizes an overall pattern. Structuring the observations this way permits us to pose a question about the market's price stability. The question is useful because it will focus our continued study; it identifies what we're really after: a systematic account for the day's events.

Investigations like these led to the development of the standard competitive model of markets. This model will be our main frame of reference in the microeconomics section of the text. Indeed, as we study the competitive model we will use examples from various financial markets to reinforce key principles.

The central task of the theoretic economist, then, is to record observations and explain. Models help with the explanations. In sum, the economist's method calls for his wearing two hats. Half the time, he dons the hard hat of the empirical scientist; the other half, he wears a theorist's thinking cap, organizing the information he has gathered into a coherent structure, a model which highlights key relationships that are sometimes hidden from view.

Economists as storytellers

When economists want to *illustrate* an economic

principle to the general public the preferred method is to tell a story. The story nearly always begins with the word "Suppose ..." For example, when someone asks a learned economist about the economic effects of taxes, the response might go like this: "Suppose sales taxes on consumer items were raised by 2%, then product prices would rise to some extent...; but if income taxes were raised by 2%, persons would have less to spend and so product prices might actually fall. In either case consumers will purchase fewer items...ceteris paribus."

Stories act as parables; they teach a lesson about some aspect of economic life. If the parable is well done, the tale will strike someone uninitiated in economics as nothing more than plain common sense. If the parable is thorough, it will reveal elements of economic theory. Though no brief narrative can render a theory in full, it can make clear the links between variables. In the preceding paragraph's example, taxes are related to the purchases of consumers. A good story must also be appropriate in detail. A story about a **barter economy** may be of little help, if our subject is an economy which uses money to consummate trades.

Economists resort to stories because they hold a special position in civil society. They are regularly called on by governmental officials, businessmen, and the media to explain the vagaries of the market. When they do so, they must be able to translate their complex theoretical idiom into publicly accessible language. Indeed, the basic function of economic storytelling is to provide a linguistic bridge between professional economists and the general public. For the models that economists use in their own study and discussion are foreign to the average person, but it is from these models that economists collect their lessons. Stories therefore provide a means to meet an underlying social imperative: that scholarly learning be grasped by interested parties and society be guided by those with wisdom.

As the course progresses, the ability to examine economists' stories critically (as one criticizes a novel) becomes more important. Not only will the story line have to be understood, but hidden assumptions will need to be exposed as well. These implicit notions

---

[3] Since the 1987 Stock Market Crash, this statement fudges the truth. But the daily limit on price variations would not produce noticeable effects nine days out of ten.

uncover other aspects of the teller's theoretic views. If they are overlooked, the story might be more deceptive than helpful.

A NOTE ON MONEY

Finally, some economists, like many non-economists, have a special curiosity about money. What's the fascination? Suffice to say: money is funny. Money gives no direct satisfaction. But it most certainly does indirectly, since it is necessary for all consumer purchases. Moreover, economists are forever debating the effects of money on national economic performance. Some economists claim that money affects prices. Others argue that it affects the production of goods. There's almost continual research into the matter of money and its impact.

Even if we did not pursue the question of money's effect on the economy, there's still much to learn. Books have been written on money's various forms and uses through the ages, and these are always fascinating accounts of man's ingenuity for generating and expediting commerce.[4]

AND IN THE END?

So what is the aim of an economist? Is he or she simply a curiosity seeker, wanting to know what makes the economic clock go tick-tock? Or is there some ulterior motive? Is she in it for her own self interest? For the money? For the Nobel Prize? Or does she work on behalf of others, in search of truth, justice, or some other noble prize? Might she even want to change the world? Is she a passive observer or an impassioned seer?

It depends which economist a person meets. Some are quite ideological and so use their expertise to influence society. Others insist on seeing themselves as non-partisan scientists. It's important at the outset to realize that economists as a group have two aims: the scientific, or **positivistic**, which we've discussed; and the moral, or **normative**, one. Each economist has a bit of both in him, despite any protestations to

the contrary.

When the economist plays the part of empirical scientist, his statements about the economic world will always be *descriptive*. He is simply making an observation. A typical one: From Monday to Tuesday the price of a barrel of oil rose from $16 to $17; in that same period the quantity purchased fell from 173,000 to 156,000 barrels.

When an economist plays the role of advisor, his statements concern what *ought* to be the case; the remarks are *prescriptive*. Such is the case when he speaks with his favorite politician--the one who pays him. (This is not the only time he makes prescriptive statements.)

For example, suppose we read the following comments in the newspaper attributed to a famous economist working for the President: "Economic analysis indicates that if we increase the money supply, then lower interest rates will follow. That's desirable because business activity will pick up with lower interest rates. But this same increase in the money supply could raise inflation. Should we increase activity at the cost of some inflation? My answer would be yes--it's worth it."

Maybe he's right. But the positivistic statements above ended with the phrase "could raise inflation." The final statement represents a moral judgment.

This moral dimension of economic work is, in the final analysis, unavoidable since economic science concerns things which have great bearing on the well being of individuals in society. Indeed, the wall between empirical and moral in economics is actually very permeable.

Examples of this permeability abound. Let us examine one carefully.

In the past decade a number of cases have arisen involving the issue of pay equity, i.e., equal pay for the same work. One ongoing drive for pay equity occurs on the nation's college campuses. Perhaps, unbeknownst to you, many classes at a given university are taught by part-time (adjunct) professors.

---

[4] See Galbraith, Money, Whence It Came, Where It Went. Boston: Houghton Mifflin, 1975.

At the same time, salaried and titled faculty frequently choose to instruct additional classes for some extra personal income. One might casually expect that for such "extra" work adjunct and full-time staff would get the same rate of pay. But that is not the case. It is not uncommon for part-time professors to receive 40% to 60% of what the salaried professor would earn. In California, a strong political movement is afoot to equalize the pay for these two groups; that is, to raise the adjunct professors' compensation to equal that of their full-time counterparts'. The movement is spreading. It may succeed.

What would that success imply? Would everything improve as a result?

To an economist, the analysis begins by first noting that the funds from which colleges and universities pay their faculty are limited. Paying higher wages to part time faculty leaves fewer dollars for other tasks. What tasks would then be eliminated? How might the institution save elsewhere in order to cover the increased costs for instructors? Would the university seek to limit the pay raises of full time professors? Would those professors agree? Would the institution seek to eliminate departments with low enrollments? Should it reduce the number of sections it offers in various courses and pack the remaining sections with more students? (Who pays then?) If it took this latter strategy, then higher adjunct pay scales would lead to *fewer* part time positions. Now who pays? Finally, what if the institution simply raises tuition in order to collect the additional income to pay the higher wages? And what if, in this instance, some students drop out?

Answers to these questions cannot possibly come from empirical science alone. The descriptive aspect of the economic science identifies these questions in order to delineate the various and likely trade-offs associated with this specific effort to raise wages and be fair. We quickly see, however, that achieving equity is not an easy proposition. It is apt to come at the expense of someone else. And in that case, how do we know whether society as a whole is better off? About such things, about the moral dilemmas we face in our economic choices, even economists disagree. But good economic science would address these sorts of issues and *alert society to the various good and bad implications of its choices*. If this much were accomplished, then our decisions, either as a society or individually, would be more intelligent ones.

Our purpose here, of course, is not to resolve the matter of pay equity for part time faculty. Rather, it is to alert the student to the overlay of the scientific and moral. In much the same way society seeks out defense experts when it tries to decide whether to engage in war, society looks to the economist for answers to certain types of questions. Now if a defense expert were to tell us we could win a war against this or that country, the follow-up question becomes inevitable: should we? Similarly, the economist's opinion holds a special legitimacy because of his or her expertise. After the economist has properly informed society what choices it faces and what ramifications those choices may hold, the moral question enters: What should we do? The economist can help there too. But we who partake in that choice need to recognize the difference between the economics instructor at the blackboard and the evangelistic preacher at the pulpit.

■■■

VOCABULARY

Scarcity – one of the most fundamental principles of the economic science; the idea that human desire vastly exceeds the ability of nature to satisfy any particular want; scarcity not only describes the condition of human life, but also, intellectually speaking, acts as a "constructive" principle in economics: as economists conceive it, scarcity is the basis for all human choice

The Market – that human institution devoted to organizing the production and distribution of goods and services made from human and natural resources

Exchange – a trade

Capital – the durable plant and equipment owned or operated by a business enterprise

Profit – the firm's earnings from the capital it owns

Growth – economic expansion of either production, income, or wealth

Recession – economic contraction of either production, income, or wealth

Political Economy – the older name for economic study, closer to the modern subject of macroeconomics

Inflation – a rise in the general, or average, price level

Unemployment – idleness of an economic resource, usually human

Empirical – observable or experiential; from the observable or experiential realm

Control – in science, the experimental trial that is used to compare results against the variable trial

Variable – in science, the experimental trial that, in conjunction with the control, tests the hypothesis

Ceteris Paribus – either real or imagined condition of the world in which all relevant and observable factors but one are constant; an operative assumption in economic logic

Normal – descriptive of the typical state of affairs; often, the average measurement over a period of time; for example, the normal temperature on a given day; in economics, the most frequently observed conditions of the market or the average measurement over a period of time

Model – a reduced form of some physical specimen

Stock Market – the market for the exchange of corporate shares

Shares – legal documents (paper assets) designating ownership of corporate assets

Barter Economy – an economy in which goods trade for goods; an economy without money

Positivistic – refers to the scientific aspect of economic study

Normative – refers to the moral aspect of economic study

Opportunity cost – the sacrifice of an item most otherwise valued in order to get a desired good; what one gives up in order to get; opposed to monetary cost/value

END-OF-CHAPTER QUESTIONS

On scarcity and opportunity cost

1. In everyday speech, the word "scarce" means rare. Why is rareness not sufficient to understand the economist's idea of scarcity?

2. Consider the following goods. Are they scarce goods in the sense discussed in this chapter? Why or why not?

    gold • water • the Mona Lisa
    automobiles • chalk • corn
    gasoline • money • air • maps of Pluto
    computers • bonds • sand • real estate

3. What resources do you possess? How much value do you place on them? If you were to trade them, what value would the market give them? Does your personal valuation coincide with the market's? Further, do you possess any negative assets: do you owe anything to anyone, any company, or bank? Develop a simple list of your positive and negative assets and estimate your economic worth.

4. Following up on question 3, why do you choose to hold the assets you possess in their present form? Why do you choose to hold the debts that you do? If you have money in the bank, why don't you buy something with it today? If you own a car, what sacrifice did you make to acquire it? What alternative asset could you hold, or would you choose to hold, in place of the vehicle?

5. How do you budget time for your school work? Do you have a job? If so, what is the opportunity cost of your employment; if not, what's the opportunity cost of not working?

6. At finals time, do you adjust your schedule for school and other activities in any way? Why? How can this change in behavior be explained in terms of (changing) opportunity costs?

7. Suppose you and a group of friends want to rent out an entire restaurant facility for one full evening to have a party. How would the manager of the restaurant determine the price to charge you? Relate his determination of price to the concept of opportunity cost.

On the economic science

1. Describe the scientific method. Outline its steps and identify exactly that point where new knowledge is acquired. What assumption discussed in the text is the economic equivalent of having a control and variable in the experiment?

2. How are economics and physics similar? How do they differ?

3. What is a model, and an economic model in particular?

4. Why do economists tell stories? What is the relationship between their stories and their models?

CHAPTER 2

ECONOMISTS AND THEIR THEORIES

In the first chapter we saw that the discipline of economics investigates the various problems associated with the material wealth of society. In other words, economists probe all the most fundamental factors governing the production, exchange, and distribution of goods and services.

That focus has been the historical constant. But as you might imagine, theories regarding production, the allocation of resources, etc. have evolved as the very nature of economic activity has been transformed. What began as a study of economic relations in a predominantly subsistence-level, agrarian society has matured into a science of decision making appropriate for consumers and producers in an economy of vast and diverse material wealth. Today, our wealth is increasingly an *invisible*, informational kind, and we face the challenge of explaining the economics of a 5,000,000 megabyte world of surplus data.

Material progress, therefore, has a way of inspiring new economic theories. Just as the evolution of society foments a tension between young and old, so too contemporary theories clash with preceding ones, creating an ongoing conflict amongst economists as they try to demonstrate whose vision and stories offer the most penetrating insights into the nature and condition of worldly ways. In the end, we arrive at economic truth through argument, research, and the lessons of history.

This chapter examines the work of the economic discipline's most influential theorists. The aim here is to provide an historic and philosophic introduction into the problems economists have studied, the explanations they've offered, the tools they've developed, and the policies they've proposed--all over the span of two and a half centuries--in an effort to come to terms with matters regarding society's material well-being. By reviewing the writings of these major thinkers, the principle lessons from the history of economic thought become the principle lessons of this text. After this chapter, no genuinely new ideas will be introduced; rather the ideas contained herein will simply be explored in greater depth.

PRE-CLASSICAL WRITERS: MERCANTILISTS

The Mercantilists wrote on economic issues during the 17th and 18th centuries. They were not quite economists, really, i.e., they did not think of themselves that way. Rather, they were a loosely-knit group of learned social observers and businessmen, conversant in the affairs of politics and commerce.

These writers were among the first to view the economic problem from the perspective of the entire society or state. Moreover, Mercantilist literature had a decidedly cosmopolitan flavor. The most frequent themes appearing in their writings consisted of the advantages of foreign trade and how it might be manipulated to expand a domestic economy.

The need to discuss economic issues in terms of the nation-state constitutes our first example of how historical forces reshape the opinions and visions of educated persons who study mankind's social relations. Previously, economic relationships had been predominantly feudal in nature: lords owned and controlled the key land resource while serfs worked the land in return for shelter and subsistence. At this stage, serious economic study had a somewhat narrow scope, with attention going to questions about fair prices and wages, the charging of interest (usury)--in a word, matters of economic justice. Absent were systematic, empirical observations and policy prescriptions.

By the 18th century, in the most powerful European nations, monarchs superseded the role of the landed gentry in the political realm and the commoner won the right to acquire private property, allowing him for the first time to be the master of his own destiny. More and more people found a trade and lived in the village. Owing to this transition, the pace of business activity picked up. People were now making more exchanges with a widening array of craftsman. In the burgeoning economy, new markets developed for "luxury" goods. People formed *wants* beyond the requirements of subsistence. And the servicing of those wants spawned a new breed of economic man: the entrepreneur. Thus, the task of the economic observer changed too. In an environment where individuals could express freedom through their choices in the marketplace, social relations lost their authoritarian tone, and questions about trade found more urgency than ones about justice. Stories about nascent industries and production took precedence over ones about subsistence and survival.

As noted, mercantilist writers were not a formal group of laboring academicians. Their analytic approach was sometimes confused, their vocabulary sometimes ambiguous and contradictory. Consequently, they are not noteworthy in the history of the science for the reliability of their conclusions. Our present interest lies instead in the topics they selected for study, for these matters helped to shape the evolving science. Three questions are most prominent: What is wealth? What is the effect of money on a nation's wealth and economic performance? What can a nation do to augment its accumulation of wealth? Let us begin a systematic review of their approach to these questions. We will take them in reverse order.

What can a nation do to augment its wealth?

Mercantilism gets its name from one of the most significant trends of the age: expanding merchant marine trade. Shipping routes to the Orient, Africa, even to the Americas provided new markets for major European countries to deal with. The trading pattern chiefly had the British, French, or Spanish sending (for payment, of course) finished goods to other nations or colonies, while bringing in raw materials from the rest of the world.

We find ourselves, then, in the realm of foreign trade, of **imports** and **exports**. The most consistent claim throughout the Mercantilist literature is that a nation's wealth can be augmented through the manipulation of the country's **balance of trade**. That balance of trade refers to the volume (in money terms) of a nation's exports vis-a-vis its imports; if exports exceed imports, the nation is said to have a favorable (positive) balance of trade; a negative trade balance results from the opposite.

What's so good about having exports exceed imports? When a domestic company sells a good to a foreign purchaser, that company collects a revenue and brings the funds into the domestic economy; when a domestic customer purchases a good from a foreign company, money travels out of the country to the foreign concern. Thus, if export receipts exceed payments for imports, the net result is an inflow of monies to the domestic economy. This result, thought the Mercantilists, makes a nation richer.

protectionism

This conclusion led to another about creating conditions to ensure a favorable trade balance. The Mercantilists claimed that shielding domestic business from foreign competition through **tariffs** would be beneficial to the protected nation's economy. For instance, if a tariff were placed on a foreign good, then domestic consumers would have to pay extra dollars for it. Whenever a domestic alternative were available, the difference in cost would discourage the purchase of the foreign item. If applied to all foreign-made products, tariffs would therefore lower imports. This would lessen the **flow** of money out of the country, as well as raise sales and employment in domestic industries. The strategy of using tariffs or other governmentally-sanctioned means to reduce imports is called **protectionism**.

Now we want to more closely examine the basis on which the Mercantilists concluded that an increase in the amount of money which a domestic economy collected from foreigners increased the welfare of the nation.

What is the effect of money?

If exports exceed imports, a nation will enjoy a **trade surplus**, a positive net inflow of currency from foreign trade.[1] Does this by itself make that nation better off? The Mercantilists maintained that it did. Those who collected the income could spend the money on domestically produced commodities and therefore encourage domestic enterprise. An increase in the amount of money in circulation had the effect

---

[1] During these times precious metals were used to settle accounts more often than paper currencies, i.e., gold or silver served as money.

of encouraging production and exchange--so they reasoned. Money fed wealth creation.

Critics disagreed. They claimed, to the contrary, that an increasing money flow from a positive trade balance would lead to higher domestic prices. The domestic economy would not be *productively* stimulated since the impact of any increased currency inflow would fall on prices, and not on the pace of activity or the final output of domestic firms. This conclusion reflected a more general opinion on the part of many writers that any increase in the supply of gold, silver, or whatever served as money, would diminish the value of a domestic currency and, hence, raise prices.

Not only that, higher domestic prices had a secondary effect on the trade balance. Increased costs for domestically produced goods would discourage foreign purchases. Thus, in time, the export sales would sink, leading to the *gradual equalization of export receipts and import payments*--a zero trade balance.

What is wealth?

If these critics were right, where did the Mercantilists go wrong? The confusion comes, according to critics, in mistaking money for actual wealth. Land, labor, and capital comprise a nation's resource base. These resources and the real goods made from them constitute a nation's true wealth. Money, on the other hand, facilitates transactions, but does nothing to augment activity. So according to the critics of Mercantilism, money is neutral. Money is like a thermometer, a means to assess relative value without affecting what it measures. Thus, if additional money were in the hands of domestic consumers, the effect would appear as though the measuring device were being tampered with--in this case, devalued.

What we can learn?

This is not the place to determine whether protectionism is good or bad. Suffice it to say here that the majority of economists loathe it. Still, some concede that there are certain times when protectionism can be justified, often with the caveat that the benefits would be temporary.

equilibrium

Regardless of which side is correct, the Mercantilist discussions stimulated an analytic approach to economic problems. Most noteworthy is the argument of the critics claiming that a favorable trade balance would tend to vanish of its own accord, i.e., would create conditions that would bring its elimination. This represents one of the fledgling discipline's earliest appeals to the logic of **equilibrium**. Equilibrium in economic study refers to a process by which opposing forces tend to reconcile themselves, like the motions of a seesaw with two children at either end. In claiming that attempts to sustain a favorable balance of trade would be thwarted by the effects of rising prices, those contesting the logic of protectionism have described an economy capable of internal adjustments which favor balance and stability. Their analysis suggests a kind of Newtonian market principle at work behind the scenes: each action produces an equal and opposite reaction.

science and politics

We can also see in the work of the Mercantilists the relation between the positivistic conclusion and the normative judgment in regards to governmental policy. An analysis has determined that a nation gets wealthier when more money flows into the domestic economy than flows out. To complement the analysis, the Mercantilists then recommended the adoption of a strategy designed to discourage domestic currency outflows. The strategy by its nature requires the support of society's political and legal institutions. Small wonder then that the science of material wealth was originally dubbed **political economy**!

shaping the discipline

Finally, we should come to some appreciation, as well, for the shaping influence the Mercantilist literature had on the emerging science of political economy. Its writers defined the crucial theoretical issues. The matters of dispute from their day remain fodder for research and controversy among today's professional economists: Can a nation help itself by manipulating its trade balance? Is **free trade** or protectionism more advantageous? What is the role of political institutions in encouraging foreign trade?[2] More generally, can governmental intervention in private enterprise improve the functioning of its domestic economy or increase its wealth? This last question brings us to the supreme normative issue in the entire field: should the role of the government in the economy be active or passive?

PRE-CLASSICAL WRITERS: THE PHYSIOCRATS

In Chapter 1, we mentioned that some economists view the economy as a sort of self-sustaining, value-making entity. The Physiocrats were the first economic "school" to view the economy this way. They argued that for economic activity to be regenerative, society's resources must be sufficiently productive so as to create in output more than was expended to produce it. They called this "extra" product society's surplus or **net product**.[3]

An example may help. Each spring a gardener plants some seeds for tomato plants he wants to harvest in the late summer. He plants 100 seeds each year, but not all of these seeds fertilize; in fact, on average, he gets 75 plants. Now at the end of the season, the gardener cannot take all the fruit from the 75 plants and serve them as food. Some fruit must be set aside from which to extract seeds and then those selected seeds--another 100 of them-- are collected and saved for next year's planting. The fruit set aside is the net product of the garden--to use the physiocratic phrase.

The unique perspective of these economists comes in their linking of one year's production with

another's. Indeed, the physiocrats described production as a continuous chain in which yesterday's output helps to determine today's; and today's, tomorrow's. If producers have a surplus, there will be sufficient resources to begin tomorrow's work and have it be as productive as yesterday's. But the net product must be put to work; it must be employed in the creation of future output.

Quesnay

The person most responsible for creating a model which could identify the net product of the economy was a French Physiocrat economist named Francois Quesnay. In an elegantly simple model Quesnay was able to depict how a surplus could be produced through the series of exchanges which occur between three classes of people: farmers, landowners and artisans. He called his model the **Tableau Economique** (Economic Table or Picture). It was one of the earliest attempts made at modeling the macroeconomy. To this day macro-models have retained elements first found in his Tableau.

the model

Diagram 2-1 replicates Quesnay's model.[4]

Pretend, first of all, that we are living in the year 1758, the year the Tableau was written. Economic life centers around the activities of three social classes, each distinguished by their economic function: farmers, landlords and artisans. Farmers live and work on land owned by landlords. They pay rent and sell their produce to the artisan class. The artisans live in the village, where they work, produce, and sell their wares amongst themselves and to farmers. Throughout 1758 farmers and artisans produce and sell goods to a degree just sufficient for their own well being. Neither group is able to accumulate savings or wealth during the year. Thus, as the year 1758 comes to a close, all three groups, landlords, farmers and artisans, will be ready to begin anew.

---

[2] These questions were most recently debated during the NAFTA and GATT trade talks. NAFTA stands for the North American Free Trade Agreement; these talks involved Canada, Mexico, and the U.S. GATT stands for the General Agreement on Tariffs and Trade; it involves most European nations and the U.S.

[3] Already we have seen the word "surplus" used in two different ways. There will be other connotations as the course progresses. The common denominator in all its applications is the idea that two variables, taken together, have produced a net positive. Similarly, "net product" will appear later in the text, but in a different context. It is only in the present discussion, then, that we adopt the Physiocratic sense of the term.

[4] Credit and thanks for his computer rendition of the Tableau goes to former student Don Gray. We are indebted.

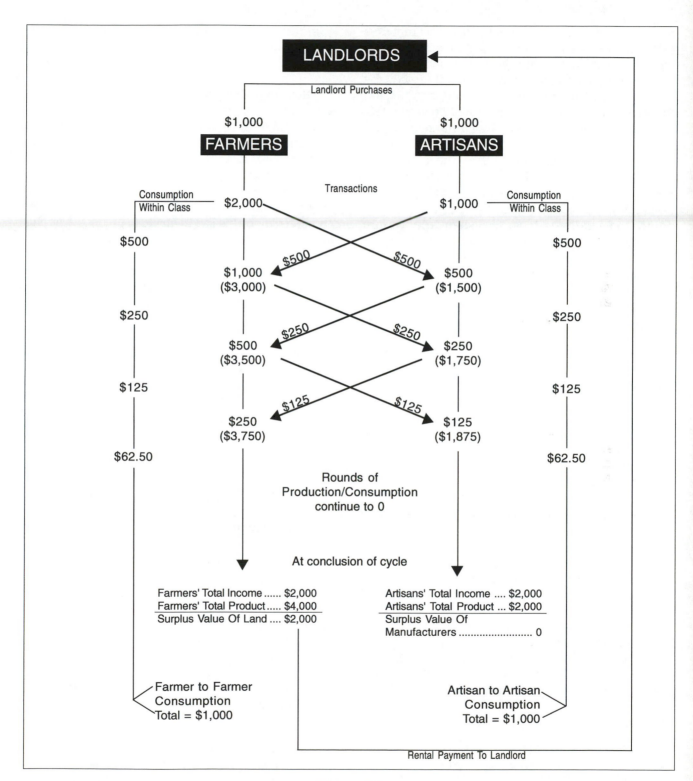

Diagram 2-1

The landlords, on the other hand, collect rent from farmers totaling 2000 francs. They allow their rental income to accumulate in their castle vaults through the year. This accumulated savings will provide the basis for initiating spending and production throughout the economy in the upcoming year, 1759. It can be viewed as **seed money** for future activity.

Let's say that on January 1, 1759 the landowners spent 1000 francs (1/2 their rental income from the previous year) on farm products and 1000 francs (the other half) on goods produced by the artisans.[5] In so doing, the landlords have just spent their entire accumulation of rent from the previous year.

Economic activity has begun. The expenditure creates income of 1000 francs for the farmers and the artisans each. Now each group can begin the new year's activity. The farmers need the money so they can maintain their farms, feed the livestock, and hire some extra labor when the heavy farmwork begins; the artisans likewise need the income to cover the costs of what they plan to produce in 1759.

At this point Quesnay makes three important assumptions:

a) the marketed value of artisan-produced goods per (franc) unit of income is 1-1.

b) the eventual market value of farm-produced goods per (franc) unit of income is 2-1.

c) the farmers and artisans will take every franc received as income and spend it as a direct cost of production.

Thus, with the 1000 francs received as payment from the landowners, the artisans will make 1000 francs worth of manufactured goods. But the farmers will produce *2000* francs worth of foodstuffs from the 1000 francs they received. They are able to produce double the value of their receipts because *the land is thought to possess special productive*

qualities. It is therefore the land which yields society's net product; i.e., the surplus is rooted in the soil!

How can this idea be justified? One has to approach the matter from the experience of a farmer. From a single seed, one gets but one plant. But the plant bears many fruit--and then each fruit bears many seeds. In the days of Quesnay, production was still agriculturally based and the ability to support all three classes of people, one of whom did not even engage in productive work, could only be accounted for by the land's ability to produce a surplus output--or so thought the Physiocrats.

Of the 2000 francs worth of food, 500 units will be used--literally consumed--by the farming sector itself. This type of **consumption** is seen on the left hand side of the Tableau, originating from the 2000 figure. Another 500 will be traded for tools, etc. purchased from the artisans. This transaction also emanates from the 2000 figure and proceeds diagonally to the right, where "500" represents the second income received by the artisan sector. The remainder (1000) goes to the landlords as an initial rental installment, but is not explicitly shown on the Tableau.

Now it's the artisans' turn. Of the 1000 received from the landlords, 500 will go to farmers to buy farm products; this is shown by the diagonal line heading down and to the left. The other 500 will be spent for the replacement of worn out manufactured goods which artisans use in their own production. This activity, shown on the right hand side of the Tableau, is analogous to the consumption of agricultural products by the farming class, since it represents an output or product which stays within the class, and hence generates no income for other groups of people.

This completes one full round of an expenditure/production cycle.

In the second round, the farmers will take the 500 received from the artisans and put it to work to create *1000* francs worth of food. During the same interval, the artisans will take the 500 received from

---

[5] The presentation here follows the example from Schumpeter, J.A. History of Economic Analysis, 5th ed. Oxford University Press, New York, 1963. p. 239-240.

the farmers and produce 500 francs worth of output. From this point, the dispensing of the product by both groups occurs in the exact same proportions as before. Thus, from the farmers' product of 1000, 500 will go as a rental payment (not explicitly shown), 250 franc units of food will be sold to the artisans (shown by the diagonal line), and 250 will stay within the farming community (shown to the left). Meanwhile, the artisans' product of 500 units will be divided amongst its own (shown to the right) and half for the purchase of food from the farm sector (shown by the diagonal line).

And so it goes into round three. The 250 the farmers receive will turn into 500 francs worth of farm goods; the 250 the artisans receive will produce 250 francs worth of artisan goods. From this point on, both groups will collect new income and make further expenditures until the values reach zero, marking the end of the period.

By the end of 1759, the farmers will have produced 4000 francs worth of food, sold 1000 worth to the artisans, used 1000 for themselves, and turned the remaining 2000 over to the landlords for rent-- all this from 2000 francs of income. The artisans, during the same period, will have produced 2000 francs worth of merchandise and sold 1000 of it to the farmers and used 1000 for themselves--all from 2000 francs of income.

The story for the year is complete but there's one more payment that really ties the knot on this physiocratic model. The farmers' 2000 franc annual rental payment is the basis for initiating activity *next year*. So that surplus, due the landlords since they own the land, is the first expenditure committed in the upcoming year. That expenditure acts as the font from which all of *1760's* subsequent activity flows. Year-in, year-out, this is how the system operates, according to Quesnay. Overall, the economic system is balanced, cyclical, and integrated.

Understanding the Tableau: what we can learn

Quesnay's creation is not perfect. For example, the model is not suitable to describe a growing economy, but only one which clones itself year to year. A second difficulty is more serious: Does the land *really* have the ability to produce a surplus in the way described? And if it does, why *wouldn't* the manufacturing sector be similarly capable of producing one? Quesnay makes heroic assumptions as to the source and proportions of the surplus in order to yield a positive net product. Yet in the final analysis, the Tableau never fully justifies the assumption.

Nevertheless the model retains instructive value. Even if incorrect in specifics, Quesnay's Tableau still blazes a trail to genuine macroeconomic understanding. We count three major lessons from it.

First of all, the Tableau forces us to think of the macro-economy as being held together by a series of interdependent exchange *FLOWS*--a flow of money and a flow of goods which occur through time. Indeed, in order to understand macroeconomics, this *is* a key insight. The macro-economy is a cyclic, flowing system that continuously directs and redirects to various segments of society the income and resources necessary to meet society's desire for goods. The macro-economy is like a machine producing and reproducing goods through time. It is like a living being sustaining and reproducing *itself* through time. It seems to realize man's dream of creating a perpetual motion machine.

In Quesnay's mind, the net product of the land is most crucial in sustaining a flow of economic activity. That's because the net product from the land yields, economically speaking, an income *to* the landlord and a future expenditure *from* the landlord. The "January 1st" expenditure leads to a series of expenditures, yielding another surplus, another rental income, another expenditure. Surplus to surplus, income to income, expenditure to expenditure. Year-in. Year-out.

Second, when the economy is viewed as a series of flow relations, an important *accounting principle* reveals itself, a principle whose implications would remain obscure were it not for the Tableau's elegance. That principle states that *ONE PERSON'S COST IS ANOTHER PERSON'S INCOME*. Not only does an expenditure *lead to* production and income in the future, *but each and every expenditure is at once expense and income*. This fundamental principle will reappear in future chapters discussing national income accounting (Chapter 8).

Finally, the Tableau is also the first explicit model incorporating economic equilibrium of the macro-economy. We mentioned earlier that the Mercantilist's critics had a groping sense of an equilibrium concept in their assessment of a nation's trade surplus. But Quesnay's concept is wider and more complete. The Tableau's economic equilibrium is contained in the economy's general ability to replicate itself. Its relations and flows are stable and predictable.

When we speak of equilibrium in the physical world we imply that physical forces are somehow arranged so that a balance exists. When a proper balance is achieved the object is often said to come to rest. For instance, after a pendulum has been struck, it will eventually return to center, practically motionless. By Newton's law of inertia, a body at rest tends to remain at rest--until it is disturbed by some other force. So, inherent in the concept of equilibrium is the idea that when a thing achieves its equilibrium, it tends to remain in equilibrium.

An economic equilibrium will have analogous properties. The motions of a well functioning economy will tend toward a stable balance. This balance entails two factors: production levels and amounts purchased. If a balance is achieved, economic inertia will tend to reproduce the balance: levels of production and purchases won't change unless outside conditions change. Hence there's stability to this economic equilibrium.

In truth the balance attained in the macro-economy is more akin to the equilibrium of our solar system than to a simple scale or pendulum. The planets revolve round the sun--so they are in motion--but they are in equilibrium as well. The fact that the planets' orbits are stable counts as evidence for their being in equilibrium. Stability is maintained because the gravitational forces of the sun and planets are themselves constant; thus they act to reproduce the previous orbit. Year in. Year out.

It is the orbits, not the planets, which are "at

rest." In Quesnay's equilibrium, it is trading "orbits," or patterns, which are at rest, not the specific expenditures or exchanges themselves.

That Quesnay saw and described such a balance constitutes his greatest achievement as an economic theorist.[6] In his model, equilibrium arises out of the *consistency* of the expenditure pattern of the three groups and the land's (assumed) consistent ability to deliver a surplus product. In economics, whenever spending behavior, income trends, and resource productivity results are consistent and integrated, then equilibrium rules the day.

CLASSICAL ECONOMIC THOUGHT

Smith

By the time Adam Smith ventured into economics, by way of moral philosophy, America was engaged in a war with England for independence. In fact, Smith's great book, Inquiry into the Nature and Causes of the Wealth of Nations, was first published in 1776, the same year the U.S. Declaration of Independence was signed.

Smith was the benefactor of more than a century's worth of literature devoted to economic concerns. He had contacts with several of the French Physiocrats, including Quesnay, and he was privy to the Mercantilist controversies by virtue of his interest in political affairs generally.

Smith himself was a proper man, who led a quiet life of academic teaching and study. He was not, however, the type to seclude himself behind the ivory towers of the university. He actively followed the events which were leading to a new economic order in the British Isles--he was, as mentioned, a native of Scotland--and throughout Europe.

While history indicates that the economic science had no clearly marked beginning and evolved slowly as entrepreneurial business practices gradually took root in the European states, present-day economists nonetheless consider Smith to be the founder of the

---

[6] ibid., p. 241.

formal discipline of economics. They bestow this honor upon him despite the fact that he introduced no original idea himself.[7] Instead, his Wealth of Nations contains the best ideas from many sources which he compiled and organized for his tome. Why for this is he so revered?

Timing had much to do with it. What was required at this juncture was someone with a special ability to synthesize the competing theories, the claims and counterclaims; someone who could identify the core truths from what had been offered and develop a technique for observing and analyzing, for economics prior to Smith had no formal *method* to conduct these basic tasks; and analyzing not just opinions, but also events themselves. As it stood, economic discussion possessed a certain disorder. Those interested in commercial affairs had a very imprecise vocabulary to describe the events they saw, and this led to some instances of slipshod logic. Thus, the science needed a capable intellect and great communicator; an expositor who was clear, illuminating, and convincing. Smith, as it turned out, was all of these. In the history of economic discourse, few have matched him. Smith's gifts for systematizing and conveying his knowledge were not just well timed, they were unique.

Two outstanding themes emerge from Smith's work. First, Smith envisioned the market as being completely *self-regulating*; i.e., as needing no independent supervision. He explained this feature of the market by using the metaphor of the **invisible hand**. Smith's second theme is predicated on the first: since the market regulated itself, it would function better without governmental intervention. Thus, Smith was a strong advocate of **laissez-faire** economics. This marks the second time we can observe how economic understanding influences the economist's view towards governmental policy, the Mercantilist controversies being the first.

Let us examine each of these themes.

self-regulation & the invisible hand

[7] ibid., p. 184. Schumpeter emphasizes "analytic" idea.

Smith attributed the marvelous ability of the market to deliver goods that people wanted--and provide them at the cheapest possible price--to what he called the invisible hand. This is no normal hand (obviously). In fact, it's not a genuine hand at all. Smith used the invisible hand as a metaphor for the direction and influence the market gives to all its participants, or **economic agents**. More precisely, the invisible hand guides the market, directing resources to their best outlet, entrepreneurs to their highest return, and consumers to their most satisfactory selection.

Smith argued that, within the limits of a nation's resources, markets are entirely adequate to provide for the wants of the community *so long as commodity prices are free to find their own level*. If prices are flexible, then they will function as *signals* indicating either (1) the changing wants of consumers or (2) changing conditions of production. Thus, prices change when circumstances in the market change; hence, changing prices *inform* participants in the market of the new status quo.

In The Wealth of Nations, Smith provided simple, intuitive examples outlining market processes. To illustrate some of those, we provide a modern "translation" of his 18th century English.

Suppose consumers, on their own initiative, decided to spend more of their dollars for pizza rather than hamburger. We would anticipate the price of pizza to rise to reflect the greater desire for it. Meanwhile, we'd expect the price of hamburger to fall. Together, these changes in individual prices suggest an increasing *relative price* of pizza, i.e., the price of pizza compared to the price of hamburger would rise. The change in relative price *informs* entrepreneurs that the *profitability* of pizza, relative to hamburger, has climbed.

When these changes occur, what is the sensible thing for an entrepreneur to do? Human nature is such that she seeks her best advantage: if pizzas have become more profitable at the expense of hamburger, then increasing pizza production and decreasing hamburger production makes the most business sense. That's where the money's going! The invisible hand points the way!

In time, entrepreneurs will devote more of their resources to pizza making and less to hamburger production. But as the entrepreneurs make these adjustments, pizza prices retreat from their highs and hamburger prices come off from their lows. Why? In trying to garner some of the increased profits of the pizza industry, entrepreneurs get increasingly competitive amongst themselves. This drives pizza prices back down. On the other hand, lessened production in the hamburger industry eliminates any gluts that existed after consumers made the switch to pizza. With the gluts gone, hamburger prices return to previous levels.

It's more than luck that accomplishes this neat trick. The pizza example traces a veiled, but still detectable, order underlying the workings of the market. The example manifests a coordination between buyers and sellers, one which maintains a market **equilibrium** where consumer purchases and firm output are equated.

According to Smith the invisible hand does its best work when persons in the market are fully able to pursue their own interest. Smith argued that *competitive self-interest is, paradoxically, a harmonizing force in a market-based economy*. How does this paradox work? How does the self-interest of thousands of individuals get coordinated? How does nitty-gritty competition for customers manage to produce social harmony and wealth?

In a famous passage, Smith explains that it is not altruism which motivates the baker to bake his bread. He is thinking only of himself and his (potential) profits. But this is fine since consumers, after all, want bread. Because one party has exactly what the other lacks, a mutual advantage arises spontaneously. Thus, the market needs no special, premeditated, directive to arrange trades. Since businesses deal very directly with the buying public, they are in the best position to know its desires; if they provide wanted commodities, they will reap the rewards; if not, they lose out. So the market reconciles the contrary self-interests of buyers and sellers and functions harmoniously because the demands of

individuals will largely translate into profits for firms.

The key to making self-interest the means for maintaining market coordination turns on the ability of the pricing system to reflect the self-interested behavior of all parties. As in the pizza example, when significant forces on the consumer side act in concert, price changes ensue. Then, other self-interested parties *respond* to those forces, eventually offsetting them almost completely. Without the price change, participants in the market lack a common indicator as to prevailing market conditions. Without the signal, adjustments are slower, less "in tune," less efficient. Flexible prices allow the market to be efficient, smooth, operative, coordinated, stable.

laissez-faire

If consumers lead the way, and the pricing system expresses their desires accurately, and firms are unfettered in their pursuit of profits, then what is the function of government in the market? None is left really. Better the government keep its hands off the market. To Smith, the market is the most appropriate human institution for solving the fundamental economic challenges that face each society, namely:

a. What to produce
b. How to produce
c. How much to produce
d. Who receives what is produced

When Smith considered the consequences of the government's directing the production and distribution of goods, he thought that it would skew economic activity toward political interests rather than the interests of individuals. Consequently, members of society would be worse off, since they wouldn't receive what they prefer for themselves but rather what the government prefers for them to have. These conclusions constitute the birth of laissez-faire economics.

Perhaps needless to say, this explanation became very popular among business people. Businesses view almost all restrictions that governments place on them as unwelcome intrusions. By popularizing this argument, Smith won the minds of businessmen for centuries to come.

That Smith's laissez-faire economics is at odds with the mercantilist view should be clear. For Smith, protectionism is a perfect example of a government's restricting the market choices of consumers. By removing competitive pressure from domestic producers, these firms have less incentive to provide the range and quality of products possible through open competition with foreign firms. Consumers lose out as they pay higher prices for less output. Laissez-faire economics suggests the exact opposite of protectionist policy: free trade.

It is impossible to underestimate the importance of Adam Smith's contributions to economics. The bulk of our present economic wisdom is easily traceable to the discussions found in his book, The Wealth of Nations.

As we advance our studies of the market, we will be relearning the lessons of Smith in a more precise way. Thus, the student should have a good command of the material just discussed, since it will make later chapters more understandable.

Marx

To adherents of laissez-faire economics, Karl Marx is the devil incarnate. He is the progenitor of the socialist ideology, which calls for governmental ownership and control of economic resources. He is the "founder" of Communism. The few remaining communist nations owe allegiance to his political and economic doctrines. Although he's dead, many would consider his ideas to be a threat to the American way of life.

An introductory economics textbook is not the place to resolve deep-seated political arguments. We're trying to focus on the economic; not produce-- nor reproduce--a manifesto. Still, a considered word is worthwhile.

Many of Marx's views have become associated with historical, political figures from the Soviet Union, etc., who in unscrupulous and devastating ways, used

Marx to justify their own political ambitions. Were these genuine labor movements as he had envisioned them, Marx would have supported them. But, it's unlikely he would have supported the dictatorships which continually evoked his name. Quite in contrast to the Communist leadership, Marx truly valued the dignity of the worker and railed against his degradation: he opposed the use of child labor; he lambasted the "sweat shops" of the 19th century which submitted the worker to ungodly conditions for paltry reward. He decried vast unemployment. Were he alive in our time, he'd support Lech Welesa, founder of the Polish Solidarity Union, winner of the Nobel Peace Prize, and eventually President of independent Poland.

The "Commie Pinko" caricature tarnishes his reputation in economics. Yet Marx, whose writing can be both rambling and dense in a single page, had compelling economic insights. These cannot be ignored. The major one we'll examine is his theory regarding the relationship between capital and money.

definition of capital

What is capital? The standard American textbook definition prescribes that only man-made resources be considered capital; so the plant and equipment of a firm are that firm's capital resources or capital stock. Capital is distinct from the other categories of economic resources, land and labor, by the fact that it's neither "of the earth," nor human. Money, on the other hand, is not considered capital. Although money is a tool of human society (i.e., man-made), American economists tend not to view money as essential for production, since their view of production takes the perspective of an engineer. Hence, most American economists don't classify money as capital, since money isn't considered to be a tool essential for production.

Marx's conception of capital, however, is different. It is more inclusive. Marx considered money to be capital, i.e., a necessary component of production of marketable commodities in a *capitalist* society. He viewed money as a kind of *circulating* capital, whereas the equipment of the firm represented *fixed* capital. What is the basis for considering money as capital? Is it legitimate?

To address these questions we should recall the opening words of this text: What's a sport? What should "sport" include? We are dealing here with definitional matters and the effect of more or less inclusive definitions on the nature of economic study. The limits set by a concept's prescribed definition—in any science, not just economics—inevitably structures that concept's relation to all other terms belonging to the vocabulary of a given science.

So, to define capital broadly such that it includes money will lead to a different conception as to how the capitalist system actually works. While Adam Smith conceives capitalism to be a system of market exchanges determined by individual self-interest, Marx emphasizes the power exerted by firms over labor through their ownership and access to capital *including financial or money-capital*. Whereas Smith believed competition for profits would bring social harmony, Marx could only see cyclic volatility resulting from firms' pursuit of profits.

But just as important, a definition cannot be capricious and arbitrary. There needs to be a practical basis for considering something to be within or outside of a certain category: there needs to be a basis for considering money as capital rather than as distinct from it. In this regard, classifying something as capital turns on the idea of what is necessary for the production of goods. For this, let's consider the following, highly typical, statements found in prominent American business periodicals:

a) from Business Week: "Investors from the U.S., Europe, and Japan are expected to put more than $30 billion into the stock markets of capital-hungry developing countries from Latin America to Eastern Europe..."[8]

b) from Inc.: "...the company had huge amounts of money tied up in raw materials and inventory for months at a time. Worse, every step along the growth path consumed capital. Fraedrich worked tirelessly on the finances, but he could never bring in as much cash as the company

needed."[9]

c) from Entrepreneur: "The financing plan describes how the desired capital will be used and how it will be repaid."[10]

Their view is that growth and development requires money; that it's needed for ongoing production; that it's a necessary condition for initiating production. In short, *they see money as capital*. Oddly then, the business people and Karl Marx operate with similar views regarding the relation between capital, money, and production in modern economies. The view implies that in order to understand the operations of Western capitalist nations (U.S., Japan, West Germany, et. al.), matters of finance and money must be a primary part of one's analysis. Perhaps this is why economic discussions in the press focus so much on debts, loans, interest rates, profits, and profit-growth.

That money is capital constitutes a primary *economic* theme of Marx's writings. There were others. He believed that historical forces shaped the organization of a given society's economic relations. He felt that capitalism was inherently unstable and would eventually collapse. He emphasized conflict in the relations between profit and wage incomes, between capitalists and labor. Marx's premonitions for capitalism's collapse, fortunately for us, did not come to pass. And most economists today consider him to have been imprecise, even confused, in much of his critique of capitalist business practice. For our purposes, however, his ideas can be considered important for the emphasis they place on money itself, the direction in which such emphasis takes us in theoretically speaking, and the counterpoint his ideas provide for other theories. This significance of money in the modern capitalist economy will be studied in later chapters on money and in Chapter 10 on the American Depression of the 1930's.

---

[8] "The Emerging Market Play Is Alive and Well" by John Pearson, from Business Week, July 11, 1994, p. 58.
[9] "Sole Survivor: Company Profile" by John Case, from Inc., June 1994. p. 56.
[10] "A Decent Proposal" by Lawrence W. Tuller, from Entrepreneur, July 1994, p. 26; from the book The Complete Book of Raising Capital by Lawrence W. Tuller, McGraw-Hill, 1994; Reprinted in Entrepreneur with permission from McGraw-Hill.

MODERN ECONOMIC THOUGHT

Marx wrote during the mid–1800's. During the latter half of that century the discipline took a decided turn in its focus. The most significant contributions developed the Smithian themes of self–regulation, pricing, competition, and market equilibrium. The two major contributors were, again, French and British. A French economist named Leon Walras sought to introduce rigorous mathematical analysis to economic study, the very thing it was lacking up to this point. He felt sure that future economic progress depended on the use of mathematical principles. The other great contributor was Alfred Marshall. His role was much like his compatriot Smith in that he synthesized the accumulating knowledge of the profession. He also introduced important analytic concepts. With both men, the concepts of **supply and demand** acquired more precise meaning.

Walras

Perhaps the major implication of Smith's Wealth of Nations is the idea that the demands of consumers would be satisfied by the production of firms *so long as prices were flexible*. Were there a surplus, or glut, of products, falling prices would remove the excess; were there a shortage, rising prices would send some shoppers home. Thus, the market result tends toward equilibrium, a balance between supply and demand.

mathematical analysis

Walras saw the possibility for a mathematical expression of Smith's conception. He devised a method to illustrate the market's balance by using simple linear equations, i.e., of the form $Y = mx + b$, one for demand and one for supply.

Economists by this time had understood some basic relationships between prices and quantities as they pertained to either side of the market. It was clear, for instance, that higher prices discouraged purchases and lower prices prompted them. To an entrepreneur, however, higher prices were an inducement to produce and lower prices deterred production. In other words *the relationship between price and quantity on the demand side was inverse,*

while the relation was positive on the supply side. These principles have come to be known as the laws of demand and supply.

Walras expressed the laws in mathematical formulations. A typical demand equation had the following look:

$$Q_d = -4P + 46$$

And the typical supply equation appeared this way:

$$Q_s = 2P + 4$$

The negative in the demand equation signifies the inverse relation between price and quantity. The positive 2P in the supply equation signifies the firms' positive response to changes in price.

The market's ability to coordinate the supply and demand forces in the market hints at a simple illustration of the equilibrium concept. Walras simply set the two equations equal to each other.

$$
\begin{aligned}
Q_d &= Q_s \\
-4P + 46 &= 2P + 4 \\
-4P + (46 - 4) &= 2P + (4 - 4) \\
(-4P + 4P) + 42 &= (2P + 4P) \\
42 &= 6P \\
7 &= P
\end{aligned}
$$

If these equations represented the conditions in a product market, then the product's equilibrium price would be $7. We can also solve for the equilibrium quantity by using the fact that the price in equilibrium is $7.

$Q_s = 2P + 4$	$Q_d = -4P + 46$
$Q_s = 2(\$7) + 4$	$Q_d = -4(\$7) + 46$
$Q_s = 14 + 4$	$Q_d = -28 + 46$
$Q_s = 18$	$Q_d = 18$

or

The equilibrium output is 18 units, which we demonstrate by plugging $7 into either the demand or supply equation.

Walras extended his work to illustrate that even in a complex world of many markets, the forces of supply and demand would find a general equilibrium such that no individual market would be faced with a surplus or shortage, at least not in the long run. The many distinct separate markets would come into balance together *so long as prices in those markets were flexible*.

Walras' influence led contemporary economists to investigate the conditions necessary for equilibrium beyond that of mere price flexibility. The nature and conditions of the kinds of *competitive* markets Walras had in mind will be explored in depth in Chapter 24. The more fundamental lessons of supply and demand will be developed in Chapters 4, 5, and 6.

Marshall

Alfred Marshall may have been a slow working economist--his influential <u>Principles of Economics</u> took over fifteen years to write--but the accomplishments he managed by sheer thoroughness far outdistanced those of many faster paced contemporaries. His methodical pace did not stem from any intellectual deficiencies. In fact, his original contributions were numerous. But Marshall saw how qualified economic truths tended to be. For instance, some people are inclined to think that if a firm raises its prices, its profits will automatically increase because it takes in more money per unit sold. But Marshall would be quick to point out that at higher prices fewer items would be purchased. Thus, if the firm loses a substantial portion of its clientele as a result of raising prices, revenues and profits can be adversely affected. The end result would depend on a number of factors which Marshall took pains to describe.

For the moment, we can examine two of Marshall's lasting contributions. The first is his diagram for conceptualizing market demand and supply; the second is the measurement device he invented to assess the strength of the price-quantity relation.

graph of demand and supply

If the laws of demand and supply can be expressed mathematically with equations, then they can be graphed in order to give a visual counterpart to the math. Marshall's <u>Principles</u> popularized the use of supply and demand curves to describe and study market events. The complete picture, called the Marshallian cross diagram, can be used to represent any market.

The Marshallian cross diagram

The figure below uses the equations developed in our discussion of Walras to illustrate the market equilibrium of $P = 7$, $Q = 18$. The supply curve slopes up and to the right to portray the positive price-quantity relation. The demand slopes down and to the right since the price-quantity relation is negative on that side of the market. (See Diagram 2-2.)

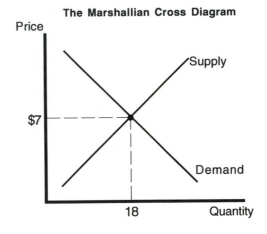

The Marshallian Cross Diagram

Diagram 2-2

Graphic illustrations such as Diagram 2-2 will be used throughout the book to illustrate new trends in the market. In Chapters 4, 5, and 6 we will rely on the Marshallian cross diagram to highlight all the major lessons about supply and demand. The crucial task at that time will be to combine words and pictures so that they tell a coherent, instructive tale.

elasticity

While the laws of supply and demand are helpful conceptual tools, they say little about the magnitude of the price-quantity relation. Often we want to know to what degree economic agents react to price changes. If prices rise *significantly*, will consumers purchase a *significantly* lesser amount? Perhaps, for some goods, buyers respond weakly to price changes; then for other goods consumer reaction is pronounced. In fact, such observations were confirmed and Marshall sought to measure and illustrate them.

Suppose the price of a good rose 10% and then, in response, the quantity bought fell 10%. Marshall took these two percentages and formed a ratio from them:

$$\frac{\% \text{ change in Q}}{\% \text{ change in P}} = \frac{10\%}{10\%} = 1$$

Marshall called the ratio the price elasticity of demand. It measures the responsiveness of quantity demanded to changes in the price of a good. Conversion to percentage changes gives a truer reading of the strength of the effect.

The example above illustrates the case of unitary elasticity. If the ratio is greater than one, then the product's demand is said to be elastic, meaning more responsive; when the ratio is less than one, the demand is said to be inelastic, meaning relatively less responsive.

As a shorthand we can use graphs to illustrate a demand which is more or less elastic. In Diagrams 2-3 and 2-4, the first picture shows a demand which is inelastic, since the quantity demanded changes only a small bit compared to the illustrated price change. But the second graph indicates a high degree of response on the quantity side, induced by a rather small change in price. We will be studying all the technical details about elasticities in Chapter 17.

Keynes' economics

John Maynard Keynes is probably the most important economist of the past century. While many of his ideas have been challenged in the past 20-30 years, the shape of modern capitalism retains more of the influence of John Maynard Keynes than that of any other economist. His prominence stems from

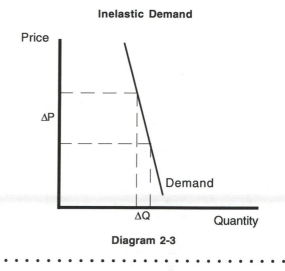

Diagram 2-3

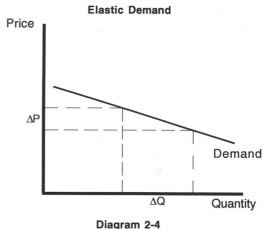

Diagram 2-4

his thoughts regarding the economic difficulties experienced in the U.S during the 1930's. In his influential book, <u>The General Theory of Employment, Interest, and Money</u>, completed in 1936, Keynes discussed the limits of "classical economics," by which he meant that body of orthodox opinion that viewed the market as a self-regulating entity. In the book, Keynes challenged the applicability of classical theory to modern market conditions and questioned the soundness of laissez-faire conclusions.

view of the depression

The Depression of the 1930's posed a vexing dilemma for the economics profession, whose masters had always relayed to the next generation the mantra of laissez-faire. Conditions in the United States were of the most serious nature: extremely high rates of unemployment, extremely low rates of investment, bank panics, destitution, hunger, and pessimism regarding the future. To the doctrinaires, the market would correct itself in the long run. Where investment had been low, falling interest rates would restore investment to its pre-1929 levels. Where labor was idle, many economists anticipated wage adjustments to reestablish incentives for firms to hire. The market had its own tools to induce recovery, they argued.

Still, the wait was prolonged.

To Keynes, viewing the American situation from across the Atlantic--he too was British--recovery would not likely be automatic. A general, macroeconomic depression can establish its own norm, if the mood of the business community were not reversed. Workers cannot impose their hiring on management when product sales are slumping and the firm cannot employ them profitably. Thus, Keynes

placed himself in direct opposition to the received wisdom. He developed a new account to explain events, which suggested that price adjustments alone might not restore the economy to full employment.

The argument led to a heretical conclusion: the government might have to intervene on behalf of society to offset the lack of spending activity which characterized the Depression. To Keynes, the abandonment of laissez-faire represented a pragmatic alternative to economic decay. To laissez-faire adherents, he betrayed the faith.

SUMMARY

The remainder of the book will be developed so as to relearn the lessons presented in this chapter in deeper and sometimes in more technical ways. It is very advisable to understand this chapter very well. Within it you have learned the chief insights of some of history's best economists. Their lessons comprise the foundation of the entire intellectual edifice called economics.

VOCABULARY

Economic Agent – a participant in the market; a person who makes economic decisions

Equilibrium – a balance between twin economic forces of some kind; the price and quantity combination at which the market would tend to settle, i.e., where supply and demand intersect

    (a) *micro* – where supply and demand intersect for a particular product or resource

    (b) *macro* – where aggregate supply and aggregate demand intersect

Supply – a relationship listing what amounts of a product a firm, or group of firms, would be willing to deliver to the market at various prices; can appear graphically or as a table of points

Demand – a relationship listing what amounts of a product a consumer, or group of consumers, would be willing to buy at various prices; can appear graphically or as a table of points

Invisible hand – the metaphor used by Adam Smith to capture the automatic tendency of a (the) market to self–adjust, to direct resources to their best, most profitable outlets and agents to their best decisions

Laissez-faire – the contention that the government ought to refrain from intrusions into the market

Exports – the sale of a domestic good or service to a foreign customer; the dollar value of such sales

Imports – the sale of a foreign good or service to a domestic customer; the dollar value of such sales

Free trade – the concept describing the trading between nations which is absent of any governmental influence, especially tariffs, taxes, or quotas (specific quantity restrictions)

Protectionism – the deliberate use of taxes, tariffs, or quotas applied to foreign imports

Trade balance – the *accounting* reconciliation between exports and imports, *in monetary terms*

Trade surplus (deficit) – condition occurring when export dollar sales exceed (are less than) import dollar sales over a certain stretch of time

Net product – the amount of output produced in excess of that amount with which society began production; amount of output representing the growth in output over time

Flow – a term to describe economic activity which occurs through time, or an economic variable which is measurable only over a period of time

Seed Money – more often called start up capital, this concept refers to initial funds or financing used to initiate business activity

Consumption – expenditures of households for the purposes of personal satisfaction

END-OF-CHAPTER QUESTIONS

1. Write a paragraph or two summarizing the contributions of the following economists:

   the Mercantilists
   Smith
   Marshall
   Quesnay
   Marx
   Keynes
   Walras

2. During the 1970's the United States experienced an "oil crisis" of relatively high prices. Much of the oil consumed during that time was imported. Would it have been wise to place a tariff on foreign oil in order to avoid (or remedy) such a problem? Try to explore some of the costs and benefits to such a policy.

3. What would you consider the major economic groups to be today? That is, if you were to follow the example of the Tableau Economique, could you divide society into different two or three broad categories? Attempt to do so and discuss how these groups interact economically.

4. Are you familiar with any example from your experience wherein the patterns suggested by the pizza and hamburger illustration were played out? Can you think of examples of fad products which saw increased competition after a rise in demand was established?

5. If you ruled the nation, what would you do if there occurred a business slowdown? Is an economic downturn avoidable? What would you do in your country to avoid one?

PART TWO

RUDIMENTS OF MARKET SUPPLY AND DEMAND

"Economics is the science of common sense."

CHAPTER 3

WHAT DOES THE MARKET DO?

It is best to include in the definition of a term exactly what a thing accomplishes, i.e., its function. So, for instance, a good definition of the word "car" mentions not only the fact that it's an object with four wheels, made of metal or fiberglass, but also the words "designed for transportation."

Similarly, we should not be satisfied with the definition of the market as a place where "potential buyers and sellers meet." In observing market phenomenon, we need to understand what the market accomplishes for society, its function in economic society.

The market does many things. But two are paramount. First, the market *informs*. Without reliable information about the true costs of amassing resources for production, entrepreneurs, in particular, would have difficulty making appropriate decisions regarding the opportunities for profit. Second, the market *allocates*. In other words, the market distributes to agents a limited supply of resources, goods, and services according to their willingness to spend.

The dissemination of information and the allocation process both rely on a flexible pricing system. Prices inform; prices allocate--so long as they are not rigid.

What prices do

We can begin by noting that *prices have both a passive and active function: their passive function is to serve as a measuring device, informing market participants of the prevailing scarcity conditions in the market; their active function is to allocate scarce goods*. Let's examine each of these functions more fully.

prices as bits of information: it's a real thing

If prices inform, what information do they contain? What's their purpose? We'll begin by making a broad analogy.

That which informs also communicates. In order to communicate we must have a means, or *medium*, of conveying information. The radio, for example, is such a medium; so are the newspaper and television. Indeed, that's why these means of communication are known generally as "the media": they represent *several* methods of relaying data between persons.

Yet, with respect to the world of communication, we haven't reached rock bottom. Each of these media employs *language* to impart information; thus, language is the common, public, communications medium. Language is our principle means for dispensing news, facts, conclusions, wisdom; for making pronouncements, sending bulletins, tidings, and assertions to interested parties.

If market prices truly *inform*, then they must communicate. And since prices speak a *language of money*, money acts as a communicative tool in the marketplace. Besides facilitating trades between agents, *money and money-prices transmit data about situations affecting the market*. Hence, when market prices change, they inform agents of altered market conditions, as words update the population on events occurring in an ever-changing world.

Now let's consider an example.

Suppose one summer drought conditions existed in an important corn-growing region. What would we expect to happen to the price of corn? Surely, we'd anticipate higher prices. Corn production would be cut due to the poorer growing conditions that summer, and price hikes would simply reflect that fact. The magnitude of the price hike would reveal the extent of the weather disturbance's effect on the market's output of corn.

The example permits the following conclusion: because of the drought, *the opportunity cost of producing corn rose*. If the drought did not wipe out a particular farmer's entire crop, it severely reduced the yield. Had a farmer irrigated the land during the season to maintain yields, then his or her expenses would have risen in proportion to the extra water used. Since more resources had to be expended, the opportunity cost of raising corn in that year increased.

Thus, the monetary price hike notifies market participants that circumstances have altered conditions of production so as to require more resources to deliver corn to market. More generally, *whenever a good's price changes we can view that change as a kind of market "communique," notifying agents of changes in the underlying factors affecting* **real** *production and exchange.* To extend the analogy, *the market's pricing system is an immense information network. Prices at once represent and communicate a complex market reality; they translate events into a language of numbers, units of measure called (in the U.S.) dollar bills. Therefore, as money prices vary through time, they manifest a corresponding real world motion--or perhaps, commotion--which bears on the market's ability to deliver goods.*

prices as bits of information: it's a relative thing

Suppose someone were to walk up to you and say, "It's 35 degrees out, celsius." If you're like most Americans, you wouldn't know what weather conditions the statement implies. Until you go out into it, soak up the rays, you have no basis to know.

Yet even this experience yields less knowledge than one might think. For if the next day somebody said, "It's zero degrees out, celsius," you'd know only that it's colder than yesterday, but not much else. You must go out, feel the chill in your bones, and observe that at zero celsius water freezes.

Now, if on the third day, someone informs you that it's 20 degrees, celsius, outside, you'd have a fix on what the weather is like that day. You'd know it's more than halfway between a fairly cold day and a rather warm one--20 degrees must be pretty pleasant. And indeed it is.

What does this example illustrate and what does it have to do with economics? Much of our knowledge in practical life is of a *relative* kind, based on comparisons. Thus, we must have information about *two* things or from *two* experiences in order to know anything. Even when there is a standard unit of measure, like temperature, the scale means little without direct comparative experience.

Knowledge of economic reality is like this. If somebody walks up to you and pronounces, "In Spain,

a two liter bottle of milk costs 3 euros," you would have no basis to understand the statement. What is a euro? What's it worth? What's it usually buy?

The euro is the new common currency used through most of Europe. This is good to know but it doesn't *connect* 3 euros to anything. Someone could say that last year the same amount of milk cost 2.9 euros. That's better, but still, economically speaking, you're very much in the dark. Unless you could *compare* milk's price with another price, it's impossible to have a handle on what is actually important for a consumer to know: is 3 euros expensive or not?

One way out of the ignorance would come from knowing the **exchange rate** between U. S. dollars and euros. The exchange rate is simply the price of one currency in terms of some other. As of this writing (late 2002) one dollar will purchase about 1 euro. So, some quick arithmetic tells us that, in Spain, a two liter bottle of milk costs approximately 3 dollars. By American standards, where two liters of milk is about $1.50 - $1.60, that's pretty expensive.

But notice: we had to know *two* prices or we knew nothing at all. We had to know the price of milk *and* the value of a euro. That allowed us to translate Spanish prices into American prices and draw the proper comparison. In economic lingo, we found the **relative price** of milk bought in Spain by comparing it to the **nominal price** of milk bought in the U.S. We can present this mathematically.

Data: (1) **Nominal price of Spanish Milk : 3 euros**

(2) **Nominal price of American milk: $1.50**

(3) **Exchange rate: $1.00 buys 1 euro**

Relative Price of Spanish milk:

$$\frac{3 \text{ euros}}{\$1.50} \cong \frac{\$3}{\$1.50} \cong \frac{2}{1}$$

As the example illustrates, we can express a good's relative price by forming a ratio between the nominal prices of two goods. The ratio above makes clear that the cost of milk in Spain is relatively high.

Relative prices tell the consumer exactly what he needs to know. And what is that? Prices offer information about the relative sacrifice attached to acquiring a good. A good's price does not exist in solitary confinement; it exists only in relation to other goods' prices. From that context, consumers make judgments and trade-offs between goods based on their relative expense (and, too, on their relative quality).

As a student of the market, you must become cognizant of the relative nature of prices, and to make a conscious habit of thinking in relative, or comparative, terms. *In economics, everything comes in pairs.* A major conclusion from many years of economic study is that relative prices, more so than nominal prices, stir market events and alter the choices of agents. What's more, the purchasing adjustments made by agents, under the influence of changing relative prices, have feedback effects which tend to alter the decisions of producers. If the habit of thinking in pairs is not adopted, the entire structure of the discipline, and the hidden patterns of market events, is apt to escape you.

distinguishing the real from the relative

Let's re-consider the example of the corn market. We said that the drought altered the real conditions of production; hence, the opportunity cost of cultivating corn in that year rose.

But rose compared to what? When we worked through the example, we implicitly assumed that the growing conditions for all other agricultural products remained the same--this is the ceteris paribus assumption. By imagining a drought under ceteris paribus conditions we can deduce a second conclusion: the increased opportunity cost of corn production alerts the buyers to the fact that corn production had become more difficult *relative to the production of all other foodstuffs.* So as real costs changed, relative costs changed too. The real and the relative are entwined.[1]

In sum, scarcity is both a real and relative thing.

A good's price gauges not only the opportunity costs associated with production and distribution, but the *relative* cost (or difficulty) of that production as well. Hence, the higher the good's price, the more scarce it is and the greater the opportunity cost to society for providing it; and the less the good's price, the less scarce it is and the less its opportunity cost.

THE MARKET AS ALLOCATOR

As price fluctuations relay information to consumers regarding the relative sacrifice required to purchase a good, they send a simultaneous signal to firms about the *relative profitability* of goods. Entrepreneurs will interpret a rising price as an indication of expanded profit potential. Drawn by this stronger incentive, existing firms will rev up production; later on, new entrants (firms) will appear. The net result suggests that a greater amount of resources will be devoted toward the production of that good whose price has risen.

An example of the allocative function

Let's take an example. Consider the markets for ketchup and salsa, two goods which serve as condiments to foods popular in the States. Both foods are tomato-based products. Twenty years ago ketchup was considerably more popular than salsa, principally because the American diet was more beef oriented and more "Anglo." Today salsa has nearly overtaken ketchup in total dollar sales. How has this happened and what changes accompanied it?

Demographic shifts have occurred. The American population is more Latinized today than at any time in its history. And tastes have changed. Non-Latin groups enjoy the very healthy Mexican and Southern American cuisines more than they did a generation ago.

---

[1] Alert students might consider this example unrealistic; if there's a drought in a certain area, then *all* the crops grown in that area will suffer, not just a single one. This point is well taken, but can be adjusted for without undermining the spirit of the example. Suppose the drought occurred in the Midwest, while weather conditions along the East coast were normal. Clearly, the *real* costs of production (for any crop) would rise in the Midwest, and remain normal back East. And just as surely, the increased real expenditures imply a growth in the *relative* cost of Midwest produce to that raised in the East.

The trends appeared in market results. Gradually, more consumer dollars were directed to salsa; ketchup sales plateaued, then declined. Price changes reflected these results. Salsa prices increased compared to ketchup prices. Makers of ketchup either reduced their prices or ran more sales. None of this escaped the attention of food manufacturers.

Today supermarkets offer more varieties of salsa than ever before. Many companies which make tortilla chips also have a line of "hot" products, from mild to very spicy. And now, Mexican restaurants are as well recognized as any hamburger or pizza joint.

All of that suggests that, compared to any time previous, society now directs more of its productive resources to the production of salsa, Mexican foods, etc. Salsa companies demand more tomatoes; ketchup companies, less (proportionally speaking). Farmers raise more hot peppers than in years before and have either expanded their fields to do so or cut out the production of some other crop. Ranchers have either gone out of business or decreased the proportion of their land devoted to cattle grazing, since along with less ketchup has come less meat. Mexican restaurants occupy more commercial real estate than in prior years.

All of these resource adjustments were prompted by changes in the relative prices of goods, ketchup and salsa prices serving as the prime movers. Through these relative price changes, the market indicated to all interested parties that it "wants" to change the distribution of resources; it used the pricing system as a mechanism to induce shifts from traditional American meals to the newly popular ethnic fare.

Perhaps now we can better appreciate Adam Smith's point when he described the invisible hand. If prices are flexible, the market will function well, and resources will be smoothly and efficiently transferred to their most profitable outlet. Changes in prices and self-interest together accomplish a coordination among consumer wants, firm production, and resource allocation. Such coordination could not be readily designed by centralized decision makers, i.e., governmental authorities.

Case study: oil market

To finally drive home the point of product and resource allocation, let's consider the case of the oil industry throughout the 1970's and 1980's. Something similar happened there.

preliminary analysis

After a fairly long period of price stability in the 1950's and 1960's, the 1970's experienced disruption in world petroleum markets. The formation of the OPEC cartel brought efforts to manipulate the market price of oil as the 13 nation club deliberately withheld oil deliveries.

1972–73 saw the first stage of the "oil crisis." Rather than try to offset OPEC's production slack, American oil companies more or less followed suit. They thought it better to wait and sell at higher prices. Inevitably, oil prices zipped up and "windfall" profits poured into the industry.

With the rise in oil prices came a greater incentive to drill for oil. This meant that the industry would have to spend more to hire drill workers, to purchase iron and steel for constructing drills, and to purchase ships for oil transport, etc. The Texas economy experienced a boom during the 70's. Louisiana and Oklahoma fared likewise. Land prices in those states rose, partly due to the higher valuations of oil itself and partly from the employment boom which brought to the area new workers with a demand for housing. Unemployment was very low in that region at the time. Frequently, one could read articles about a large shift in the American population to the Sun Belt.

By 1986, things weren't so sunny there. Oil prices leveled off in the early 80's and collapsed by mid-decade. OPEC's ability to enforce production quotas on its members broke down, largely because Iran and Iraq, two key members of the cartel, fought a war with each other and paid for it from sales beyond their respective quotas. But falling oil prices meant decreased revenues for everybody else in the industry, especially in our Southwest.

The consequences of these falling prices and

revenues can be viewed in a couple of ways, both of which suggest that we should anticipate less activity within that sector of the economy. In the words of Smith, we would say that the lower prices for oil indicated *less* profits to that industry and a *disincentive* for capital expansion--the invisible hand steered a course away from oil production. A Texas oil industry magnate would be more liable to say that with revenues down he can no longer maintain current production levels at a profit. So he cuts back. He lays off workers. He caps oil wells.

Whether one prefers Smith's terms or the businessman's, the bottom line is plain: less drilling within the oil industry. Price and profit results from the mid to late 1980's could not justify production levels appropriate for the 1970's, when relatively high prices existed.

deeper analysis

There are at least two inter-connected re-allocations that we can point to in the oil case above. First is the series of resource adjustments by firms. We mentioned some of these in terms of increased oil drilling in certain states during the 1970's, followed by production cutbacks after 1986. Not discussed was the re-allocation of household expenditures. Consumers made adjustments too. During the 1970's households reduced their consumption of oil and gasoline in response to higher prices. They were more liberal in their spending by the late 1980's. It is time to examine these trends more carefully.

Let us begin with the earlier decade. When oil prices climbed, the oil industry was not the only sector of the broader energy market to increase capital expenditures for production. There was considerable interest in solar energy and natural gas; nuclear energy felt a boom; coal mines increased production as electric utilities converted to coal as a source of energy generation. Kerosine, ethanol, methanol, firewood, even hydro and wind power attracted investment monies for real capital expansion.

Consumers reenforced some of these trends as more homeowners selected solar or natural gas energy sources for heating and electricity. But perhaps the largest impact on the average person came through the auto industry. By the mid-70's new-car buyers, to a significant degree selected a larger proportion of smaller cars, often foreign-made. The gas guzzlers faded in popularity.

Changes in consumers' choice patterns should have prompted a changing resource allocation from big to small car production on the part of every manufacturer. But American corporations, thinking that the U.S. consumer would continue to purchase the bigger vehicles with little regard to the price of a gallon of gas, were dilatory in their adjustments. Foreign firms, especially Datsun (now Nissan), Toyota, and Honda filled the gap. Chrysler nearly went out of business as a result (and would have were it not for a government loan). American Motors did fold. In short, the American car market has been forever altered and the "Big Three" domestic producers, especially General Motors, cannot be expected to dominate the market to the degree they once did. Perhaps none of this would have happened if the average consumer had not re-allocated his new car purchases toward the gas-thrifty type. But that's exactly what we can expect to happen when the price of a key commodity doubles and triples in the space of eight years.

So much for the 1970's. What of the 1980's?

We mentioned earlier that on the production side, as oil prices fell through the decade, oil producers cut back on drilling, etc. In doing so oil firms freed up resources which could be devoted elsewhere. But where to? Not to other energy sources, though that might seem plausible. With the relative prices of oil and gasoline lower, those energy sources would have been less alluring to investors. We couldn't expect a sustained interest in the energy market once the "crisis" had passed.

In well-functioning, Smithian markets the re-allocation of society's *real* resources takes its cue from households. With a lower price of oil, consumers enjoy a benefit every time they buy oil and gasoline products. This implies that the actual percentage of their income devoted to expenditures on, for example, home heating and transportation, will decline. What is to be done with the income that gets "freed up?"

By and large consumers can be depended on to spend it, especially since those consumers had already budgeted that portion of their income as part of their normal expenditures. Obviously, since the percentage of income spent on heating and transportation fell, then the percentage of income spent on such items as food, clothing, and education would rise. Diagram 3-1 illustrates a hypothetical example of general consumer spending re-allocations, precipitated by decreasing energy costs.

oil to cars and trucks.[3] As reported by the Bureau, between 1980 and 1986 the percentage of income spent on gas and motor oil fell to 4% from a 1980 level of 7.4%. During the same period, the percentage of income used to purchase cars and trucks grew from 7.3% to 10.3%. As the direction of money expenditures changes we should expect relatively more resources being called upon by the market to build cars and relatively less to operate oil rigs, explore for new drill sites, etc. We should expect, too, somewhat stronger

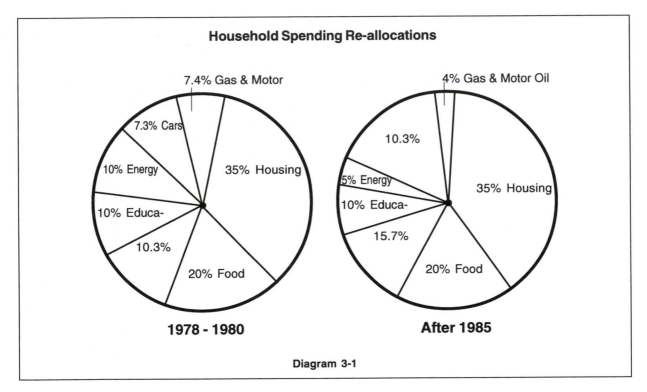

Household Spending Re-allocations

7.4% Gas & Motor
7.3% Cars
10% Energy
10% Educa-
10.3%
20% Food
35% Housing

1978 - 1980

4% Gas & Motor Oil
10.3%
5% Energy
10% Educa-
15.7%
20% Food
35% Housing

After 1985

Diagram 3-1

This is not to say that this diagram conveys every detail regarding how consumers altered their spending patterns though the 1980's period of descending world oil prices. Even within specific slices of the pie, as it were, spending adjustments took place.

some statistical support

One of the mainstays of economic data collection is the Bureau of Labor Statistics. This branch of the Department of Labor keeps track of, among other things, consumer spending.[2] Its data indicate that consumers shifted dollars from gasoline and motor

interest in the luxury cars which consume more gas and less consumer spending on cars which run cheaply. This indeed occurred. And as before, foreign car companies adapted more quickly to changing market conditions and upgraded their models toward the higher end of the market. Once again they beat the Americans to the punch.

---

[2] Such data is critical when the Bureau wants to assess inflation. The Consumer Price Index, used in determining the rate of inflation for final goods and services, relies on information regarding consumer spending patterns.

[3] Trish Hall. "As Values in U.S. Shift, So Does Spending," The New York Times. October 26, 1988, Section C, Page 1.

summary

The oil industry's story of the 70's and 80's reflects a simple swing of the economic pendulum. OPEC's assertion of market power that had shaped the 70's market, and its later slippage in market dominance, together provide an unmistakable example of how the phrase "every action creates an equal and opposite reaction" applies in real world economics. We have interpreted these actions and reactions as part of a two-sided re-allocation process. The adjustments occur on several levels. They are both real and monetary. They entail both firms and households.

Diagram 3-2 outlines these changes in the form of a flowchart, an extremely useful learning tool in economics.

To complete the story of the Sun Belt boom and bust, while the economies of Texas, Louisiana and Oklahoma suffered a tremendous setback because of the oil price fallout, the northeastern section of the country made gains. Those gains reversed the ill fortune the Northeast suffered back in the 1970's when higher petroleum prices contributed to slowdowns in business activity. Thus, the 1970's and 1980's marked a period of two massive geographic re-allocations: first, from the Northeast to the West and South; then back to the Northeast, as the oil-dependent regions went into an economic tailspin.

The efficiency of the economy as a whole depends on shifts of resources and spending as just described. If freed up resources remain unemployed, society cannot possibly be extracting the greatest possible wealth (or production) from its resource base. If companies fail to respond to market forces, they'll be gone.

As we continue our study we will be examining the ability of market prices to signal and prompt all the adjustments which need to be made in order for the macro-economy to operate at full throttle. But first we need to cement our fundamentals in market dynamics and then develop a vocabulary for macro-economics.

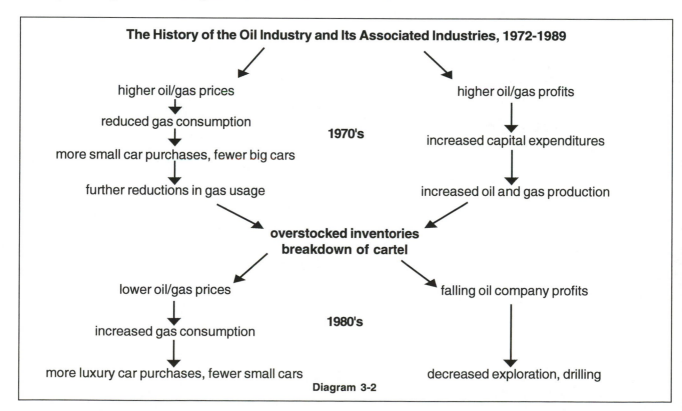

The History of the Oil Industry and Its Associated Industries, 1972-1989

higher oil/gas prices

reduced gas consumption

more small car purchases, fewer big cars

further reductions in gas usage

1970's

higher oil/gas profits

increased capital expenditures

increased oil and gas production

**overstocked inventories
breakdown of cartel**

lower oil/gas prices

increased gas consumption

more luxury car purchases, fewer small cars

1980's

falling oil company profits

decreased exploration, drilling

Diagram 3-2

VOCABULARY

Real – refers to the *concrete* products which consumers or firms purchase and consume; the purchasable goods from a monetary figure, as in the phrase "real income"

Exchange rate – the amount of foreign currency a given nation's domestic currency will buy in the open market

Nominal price – a good's price in dollars, or other currency

Relative price – a good's price in terms of a second good's price; arranged mathematically in ratio form, e.g., $6/$2 = 3 is the relative price of one six pack of good beer to another brand of lesser quality

. . . .

END-OF-CHAPTER QUESTIONS

On relative prices

1. In Spain, a loaf of bread costs approximately 50 pesetas. By American standards, is that expensive or not?

2. In Ireland, a night's stay at a bed and breakfast place is about 20 Irish pounds. In the States, the same amenities would cost $100. Given that the exchange rate between U.S. dollars and Irish pounds is 1.5 to 1 (a $1.50 buys 1 Irish pound), are nightly accommodations of this sort more or less expensive in Ireland than here?

3. Why is labor relatively cheap in China? India? Why is it relatively high in Germany and the U.S?

CHAPTER 4

THE DEMAND SIDE OF THE MARKET

Alfred Marshall's <u>Principles of Economics</u> introduced an original approach conceptualizing market phenomena. Since then nearly all economics students have had to use the "Marshallian cross diagram" to analyze the events of the marketplace. Today it's almost a rite of passage in the American collegiate experience.

Marshall used his diagram to understand particular markets; that is to say, his invention represented a microeconomic tool. In Chapter 2, we pointed out that Marshall's contribution actually was an outgrowth of Walras' mathematical expression of the laws of supply and demand. In this and the following two chapters we undertake a thorough examination of these principles.

THE LAW OF DEMAND

You don't need an economist to tell you that if prices rise, people will tend to buy less of the product; and by the same token, should prices fall, then more items will be sold. This observation leads us to the law of demand: the relationship between prices and quantities, on the demand side of the market, is negative.

The real world presents hundreds of examples of this principle everyday. Consider the effect of a simple coupon, one which offers a 20% discount. No doubt, the effect of the coupon will be to induce purchases. Perhaps some who hadn't previously considered buying the product will buy. Perhaps some who were planning to make a purchase later will make it sooner. Maybe some will buy two items instead of one. Whatever, the effect is the same.

We can observe the law of demand at work at the ballpark: "Pretzels here; pretzels! Pretzels, here! 50 cents, two for 75!" The vendor recognizes that a person is more inclined to buy two when the price per unit drops. (One pretzel for 50 cents, but two cost 37.5 cents each.) Table 4–1 and Diagram 4–1 draw out the implications of the pretzel example.

The inverse relation between price and quantity is unmistakable in the drawing, which follows the information from the **demand schedule**.

Demand Schedule

Price	Quantity
$0.50	1
$0.375	2

Table 4-1

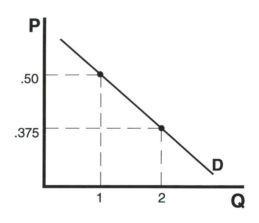

Demand Curve

Diagram 4-1

None of this would be different had we considered an example in which a good's price rose. Let's say that a certain popular retailer of clothing decides to raise its prices for cotton shirts and pants. The volume of sales (i.e., number of units sold) will diminish as a result. The greater the price hike, the greater the decline in units sold. Diagram 4–2 depicts this, following the demand schedule in Table 4–2.

Demand Schedule

Price	Quantity
$ 10	200
$ 14	190
$ 18	180
$ 22	170
$ 26	160
$ 30	150
$ 34	140
$ 38	130
$ 42	120
$ 46	110
$ 50	100

Table 4-2

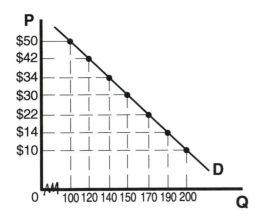

Demand Curve

Diagram 4-2

If the average price of cotton clothing were $26 and rose to $30, ceteris paribus, the retailer could expect a loss of 10 units sold, say, during an average week. If the price were lifted more, even fewer items would be sold. Of course if the price were $22 or $18 instead of $26, consumers would snap up more articles of clothing. Regardless the direction of the price shift,

the quantity side moves oppositely; regardless of the way we travel along the schedule, the basic relation is negative.

A CHANGE IN DEMAND: A SHIFT IN THE CURVE

Demand can either rise or fall. When we speak of either event, the graph will have to reflect the change in demand conditions. Yet demand will always bear a negative slope. How does all this work in the illustration?

An increase in demand

Not long ago, medical researchers published evidence from scientific experiments which showed that diets with more roughage, more raw vegetables and fruits, were linked to fewer instances of cancer in humans, particularly colon cancer. Having oats in the diet seemed especially advantageous.

Given this, what is likely to happen to the demand for oats, for example? As we might expect, it increased. As buyers scour the market for more oats, they put pressure on prices. Thus, a rising demand suggests that steeper prices and greater purchases will be observed together.

On the face of it this seems to contradict the law of demand. But in Diagram 4-3 and the accompanying two schedules we can resolve this superficial contradiction.

A rise in demand is shown in the graph by a rightward shift in the position of the curve. Any increase in demand would be shown the same way. The product might be something besides oats; the numbers on the demand schedule might differ. But the picture serves as a general one.

The fact that the new demand curve is negatively sloped shows that the law of demand remains intact. So an increase in demand does not contradict the law of demand; rather *it suggests that more units of a good will be bought at every possible price compared to some previous period; i.e., buyers intend to acquire more than they used to whatever the price happens to be.* But why? The higher demand simply expresses

Demand Schedule (before)		Demand Schedule (after)	
Price	Quantity (lbs.)	Price	Quantity (lbs.)
$1.10	60	$1.10	90
$1.15	58	$1.15	88
$1.20	56	$1.20	86
$1.25	54	$1.25	84
$1.30	52	$1.30	82
$1.35	50	$1.35	80
$1.40	48	$1.40	78
$1.45	46	$1.45	76
$1.50	44	$1.50	74
$1.55	42	$1.55	72
$1.60	40	$1.60	70

Table 4-3

A Rise in Demand for Oats

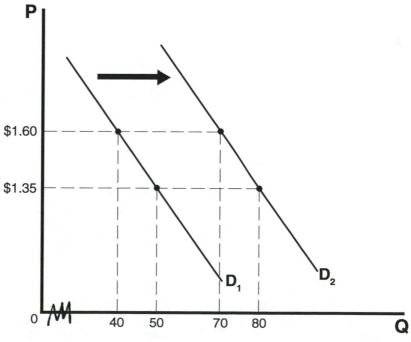

Diagram 4-3

the consumers' reaction to the news about health and diet. They now find it wiser to eat more oats (and less of something else, incidentally) on the basis of the doctors' report.

The example here points out a crucial distinction between the way the word "demand" is often used in ordinary speech and the way economists use the same word. Economically speaking, *demand refers to a series of price and quantity combinations.* Demand is not the amount sold in the market; *demand is a set of price-quantity pairings.* Thus, when we conceive of *a rise in demand*, we refer to a shift in the entire demand curve such that more quantity is bought at every single price. The two demand schedules in Table 4-3, and the accompanying diagram, convey this point most explicitly.

To draw an analogy, consider what it means when we say "income taxes have risen." It means that at *every* income level, the tax obligation is higher. That is a very different thing than someone's income going up or down and having to pay a different amount as a consequence. In the first case, everybody pays a different amount because the "universal" tax rate is different; in the second, one person pays a different amount because his/her income changed, although the rate of taxation is the same.

Similarly, if the desire for oats is universally stronger, the amount of oats consumers are willing to buy will be greater at all price levels. That is different than having the price of oats change and adjusting the amount one buys, given a certain liking or disliking for oats. Notice: price is *not* the causal factor pushing up demand after the doctors publicize their results; consumer preference is. But when we discuss changes in purchases according to the law of demand, price *is* the causal factor.

A decrease in demand

Demand can fall as easily as it can rise. There are zillions of familiar cases when it does so: the demand for Christmas trees in January, for bathing suits in September, for roses after Valentine's Day. Let's examine a decrease in demand.

What if by some crazy confluence of the stars, buyers in the market reduced their demand for gasoline? What would be the effect on market prices and the number of units purchased? Both would fall in this case, the reverse of price and quantity trends when demand rises. The schedules in Table 4-4 and its companion diagram depict the changes.

Consumers buy a reduced amount at every price. There might be several reasons why consumers would decide to reduce their demand but, regardless, the shift in the demand shown in Diagram 4-4 and the adjustments on the schedule would appear similar to this example: a fall in demand will always shift the entire curve to the left.

What's most important at this stage is to clarify the meaning of a change in demand. That phrase refers very specifically to a change in the willingness of the consumer(s) to obtain desired goods. A change in demand can be properly illustrated only by drawing two curves, since demand itself refers to the series of price-quantity combinations depicted by a single curve.

DISTINGUISHING INDIVIDUAL AND MARKET DEMAND

We can describe a price-quantity relationship for a particular product with respect to a particular individual or to a group of them. We will, throughout the book, need to use demand curves for both purposes. When the demand is said to represent a collective consumer demand, we'll generally use the phrase **market demand** to convey the idea.

Basically, the market demand is said to be equal to the demand of all the individuals put together. Table 4-5 is an illustration. The graphs in Diagram 4-5, a-d make it clear that the market's demand curve is a summation of quantities, not prices.

Nothing fancy went on here. It's clear that Mary, Bill, and Sam have different patterns of buying this product. Mary likes it best presumably, although other factors might account for the higher quantity figures that her demand schedule indicates. Meanwhile, Sam

Demand Schedule (before)		Demand Schedule (after)	
Price	Quantity (gal.)	Price	Quantity (gal.)
$ .90	650	$ .90	580
$ .93	645	$ .93	575
$ .96	640	$ .96	570
$ .99	635	$ .99	565
$1.02	630	$1.02	560
$1.05	625	$1.05	555
$1.08	620	$1.08	550
$1.11	615	$1.11	545
$1.14	610	$1.14	540
$1.17	605	$1.17	535
$1.20	600	$1.20	530

Table 4-4

A Fall in Demand for Gas

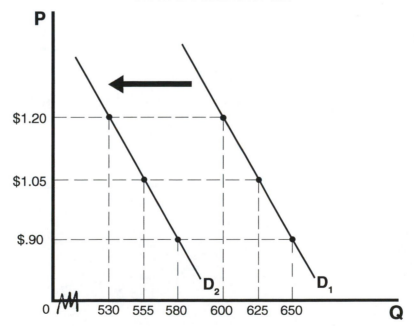

Diagram 4-4

Mary's		+	Bill's		+	Sam's		=	Market	
P	Q		P	Q		P	Q		P	Q
4	20		4	10		4	15		4	45
5	18		5	9		5	12		5	39
6	16		6	8		6	9		6	33
7	14		7	7		7	6		7	27
8	12		8	6		8	3		8	21

Table 4-5

From Individual to Market Demand

(a)

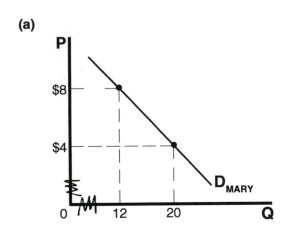

(b)

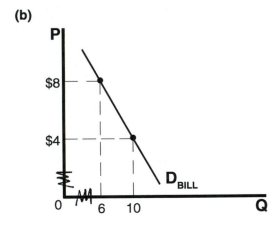

(c)

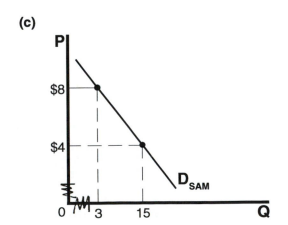

(d)

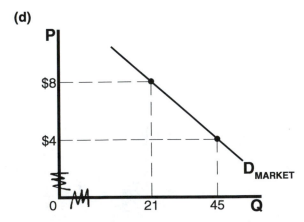

Diagram 4-5,a-d

is more sensitive to the influence of price changes than either Mary or Bill. We can see this from the fact that for every dollar change in price, Sam varies his purchase by 3 units.

More important is the way market demand is constructed on the basis of the three individuals. We calculate the market demand by adding each individual's **quantity demanded** at specific prices. Thus, we added 20, 10 and 15 to get the market's quantity demanded of 45 at a price of 4. We added 18, 9 and 12 to get the quantity demanded of 39 at a price of 5--and so on.

Prices, on the other hand, do not vary across the four schedules: the prices the individuals face in the market are, of course, market prices, so no alteration is necessary.

FACTORS WHICH SHIFT THE DEMAND CURVE

It would be nice if product prices were the only influence on consumer demand. Economics would be much easier in that case. But prices are just one of several factors which can alter demand conditions in a market. Economists collectively call those factors the **determinants of demand**. They include (but aren't necessarily limited to) five key ones whose effects on demand we will study closely: consumer preferences, income, the number of buyers in the market, the prices of related goods, and the expectations of consumers regarding future prices.

Number of buyers

Suppose in the year 2004 Mary, Bill, and Sam (same people!) comprised the entire market. But one

Former Market Demand		+	Joe		+	Kay		=	New Market Demand	
P	Q		P	Q		P	Q		P	Q
4	45		4	30		4	17		4	92
5	39		5	25		5	16		5	80
6	33		6	20		6	15		6	68
7	27		7	15		7	14		7	56
8	21		8	10		8	13		8	44

Table 4-6

An Increase in Demand Due to a Larger Number of Buyers

Diagram 4-6

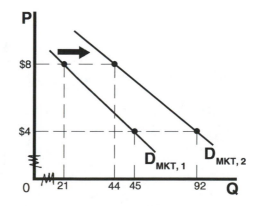

year later, two new consumers entered. Clearly the demand in the market would rise. The extent of the rise would depend on the strength of the demand of the two new individuals. If their demand schedules were like the ones in Table 4-6, then the market's demand would increase accordingly.

If the addition of consumers to the market raises market demand, then logically the exit of consumers from a market would reduce demand, ceteris paribus. Picking up from the new market demand from Table 4-6, suppose Bill (from Mary, Bill, and Sam) dropped out, then the following adjustments would be seen on the schedule and graph.

The graphic result is again most logical. Since a

rise in demand implies a rightward shift, then a leftward shift depicts a reduced demand. The schedule makes literal what the graph conveys: less would be purchased at every price. As before, these adjustments to the picture and schedule will apply regardless of the cause of the demand shift.

Consumer preferences

Some people like eggs; others avoid them. Some go for flashy clothes, but all of us know a plain Jane. Some people listen to classical music; others want just pure rock and roll. According to economists, consumers have a decent idea as to what they prefer when they enter the market: people tend to rank their preferences.

Market Demand w/Bill		-	Bill		=	Market Demand w/o Bill	
P	Q		P	Q		P	Q
4	92		4	10		4	82
5	80		5	9		5	71
6	68		6	8		6	60
7	56		7	7		7	49
8	44		8	6		8	38

Table 4-7

A Fall in Demand Due to a Drop in the Numbers of Buyers

Diagram 4-7

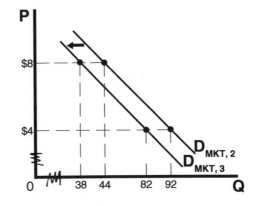

When consumers arrive at the market and see what vendors actually have available, they then take note of prices. Shoppers look for bargains, but some bargains aren't worth it because the product is not to the buyer's liking. Thus, prices and preferences together influence the choice of a given purchase.

But of course, preferences change. It is a rare woman or man who buys the same sort of clothes throughout her or his life. We find new pastimes to enjoy--travelling, for instance--and begin to purchase products appropriate for the new activity. Even during the day one's inclinations can change, so that a person who said no to ice cream in the afternoon might turn around and buy it in the evening (even though the price was the same). Perhaps the preferences of individuals fluctuate continuously.

How shall we incorporate preference changes into our developing account of demand-side forces? The preferred means is to tell a story.

Suppose we are given a demand schedule for Susan. Suppose it represents Susan's demand for a popular breakfast cereal. Then Table 4-8 and Diagram 4-8 fit the bill.

Suppose this cereal were made of oats and that Susan was very health conscious. When the doctors released the results of their cancer study, which showed that oats were particularly beneficial for diminishing the risk of cancer, Susan switched from an occasional buyer of oat flakes to a frequent buyer. If we make the proper alterations to her demand schedule, they would resemble those in Table 4-9.

Demand Schedule/Curve for Cereal

Price	Quantity
$2.15	1
$1.85	2
$1.55	3
$1.25	4
$.95	5

Table 4-8

The Effect of an Increased Preference on Demand

Price	Quantity
$3.05	1
$2.75	2
$2.45	3
$2.15	4
$1.85	5

Table 4-9

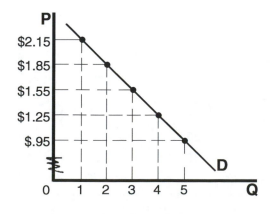

Diagram 4-8

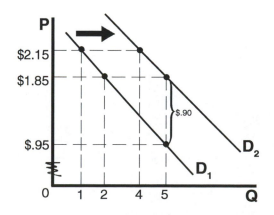

Diagram 4-9

The increase in demand is indicated by the higher (per unit) prices Susan would be willing to pay. In this case, the amount happens to work out to 90 cents more per box. Diagram 4–9 conveys this in a manner consistent with the example of increased demand when new consumers enter the market.

Of course, preferences can change in the opposite direction. If the doctors had reported that oats cause cancer, rather than prevent it, the same oats cereal would have fallen even further into Susan's disfavor. Then changes like those seen on Table 4–10 and Diagram 4–10 would have been in order.

The Effect of a Diminished Preference

Price	Quantity
$1.25	1
$.95	2
$.65	3
$.35	4
$.05	5

Table 4-10

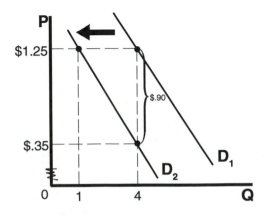

Diagram 4-10

The table and graph plainly indicate Susan's decrease in demand due to a weaker preference for the product. The graph is, again, consistent with the earlier example of reduced demand.

Income

It should be equally obvious that a person's earnings would highly influence the demand he or she has for a product. A multi-millionaire can easily afford what average wage earners cannot. Thus, changes in income certainly produce changes in demand.

Suppose, then, a person of average salary earns a promotion at work. The promotion entails a $5000/year increase over his/her present income. What would we conclude about this person's demand for, say, air flights? Or meals at restaurants? Or high fidelity stereo equipment? The intuitive answer is that the demand for these items would rise. Of course, no economist would dare contradict such pure common sense.

Now we need to reflect on that assessment. If we're considering Sam's demand for clothing (say, dress shirts) both before and after the salary increase, then the following demand schedules would convey our common sense.

Demand for Shirts Before Raise		Demand for Shirts After Raise	
P	Q	P	Q
$15	7	$25	7
14	8	23	8
13	9	21	9
12	10	19	10
11	11	17	11
10	12	15	12
9	13	13	13
8	14	11	14

Table 4-11

Sam's Increased Demand Due to Higher Income

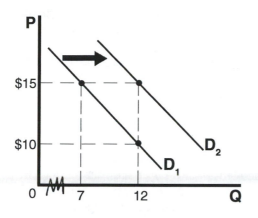

Diagram 4-11

What would be the consequence of a fall in income? For the same dress shirts, we'd anticipate a decrease in demand in line with the degree of decrease in income. The demand curve would shift left to convey the idea.

normal and inferior goods

Thus, we typically expect consumers to adjust their purchases in the same direction as the change in income. Whenever this is the case, as we assumed for dress shirts, the good is considered to be a **normal good**. For all normal goods, demand rises when income climbs; it falls when income declines.

But not all goods are normal. Certain goods--for instance, used cars--have a demand which moves in the reverse direction of the income change. Used cars will be in demand *less* when income rises, and *more* should income fall. Any product similar to used cars in this respect is classified as an **inferior good**. Let's develop an example more fully.

Certain brands of beer are inferior goods, though it may be difficult for the average college student to see why. Nonetheless, when an individual graduates from college, and begins to earn a regular salary from a "real" job, he or she will probably have a *decreased* demand for Label XYZ beer. With greater income the person will more likely quaff the finer brews, which weren't so easily affordable in college. The following

pair of demand schedules capture this change. The student should (soberly) draw the appropriate diagram.

Demand for XYZ Beer During College		Demand for XYZ Beer After College	
P	Q	P	Q
	(six pack per week)		
$4	10	$4	.5
3.50	11	3.50	1
3	12	3	1.5
2.50	13	2.50	2
2	14	2	2.5

Table 4-12

Implicitly we know that as income rises and the demand for the inferior product diminishes, the consumer is choosing some other product, a normal good, in its place, ceteris paribus. Thus, one can infer that income changes set off a simultaneous shift in demand for two goods, one normal, the other inferior.[1]

Yet another possibility remains. Suppose our hungover college student, dissatisfied with his first real job and post-collegiate income, decided to return to graduate school with hopes of acquiring a specialized degree and even greater income further down the road. In that case, income would immediately fall, the demand for the finer beers will slacken, and the demand for XYZ beer, peanut butter and jelly sandwiches, and other assorted inferior goods would *rise*. Such is the opportunity cost of graduate school.

Expectations concerning future prices

If we can assume that consumers are trying to make the most of every dollar they earn, then we can reasonably say that consumers will try to anticipate events of the future in order to gauge the right time to buy. In other words, consumers will, at least to some extent, try to time their purchases for maximum benefit.

---

[1] Eventually the reader should come to see that we needn't always record exact prices and quantities on the graph to make the point that demand has increased or decreased. Truly, the picture says a thousand words.

For instance, a woman might see a pocketbook that she likes selling for $35 currently. Feeling that it is a fair price, she buys the pocketbook. But if she were to find out that just one week after her purchase the same store had a sale on the same pocketbook, she would certainly feel as though she had lost out. She did, in fact: if the sale price were $25 dollars, then the woman's mistaken impression that there would be no sale had an opportunity cost of about $10.[2]

But now suppose the lady saw the pocketbook but had asked a clerk to see it. While they conversed, the very polite sales-person informed the lady that the item would be priced at $25 *next* week. The woman would be, consequently, less apt to buy the pocketbook that very day. This implies that her current demand for the good was reduced.

More generally, any time consumers *expect* that tomorrow's price will be lower than today's, their present demand for the product will decrease. This we see in Diagram 4-12. The extent of the reduction in present demand would depend on the length of time one expects to wait for the price reduction, the opportunity cost of postponing enjoyment of the good in the meantime, and the size of the monetary saving expected.

Effects of Changes in Expectations on Demand

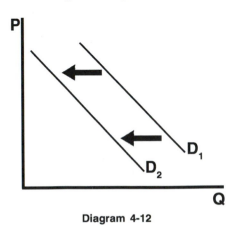

Diagram 4-12

Conversely, if consumers hear that tomorrow prices will be higher, then today's demand will rise, since consumers perceive *today's* price to be relatively low.

expectations and financial markets

Financial markets--which include the markets for stocks, bonds, currencies, and futures contracts--offer a constant reminder of the power of agents' expectations to influence market demand and, ultimately, market prices. Financial markets are those in which "investors" buy paper assets, like stocks or bonds, with the prospect of accumulating wealth. Let's consider an example of how changes in expectations can affect the purchases of stock.

Suppose we had some spare money and, rather than place it in a bank, we decided to look into purchasing stock. Our attention is drawn to a particular corporation named BIG, Inc., a maker of giant rubber bands. While we conduct our research into the business, the price of the company's shares is $45. If we were to purchase the shares at this price, we would hold the particular hope that the shares' price will rise. If it did, we would sell, and thereby reap a reward called a **capital gain**.

After a week, we decide to follow through and purchase BIG shares. But then on our way to the brokers' office we hear a radio report that tells of an ongoing feud in management, a drop in company sales, and the company's increasing tardiness in paying its bills. How do we react?

Clearly the news suggests that the company is in trouble; in that case, the value of an individual share is likely to decline--or so we would expect. As a result, we change our mind. We turn around and put the money in the bank after all.

The news over the radio changed our expectations regarding the direction of the price of BIG shares in the future: we turned from optimist to pessimist, or from bull to bear in Wall Street lingo. Either way we put it, the picture looks the same: a shift to the left of the demand curve.

---

[2] Actually, a little less than $10 since she did use the item for a week and that usage represents some value to the woman.

Of course, a change in expectations can raise the demand for a company's paper assets. Suppose your economics teacher appears on a prominent weekly financial news program and declares that the price of company Z's shares will climb 100% within the next six months. If enough people accept this prophecy (sophistry?), then the market demand for company Z's shares will soar, leading to the *realization* of the *expected* higher share price.

This second example highlights the self-fulfilling nature of expectations as they play themselves out in the decisions and purchases of market agents. Should everyone expect an asset's price to rise, it almost certainly will rise because, in financial markets especially, purchasers will direct their dollars towards those assets which they perceive as having a strong potential for capital appreciation.

Equally important, the very fact that expectations *can* and *do* influence market events should not seem strange, for the principle of self-fulfilling expectations applies to life itself: if we expect to get an A in economics, we will more likely conduct ourselves in a manner which realizes that outcome; and if we expect to fail, we tend to "prepare" for that, too, making the undesirable result all the more probable. In the final analysis, it should surprise no one that principles of human psychology manifest themselves in the economic sphere, for economics is, at bottom, a science of human behavior.

Prices of related goods

Throughout these first few chapters, we have emphasized the role of relative prices in the market. Relative prices guide the consumer and the entrepreneur to a production and purchasing equilibrium. But a relative price implies a comparison between the prices of *two* goods. And these two goods must somehow be related.

Most, if not all, of the products we buy as consumers bear some relation to other goods. We use the goods we buy either in combination with some other product or in place of another product. Products used jointly somehow are called **complements** of each other. Goods used in place of another are called **substitutes**. Examples of each group are plentiful. Belts and pants are complementary goods, as are tennis balls and tennis rackets. But apple pie and cherry pie are substitutes. So are whole milk and skim.

It's possible through economic analysis to relate the price of any single good and the *demand* for the good with which it is associated. Thus, the price of tennis rackets affects the demand for tennis balls. The

The Effect of Rising Coffee Prices on Demand for Cream

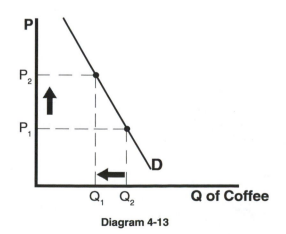

Diagram 4-13

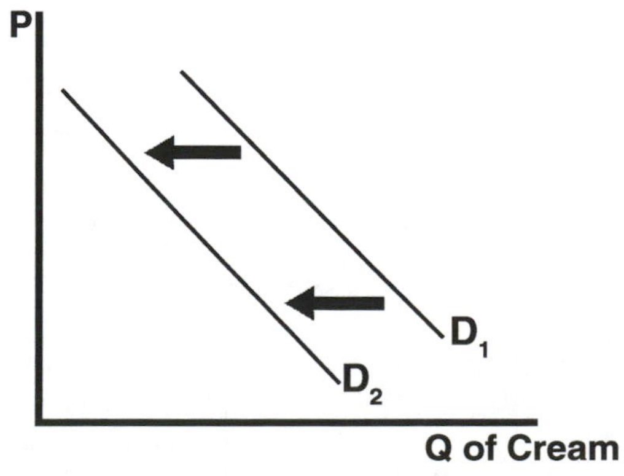

Diagram 4-14

price of video cameras influences the demand for VCR's. Meanwhile, the price of beer can affect the demand for wine and the price of orange juice can alter the demand for grape juice.

complements

Let's consider the complementary goods cream and coffee. If a leap in the price of coffee occurred, the law of demand suggests that less coffee will be purchased. But if less coffee is bought and drunk, consumers will have less inclination to purchase cream, ceteris paribus. Thus, *the increase in the price of coffee leads to a decrease in the demand for cream.*

Now, if the prices of coffee were to *fall*, exactly the opposite reaction would be induced: *consumers would* purchase *more* cream since the lower coffee prices would bring an increase in the amount of coffee purchased. (The student should draw the appropriate diagrams for this case.)

These two examples with coffee and cream demonstrate that with respect to *complementary goods, the relationship between price changes and changes in demand is inverse: when the price of one good rises, the demand for the other falls; when the price of one good slumps, the demand for the other rises.* The inverse relation is highlighted by the directional arrows in Table 4–13.

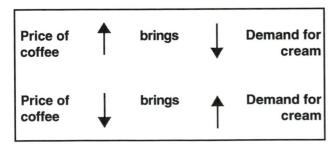

Table 4-13

For practice, let's consider another pair of goods: camcorders and VCR's. If the price of camcorders rose, then the demand for VCR's would fall; if the price of camcorders fell, then the demand for VCR's would rise.

Fair enough. By the same token, the basic inverse relation is preserved even if the positions of the goods were switched. So if we say that the demand for *VCR's* will fall when *camcorder* prices rise (because the goods are complementary), then we can equally well say that the demand for *camcorders* will fall if the price of *VCR's* should rise. This example goes to show that the inverse relation between price changes and demand changes is (partially) *symmetrical*, as Table 4–14 highlights.[3]

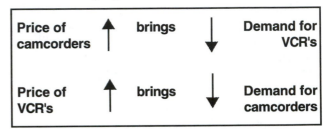

Table 4-14

The arrows head in opposite directions, irrespective of which good experiences the price ascent, and *that* establishes the paired goods' complementarity. (Some questions which follow this chapter will consider similar aspects of the relationship between complementary goods.)

substitutes

We've just seen that when a pair of goods is complementary, a change in the price of one good causes an inverse shift in the demand for the other good. We also know that complementary and substitute goods bear an opposite relation to each other: the former are used together; the latter represent goods alternately chosen.

So given these things, it would be logical to think that with respect to substitute goods the price–demand relation is *positive*. And that's exactly right. Thus, if the price of coffee rose, the demand for tea would increase; and if the price of coffee fell, then the demand for tea would fall too. Diagrams 4–15 and 4–16 and Table 4–15 depict the relationships in various ways.

---

[3] The symmetry discussed here concerns the *direction*, not the *degree* or strength, of the changes.

The Effect of Rising Coffee Prices on the Demand for Tea

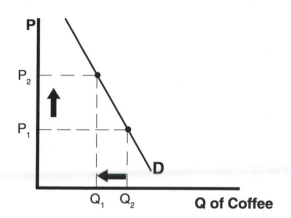

Diagram 4-15

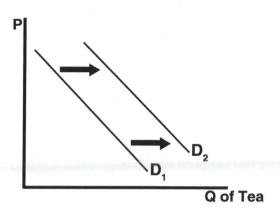

Diagram 4-16

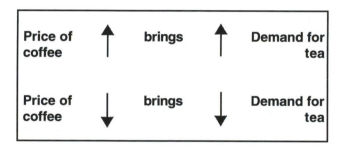

Table 4-15

We could reverse the places of coffee and tea, but we'd still wind up with a positive relation. So, if the price of tea rose, the demand for coffee would increase; and if the price of tea fell, the demand for coffee would decrease.

The role of substitute goods in the marketplace cannot be over-emphasized. We cannot, however, cover in one chapter all the subtle lessons of the market-place which are attributable to the availability of substitutes. Suffice it to say that many upcoming topics concern substitutability, including elasticity, competition and market structure, consumer theory, equilibrium concepts, and more. And most of these topics tiein with something already discussed, namely relative prices. Truly, an entire text is needed to cover all the related issues.

CONCLUSION

In the end, the vocabulary from this chapter matters most. Two terms take precedence over all others here: demand and quantity demanded. The distinction is worth some review.

Three ways to distinguish demand from quantity demanded

a set of numbers vs. a number

Let's take again a simple demand schedule, the one shown on Table 4-16.

Price	Quantity
$ 9	100
$ 10	95
$ 11	90
$ 12	85
$ 13	80
$ 14	75
$ 15	70

Table 4-16

The table of prices and quantities allows us to draw a unique demand curve. This is what economists have in mind when they say "demand." *Demand, then, refers to an entire set of price and quantity combinations.* Demand refers to the curve, or the schedule, not to any particular number under the quantity column, nor to any particular pairing of price and quantity.

"Quantity demanded" is the more narrow concept. Table 4–16 lists seven quantity demanded figures, from 100 to 70. Each quantity demanded attaches itself to a particular price. So, *quantity demanded is simply a number, an amount of units bought given a certain price.* If the price were $15, then 70 units would be purchased by those in the market. If the price were $12, those same consumers would have bought 85. And so on. Notice: each quantity demanded, like each price, is hypothetical. (In the real world, at any given time and place, there could be only one price per good, not seven.)

distinguishing price as a cause and effect

As we use the table and change the hypothetical price of a good, we implicitly assume ceteris paribus conditions. Thus, the reason why customers decide to buy 85 instead of 70, or 100 rather than 85, has to do with price changes. *Whenever a change in the price motivates a change in the amount purchased, then we are thinking in terms of quantity demanded, not demand.*

Price changes do not affect "demand," per se; that is, they do not shift the curve. Only those factors other than the good's own price (income, preferences, etc.) can potentially shift the curve, i.e., raise or reduce demand. When those factors change, we can then correctly speak of a "change in demand," when *every* hypothetical price and quantity combination gets re-written.

Such a change in demand will affect the market's price. But in this case price changes occur as a consequence, not a cause, of changes in the patterns of consumer purchases. Christmas tree prices escalate in November and December not because they cost more to produce at that time or because there's less competition in the market; rather, demand is asserting itself so as to change prices and quantities sold.

the law of demand

Connected to the idea of cause and effect is the very idea of the law of demand. When discussing a change in some good's price, and claiming the change has an effect on the amount of items purchased, we make an explicit appeal to the law of demand. That law means, of course, that the number of items bought changes--inversely--due to price changes. Clearly, this sort of change involves quantity demanded, not the broader concept of demand. Indeed, if a genuine change in demand occurs, there is no test of the law of demand, because, once again, the change in consumer purchases stems from a factor other than the good's own price.

Attaining a mastery of the vocabulary of economics equips the student with the essential tools for analyzing market trends. But as with any language skill, practice and perseverance are paramount in achieving that mastery. The distinction between demand and quantity demanded cannot be mastered, let alone appreciated, without an effort on your part to apply, very consciously, these key terms.

VOCABULARY

Demand – a set of price and quantity pairings, descriptive of consumer purchasing patterns in the market

- (a) *demand schedule* – refers to the table of price-quantity pairs
- (b) *market demand* – refers to the combined demand of individual consumers
- (c) *determinants of demand* – factors affecting consumer demand

Quantity demanded – the (hypothetical) amount of units purchased by a consumer, or group of them, at a specific price

Normal good – a good whose demand changes in the same direction as a change in income

Inferior good – a good whose demand moves in the opposite direction of a change in income.

Capital gain – the increase arising from the market's re-valuation of an asset; refers to stocks, bonds, and assorted financial assets

Substitutes – goods used in place of each other

Complements – goods used jointly

END OF CHAPTER QUESTIONS

1. Can you think of any other factors which could shift the demand curve, i.e., any other determinants of demand? Consider whether some suggestions you have might be covered by the five mentioned in the chapter or whether they're genuinely distinct. Discuss.

2. Consider the complementary goods tennis balls and tennis rackets. Suppose the price of tennis rackets doubles. What would happen to the demand for tennis balls? Would the effect be strong or weak? Why?

3. Consider and discuss other pairs of complementary goods and work through the same set of questions as in #2; examples: pizza and beer, movies and popcorn, gym club memberships and athletic apparel, cars and gas.

4. Suppose the price of cars doubles. What would happen to the demand for bicycles? Would the effect be strong or weak? Why?

Do the same exercise for these substitute goods: margarine and butter, long distance phone service and stamps for first class postage.

5. Illustrate on separate graphs the effect of a drop in personal income on the demand for an inferior good and a normal good.

6. At a department store, a voice suddenly breaks through the muzak to announce, "We have a blue dot special going on in the women's department...For the next fifteen minutes you can buy cotton blouses for just $9.99!"

Will this induce a change in demand or a change in quantity demanded? Why?

7. True or false and explain: Desire = Demand.

8. At the local restaurant, the menu is the same for lunch and dinner, and all service is buffet style. Lunch is $6.95, but dinner is $10.95. What accounts for the difference?

MOCK TEST

1. Briefly discuss the relationship between scarcity and opportunity cost.

2. Are the following goods scarce according to the economist's use of the term? Explain.

   a) tap water
   b) bottled water
   c) breathable air
   d) Maps of the U.S. in the U.S.
   e) Maps of South America in the U.S.
   f) Maps of Jupiter in the U.S.
   g) pencils
   h) cars

3. Invent a story which helps explain how price expectations can affect market demand.

4. Of the following two, which schedule represents demand?

P	Q	P	Q
5	14	5	22
6	16	6	20
7	18	7	18
8	20	8	16
9	22	9	14

5. What things could conceivably lead to a rise in demand? List four and briefly explain each. Draw a single graph which depicts a rise in demand, being clear about the price and quantity effects.

CHAPTER 5

THE SUPPLY SIDE OF THE MARKET

In order to understand the economist's view of the market's **supply** side, we must once again return to the concept of scarcity. The link between scarcity and supply has to do with costs. In a nutshell, we'll see from this chapter that it's usually possible for companies to produce more of a good, say, if demand were to rise. But within any given stretch of time, there's a limit. Moreover, as a given firm's production limit is approached, new output usually entails an increasing *per unit* cost. To convey this lesson, we will need to think carefully about the efficiency of production. We will use several examples that illustrate a link between productivity and costs, together leading to the law of supply.

After all that is complete, we can discuss the determinants of supply in much the same manner that we examined the determinants of demand.

THE LAW OF SUPPLY

Demand slopes down and to the right, a relation which seems eminently intuitive. Supply slopes up and to the right, an idea which needs a bit more explanation.

Inputs and outputs

Anything that gets produced by a firm requires the real expenditure of resources; i.e., land, labor, or capital must be sacrificed in order to deliver a good to market. The very idea that resources must be employed for production suggests a certain relation between resource usage and output: productive inputs, the resources, generate output with a certain efficiency, or productivity.

Productivity is everywhere. An orchestra practices umpteen hours to prepare for a performance. Its efforts in rehearsal contribute positively to the quality of its output. Students must spend time in order to do well on tests and the amount of time spent in study (input) correlates highly to points scored (output) on tests. Manufacturing firms modernize their factories in order to improve the efficiency of production.

But during any *given* input-output process, productivity seldom runs a constant course. Instead it varies. It varies precisely because limits to production exist, which is to say, the productivity of inputs is also limited. We cannot expect machinery to operate at the speed of light and provide us with more toys, teapots, and televisions than we could ever possibly want. That, after all, would mean the end of scarcity.

the efficiency of a car

We are going to consider a familiar example of an input-output relation that exhibits a variable productivity trend. Our example is that of a car, the input to which is gasoline. The illustration is not, obviously, about producing for the market. We're steering away from the market for the time being only because that permits us to see the input-output relation outside the complications of market forces. We will develop an analogy to production for the market with a second example.

The heart of an automobile is its engine. Manufacturers today make engines that can reach 120 miles per hour(mph), is their absolute limit. The components of the engine and the laws of physics don't permit anything faster, at least for the standard automobile.

When a car speeds at 120 mph, it isn't performing

The Productivity of Gas Usage, 0 to 120 mph

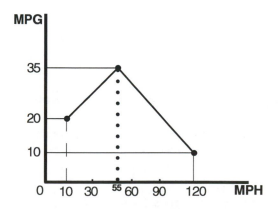

Diagram 5-1

at peak efficiency. The strain on the engine is quite severe. Its consumption of gas is relatively high. Clearly, a car travelling at top speed would have a relatively low miles per gallon(mpg).

Today's cars get their highest mpg at 55 mph. This implies that the productivity, or efficiency, of the car's use of gas peaks at 55 mph. Beyond that point the productivity of gas consumption trails off; before that point the productivity of gas consumption improves steadily. Diagram 5-1 traces this variable trend in mpg against velocities zero to 120 mph.

the cost trend

Now if efficiency increases, then costs decline; and if efficiency decreases, costs rise. This is why firms continually seek for more efficient means to produce goods: costs decline and thereby leave the firm with more profit, all other things being equal.

Since cost trends run opposite to productivity trends, a chart showing the costs of running a car at speeds zero to 120 would flip Diagram 5-1 on its head. The lowest per mile cost of operating the car occurs at 55 mph. The per mile cost dives initially; but beyond 55 mph, gas costs climb quickly. All this

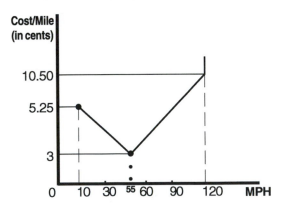

Per Mile Gas Costs, 0 to 120 mph
Diagram 5-2

is seen in Diagram 5-2.

The point here goes beyond the inverse relation between productivity and costs. The illustration shows that it's possible to get greater velocity, or

"output," from an automobile, given the technology of the engine.[1] But greater speed implies a varying rate of "efficiency" and therefore, too, a changing rate of costs. Beyond a certain point (55mph), the greater demands placed on the engine incur rising costs per unit of "output." Hence, we would not be able to run the engine full blast and operate the vehicle cheaply at the same time.

Expanding markets and rising costs

The rising costs associated with increased output constitute the most direct link between a firm's contribution to market output and market prices. Just as the rising demand placed on the car's engine at speeds greater than 55 mph leads to rising gas payments, greater demand for goods and services tends to lead to increasing use of a firm's resources. Thus, companies frequently confront higher costs as they attempt to satisfy the expanding desires of consumers. The following example tries to clarify this link.

Let's suppose that the market for fast foods is experiencing a gradual, measurable, positive growth in demand. Additionally, let's assume that the pool of labor which works in the fast food industry is fully employed. In a robust economy, these conditions will hold, roughly speaking, in many parts of the country.

Now suppose a major fast food chain decides to build a new outlet in an area where growth is particularly strong. Once the building is complete, where will the business find labor to operate the establishment? If the potential pool of workers is gainfully employed already, how will the firm get people to flip hamburgers and take orders?

In a competitive market for resources as we've described, the firm has but one recourse to attract workers: higher wages. More attractive wages can induce workers to switch from their present positions to newer ones opening up due to growing industry output.

---

[1] To be complete, we'd have to define a certain gasoline type or octane level as well.

But what would that imply about the price of the service, e.g., the typical hamburger, french fries, and soda, provided by the firm? Clearly, the price of its service will tend to rise. Market prices will sooner or later have to reflect the underlying resource cost trend stemming from the increasing demand on inputs. It's practically inevitable.

Perhaps the best example of cost–price–output connection occurs when the only alternative for a firm in a booming industry is to offer overtime pay to its workers in order to keep apace of swelling demand for its product. Whether it's time and a half or double time is immaterial: the extra units of production cost more to produce *per unit* than previous output.

These cost trends, therefore, mimic the trend in higher costs for operating a car at speeds greater than 55 mph. Progressively higher output, performance, or production, run into progressively higher input costs, because, in the final analysis, the availability and productivity of those resources are limited.

So finally we can state the law of supply: *on the producers' side of the market, prices and quantities are positively related.* Higher prices act partly as an inducement for firms to deliver goods to market; but even more essential, they compensate firms for added and often accelerating expenses associated with increased production.

Supply schedule and graph

The positive relation can be easily illustrated. As with demand, we can draw up a **supply schedule** of prices and quantities. Below is a schedule for sneakers.

Once again, the *concept* behind the supply schedule must be distinguished from the numbers listed in the quantity column. By "supply," economists have in mind the entire series of prices *and* quantities exhibited in the table. We can depict the supply relation with a supply curve like the one shown in Diagram 5-3. On the other hand, the number of units which are sold by a firm, or by the market generally, is called the **quantity supplied**. Quantity supplied is always referenced by a specific price, so that in Table 5-1, 21 represents the quantity of sneakers supplied at $70; at $90, quantity supplied swells to 27. Quantity supplied is a number; supply is a set of paired numbers, i.e., a relation.

A CHANGE IN SUPPLY: A SHIFT IN THE CURVE

An increase in supply

Since supply refers to the entire relationship between prices and quantities, an increase in supply refers to a shift in the entire supply curve shown in Diagram 5-3. Let's draw up a new schedule in order to understand the basis of this shift.

Supply Schedule

Price	Quantity
$50	15
$60	18
$70	21
$80	24
$90	27

Table 5-1

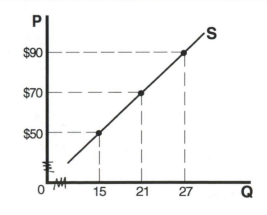

Diagram 5-3

Sneaker Supply (Before)		Sneaker Supply (After)		Corn Supply (Before)		Corn Supply (After)	
P	Q	P	Q	P	Q	P	Q
$50	15	$50	24	$1.50	2500	$1.50	1700
60	18	60	27	1.75	2600	1.75	1800
70	21	70	30	2.00	2700	2.00	1900
80	24	80	33	2.25	2800	2.25	2000
90	27	90	36	2.50	2900	2.50	2100

Table 5-2   Table 5-2

An Increase in the Supply of Sneaks

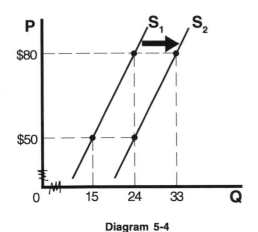

Diagram 5-4

A Decrease in the Supply of Corn

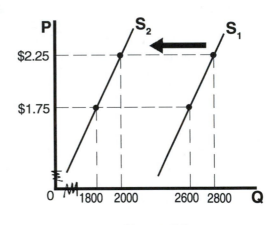

Diagram 5-5

Table 5-2 indicates that firms are willing to deliver more goods to market *at every single price on the schedule.* There could be any number of reasons for this, but regardless of the source of the change, the supply curve shifts to the right. That would be the only possible way to convey the very meaning of an expanded supply.

A rightward shift represented an increase in demand also. So we can develop a simple rule of thumb for illustrating an increase in either supply or demand: each *rises to the right.*

A decrease in supply

Now, the other case: a decrease in supply. We

discussed an instance of a decrease in supply in chapter iii when we considered the effects of a drought on corn production. Few examples could be so clear cut.

The market supply of corn is reduced since arid conditions prevented proper germination and reduced crop yield. The new supply schedule indicates that less corn is available at every price. The supply curve shifts to the left to reflect the change. Indeed, any shift to the left would indicate a decrease in supply, irrespective of the reason.

Thus, the supply curve can move as a demand curve--either to the right or left--and the direction of the shift has the same interpretation in either case:

DISTINGUISHING INDIVIDUAL FROM MARKET SUPPLY

to the right is an increase; to the left is a decrease.

The market is composed of individuals and on the supply side this means individual firms or entrepreneurs. The broad market supply will be calculated by simply adding the quantity supplied from each firm at the various prices. This is the same procedure we used for demand. Three hypothetical firm-supply schedules appear in Table 5-4, together with the market schedule. The corresponding graphs in Diagram 5-6 a-d, also illustrate the relation between the firm-supply and market supply.

Jane's Juice		+	Jerry's Juice		+	Jim's Juice		=	Juice Market	
P	Q		P	Q		P	Q		P	Q
2.50	3		2.50	7		2.50	5		2.50	15
2.55	4		2.55	9		2.55	8		2.55	21
2.60	5		2.60	11		2.60	11		2.60	27
2.65	6		2.65	13		2.65	14		2.65	33
2.70	7		2.70	15		2.70	17		2.70	39

Table 5-4

From Individual to Market Supply

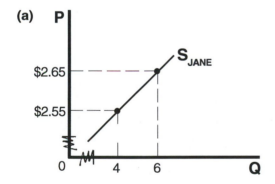

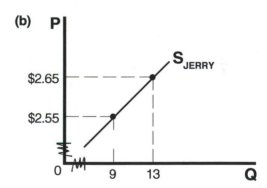

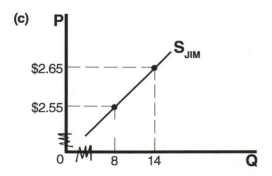

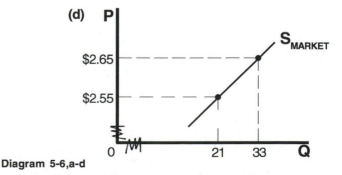

Diagram 5-6,a-d

FACTORS WHICH SHIFT THE SUPPLY CURVE

Supply in a specific market is rarely the same year in, year out. Markets are dynamic: firms leave and enter; costs of resources can suddenly change; new inventions can affect both product and production efficiencies. The list continues. In fact we will now study seven key factors which affect supply, the position of the curve and, hence, market prices and output.

Number of sellers

Any increase in the number of firms will lead to an increase in the number of products delivered to the market *at every price*. We can use supply schedules and curves to see these effects very concretely.

Suppose some entrepreneurs felt opportunities for profit-making were ripe in the just-mentioned juice

Former Market Supply		+	Gene's Juice		+	George's Juice		=	Juice Market	
P	Q		P	Q		P	Q		P	Q
2.50	15		2.50	4		2.50	7		2.50	26
2.55	21		2.55	6		2.55	9		2.55	36
2.60	27		2.60	8		2.60	11		2.60	46
2.65	33		2.65	10		2.65	13		2.65	56
2.70	39		2.70	12		2.70	15		2.70	66

Table 5-5

An Increase in Supply Due to a Larger Number of Firms

Diagram 5-7

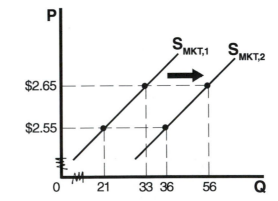

market. They then would feel a strong inclination to enter the market. Suppose two more did so. Table 5-5 and Diagram 5-7 show the results.

Clearly, market supply rose as a consequence of the entrance of new firms. The lesson here is analogous to the idea that the number of buyers helps determine the level of demand and that an increase in the numbers of buyers raises demand. Now, on the supply side, we see not only that the market supply consists of all the individual supplier's output added together at various prices,but also that the entry

of new firms means more output *at every price*.

If a greater number of sellers raises supply, then an exodus of firms will reduce that supply and the curve will shift to the left. Starting from Table 5-5's market supply, suppose Jane and Jim depart. That leaves only Jerry, Gene, and George in the market. Market supply gets commensurately reduced--as seen in Table 5-6 and Diagram 5-8.

The graphic result is very sensible: it follows our "rises to the right, lowers to the left" rule.

Jerry's Juice		+	Gene's Juice		+	George's Juice		=	Juice Market	
P	Q		P	Q		P	Q		P	Q
2.50	7		2.50	4		2.50	7		2.50	18
2.55	9		2.55	6		2.55	9		2.55	24
2.60	11		2.60	8		2.60	11		2.60	30
2.65	13		2.65	10		2.65	13		2.65	36
2.70	15		2.70	12		2.70	15		2.70	42

Table 5-6

A Decrease in Supply Due to Firms' Exodus

Diagram 5-8

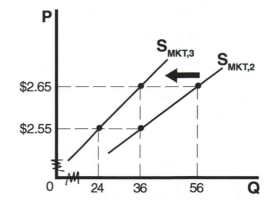

Technology

Modern capitalist market economies have been wondrously prolific in their ability to create new wealth. The catalyst for the new products we enjoy, from computers to compact discs, is advancing scientific and technical know-how. In a very concrete way, technological improvements increase our productive efficiency: we can do more with the same amount of resources.

Some improvements in production can be universally applied. This is indeed the case for advancements like the computer. Diagram 5-9 shows a rise in supply for manufactured goods because computerization creates efficiencies in the production process. Examples include the use of computer design techniques in the car industry, in the airline industry for navigational purposes, even food manufacturing to gain efficiencies in inventory and distributional activities.

An Increase in Supply Due To New Technology

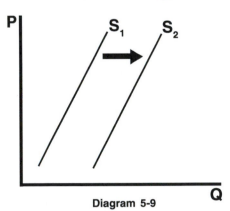

Diagram 5-9

Not all advances apply so generally, however. Not long ago agricultural scientists developed a hormone that could be given to cows with the effect of increasing milk production. Such an advance has no direct effect on, say, cotton production and perhaps none at all on car manufacturing. But the improvement might free up resources, especially land, and bring growth to other markets. For if fewer cows are needed to produce milk, then less land is required for grazing. A bio-technical advancement such as this can be depicted with an increase in supply as in Diagram 5-9, but a specific market (milk in this case) ought to be cited.

Technological advances depend on the progress of science, or the stock of knowledge about the physical universe. Since this stock of knowledge never recedes, we really can't discuss a "decrease in technology." But if there is an opposite case, it might be this: Suppose a firm dependent on capital equipment for production allowed its facilities to age without proper maintenance. We would eventually see a loss in productiveness and a fall in supply because of the effects of usage and wearout. Like a car that must be kept in good working order or its mpg will plummet, factories need to be maintained in order to realize the benefits of whatever technology the capital equipment embodies.

Natural phenomena

Throughout much of the 1980's unusual weather patterns affected agricultural production. Droughts appeared in the Midwest and California; frosts occurred in the Southeast. Each of these areas have specific cash crops on which farmers rely heavily.

A Decrease in Orange Supply Due To Frost

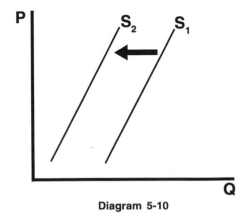

Diagram 5-10

Let's look at the case of orange production in the state of Florida. Five years during the 1980's experienced sub-freezing weather in that state's important orange growing regions. Damage to the crop was pervasive. Yields on some farms fell as much as 50%. Obviously, since this happened to a substantial number of orange growers, the market supply of oranges dropped suddenly. Diagram 5-10 illustrates the effect of the frost.

Of course weather is not always bad. In fact, people involved in agriculture can speak of good years, bad years, and normal years as far as crop yields go. These cases can easily be depicted graphically. Years of a bumper crop will have a supply curve to the far right; drought years, etc. would have supply furthest left; and an average yield, reflecting a normal growing season, would lie in the middle. All this is seen in Diagram 5-11.

Good Years, Bad Years, and in Between

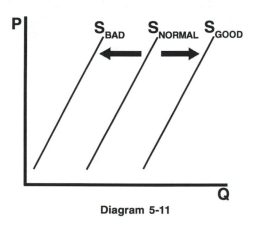

Diagram 5-11

Cost of resources

What about those commodities *made from oranges*, for example, orange juice? Won't that market be similarly affected?

Good question! Orange juice companies would surely have to pay more for oranges as a result of the frost. In that case, whatever dollars have been set aside to sustain production will be inadequate to purchase the same amount of oranges as before. The orange juice firm would find itself in a bind. It could borrow money from a bank so that it could maintain a certain production level and satisfy its customers; but that introduces new interest costs and other opportunity costs which reduce profitability. And if

the firm tried to raise its prices in order to maintain profit, customers would be apt to buy less orange juice. Most likely, the firm would adjust production downward, i.e., purchase fewer oranges and make less orange juice. Diagram 5-12 displays the result, which fits the case for a single firm or the orange juice market overall.

A Decrease in Supply Due To Higher Resource Costs

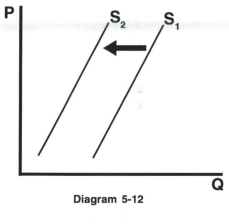

Diagram 5-12

a second case

The case above is fairly straightforward and intuitive. It will be worthwhile to consider one more. A tad more complex, it covers the airline industry through the 70's-80's and brings up the matter of supply in relation to different cases of rising input costs.

Petroleum is a critical input for the production of many things, but nowhere is its role more obvious than in the airline industry. As discussed in chapter iii, the past two decades have seen significant gyrations in the price of oil, fuel, etc. How would the airline industry be affected by these shifting costs?

When oil prices rose in the 1970's, airlines reduced their in-plane services, laid off workers, cut back on the number of flights per day on some routes, and sometimes eliminated routes altogether. The 1970's oil price-spike, by itself, reduced the supply of airline travel. Higher costs reduced airline companies' ability to deliver their services profitably, ceteris paribus.[2]

In the mid-1980's oil prices fell. Airlines increased supply across virtually all routes. Ticket prices fell and the consumers took advantage of the cheaper fares in droves. Good bargains didn't necessarily last forever, however, as other competitive factors forced many firms to drop out of the market. That in turn led to rising prices late in the decade. Still, the logic of falling input costs is the same. Diagram 5-13 below depicts an increased supply of air travel as a consequence of falling oil resource costs, as occurred in the winter of 1985-1986.

Increased Supply Due To Lower Resource Costs

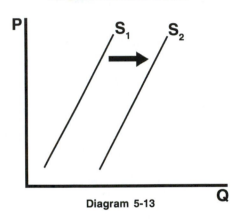

Diagram 5-13

Now, students might at this point detect some inconsistency between the current example of oil price effects on the airline industry and the higher wage resource costs discussed earlier in the chapter. In the present example, oil price changes shift the supply curve *because oil-based fuels are a resource that firms must purchase in order to provide the product.* But before, when we discussed higher wages to attract teenage workers and overtime pay in order to have workers increase a firm's output, there was no shifting supply. In fact, we used those examples to explain the shape of a *single* supply curve--no need for shifting there.

How come?

---

[2] To be sure, all other things were not equal: in particular, President Jimmy Carter allowed for the de-regulation of the airline industry in 1978. Still, higher oil-fuel prices made it more difficult for any airline, established firm or new entrant, to be successful. We will be studying some of the recent history of the airline industry in chapter xxii.

The fact is that these cases are different. To explain the distinction we need to isolate causes from effects.

In the examples which opened the chapter, we spoke in terms of rising production to meet increased consumer purchases. So the source of the market movement was something emanating from the demand side. We even explicitly mentioned growing demand. That would lift product prices, *then* lift resource costs. Higher resource costs are, in that case, an end result.

In the case of rising oil/fuel costs, we assume a given level of demand. We use the ceteris paribus assumption to consider the *consequences* of rising fuel costs. Thus, the change in resource costs becomes the cause of other market fluctuations, not the effect. Now the chain of events will be from costs, to the position of the supply curve, to market prices for the **final good**, to a change in the amount consumers purchase (quantity demanded).

Expectations concerning future prices

How would a supplier react if she came across some information which prompted her to think that the price of the product which she delivers to market will, in the very near future, experience a sudden jump?

This answer is not as obvious as it might seem. We must be clear in our distinction between a firm's *present* supply and what it *anticipates*. Normally, demand and supply curves (or schedules) refer to the present period's actual conditions. Our precise question is, therefore: if a firm anticipated higher product prices "tomorrow," how would it adjust today's offerings to the market, ceteris paribus?

Present supply is liable to fall. For if one were to sell today what could have been sold tomorrow at an even higher price, then in fact, an opportunity for gain will have been lost. If someone sells a Christmas tree on September 15th for $20.00 that could have been sold for $60.00 on December 15th, then she lost the opportunity to gain $40.00. By the same reasoning, if conditions change such that we can expect Christmas tree prices to rise to $100, there's even *less* incentive to sell in September. Thus, any time price increases are expected, a supplier is less likely to deliver her product to market today. This translates into a leftward shift in supply as seen in Diagram 5-14.

Fall in Supply Due To Expectations for Higher Prices

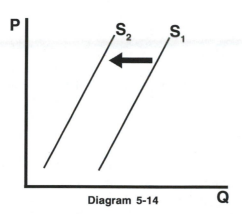

Diagram 5-14

Expectations regarding future prices is a determinant of demand too. In Chapter 4 we looked to the financial markets for examples of changing expectations leading to changes in demand. Now in chapter v, we return to the financial industry to provide us with the best examples for illustrating the common sense behind the connection between expectations and supply.

Suppose a **speculator** in the stock market owns shares in a corporation called SUNSET. Suppose he has heard from a reliable source that SUNSET plans to report to its shareholders next week a disappointing profit result. How would this speculator react, assuming he already holds shares in the corporation?

He's *more* inclined to sell. Loaded with advance information of "market moving" import, he finds himself with an asset whose price, he thinks, will drop. Self-interest compels him to get rid of his shares. But the impetus to sell today is weak if he anticipates a rising share price because the stock value is likely to fall. If the stock price does indeed go south, the price of inaction will be a loss of personal wealth.

Technically speaking then, the speculator raises his supply, indicating a greater willingness to sell, based on the expectation of a price reduction in the future. On a graph, the supply curve would shift to the right.

Tax policy

In 1990, the then governor of the state of New Jersey, Jim Florio, proposed, and successfully engineered through the state legislature, an increase in the state sales tax by 1%. The new levy also broadened the range of products covered by the tax. In particular, paper products, which had been exempt from sales taxes when the rate was 6%, were now assessed a 7% tax.

Many New Jerseyans, perhaps recalling their elementary school lessons about the Boston Tea Party, raised havoc in response to the tax hike. Much attention was drawn to the fact that taxes now had to be paid on toilet paper. Apparently, Governor Florio had touched a sore spot.

What would the effect of such a tax be, economically speaking? Sellers of toilet paper would surely want to raise prices, for if they do not raise the price at all, they will be left with less after-tax revenue and thus less profits. But then the situation becomes similar to the earlier case of higher costs for oranges in the orange juice market: higher prices occasion a decline in the quantity demanded, which might in turn reduce revenues and profits. So regardless of whether the firm absorbs the tax hike or tries to transfer it to consumers, it loses something that it could formerly call its own. Supply will be reduced. The graph would exhibit a leftward shift.

but isn't toilet paper different?

Some might resist this conclusion. Indeed, this example has been included for exactly that reason. Isn't it likely that consumers would buy the same amount of toilet paper as before? Toilet paper is a "necessity," right? And if they bought the same amount of toilet paper, couldn't firms selling toilet paper raise prices by 7% (the rate of the tax), see no loss in the quantity demanded, and thereby pass the entire burden of the tax on to consumers? (Is this why the people of New Jersey were up in arms!?)

Another good question! An instance of higher prices for toilet paper acts as a test case of the law of demand. It is true that in our society we regard toilet paper as a necessity. So it's entirely reasonable to surmise that raising the price of a 40 cent roll of toilet paper by 7% will negligibly affect the amount bought by consumers.

On the other hand, if the price of toilet paper rose 15%, 50%, 100%, or 500% through higher taxes, can we be so certain that the amount purchased would never vary? Most economists would argue that eventually users of toilet paper would either "conserve," find cheaper substitutes, or maybe even do without, and thereby reduce their purchases of toilet paper, as predicted by the law of demand. Even our willingness to buy toilet paper has its limits.

We should note here that we have a specific group of taxes in mind. In particular, sales taxes, property taxes (for, say, the land owned by a firm), and income taxes on company profits affect both firm and market supply. Excluded are income taxes placed on households, the kind withheld on our paychecks. Such taxes affect the demand side, as they leave households with less **disposable income**.

subsidies

A **subsidy** can be considered a negative tax: the government pays the producer to produce and deliver to market. Therefore its effect on market supply is opposite that of a tax: subsidies give an incentive to entrepreneurs to boost production. Hence, firm and market supply increase wherever subsidies are available.

Specific subsidies can vary in procedural details: some pay a fixed per unit rate against what the firm produces; sometimes the subsidy is forwarded before production begins; still other ones can be applied against taxes owed, i.e., like a tax break.

Many economists argue that subsidies overdo it,

i.e., create unbalanced conditions in the market-- unbalanced with respect to the amount sold and supplied, given available prices. In a case that typifies some of the difficulties that might ensue, we can examine the article below from the Wall Street Journal, June 26, 1990. We will refer to this example in our discussion of **surplus** in Chapter 6.

. . . .
: **WSJ on** :
: **BEETS** :
. . . .

Expected long run profitability

Imagine a farmer who uses 100 acres of arable land. She raises two crops: tomatoes and corn. 50% of the land is devoted to each crop during the summer of 1995.

Suppose during that same summer a doctor's report came out to the effect that tomatoes prevent skin cancer. We might well predict a significant rise in the demand for tomatoes to follow. If so, the price of tomatoes would surely rise.

Now a question: would the farmer at the end of the season be happy or sad with her profits? Would she be pleased with the decisions she made in the spring as to how much land to devote to each crop? Or does she harbor some disappointment?

Since she sells tomatoes and the price of tomatoes rose during the year, she is, *in part*, extra-satisfied. She earned more profit from the tomatoes than she anticipated at the start of the season. On the other hand, she feels a loss. Not a direct loss, but the loss of an opportunity. The farmer realizes that had she planted a greater percentage of the land with tomatoes she would have made even more than she actually did--good as it was.

The important point is this: the sense the farmer has that she could have done better prompts adjustments in her production plans *for next year*. In the spring of 1996, she might plant tomatoes on 60 acres and corn on the remaining 40 acres. The farmer is assuming that at least some of the increased demand for tomatoes will stick and prices will remain high, compared to those prices from previous summers. If she's right, she'll be able to take maximum advantage of the profit opportunities that should prevail next year.

Economists would generally recognize the expectations created by 1995's higher prices and profits as the direct cause of an increase in the farmer's 1996 supply of tomatoes. The increased price sent a signal to all growers of tomatoes that consumer dollars are moving in the direction of that market. Farmers would want to take advantage of the demand shift immediately, but the nature of the agriculture business is that major adjustments are virtually impossible in the **short run**. In the **long run**, however, when the farmer gets the chance to replant, she'll make the change in her continual attempt to make the most money possible.

Obviously, the opposite case can occur. Producers will experience dwindling profits in those markets where prices make a descent. This strongly suggests that come the next round of production, they will reduce supply and seek other outlets for their productive resources. Notice how the tomato/corn example fits this scenario. Since corn prices are falling relative to

tomato prices, our farmer would observe discouraging corn profits results from the summer of 1995. Thus, the market is sending a signal to reduce corn production. This, of course, is exactly what our farmer did for 1996 in changing the proportions of tomato/corn from 50/50 to 60/40.

CONCLUSION

As in the previous chapter, vocabulary matters most in this chapter. Understanding the economist's use of the word "supply" is most essential of all. Supply represents a list of quantities that the firm or market will make available at various prices. Price changes induce small, marginal adjustments in the number of units a firm will happily deliver to market. But changes in the other determinants of supply actually change every price and quantity *combination* on the supply schedule. The graph showing such a change will therefore display two supply curves.

We now have some tools for the study of supply and demand. We will need these throughout the course. The next chapter combines the tools from this and the previous chapter for a more complete view of market equilibrium.

VOCABULARY

Supply – a set of price and quantity pairings which reflects the number of units a firm is willing to provide at various prices

    (a) supply schedule – refers to the table of price-quantity pairs

    (b) market supply – refers to the combined supply of individual firms

    (c) determinants of supply – factors affecting firm and market supply

Quantity supplied – the (hypothetical) amount of units provided either by the market or an individual firm at a specific price

Final good – a good purchased by a household for consumption purposes; a good bought at a retail market

Speculator – a person who trades financial assets, usually stocks, bonds, and other paper assets, for the purpose of accumulating personal wealth

Subsidy – a monetary benefit provided by the government to a firm in order to stimulate production; may also be forwarded to individuals for other purposes

Disposable income – remaining household income after taxes

Surplus – an excess of quantity supplied vis-a-vis quantity demanded

Short run – period of production time during which some constraint exists in the employment of resources

Long run – period of production after resource constraints have been removed

• •

END OF CHAPTER QUESTIONS

1. A person observes that a slice of pizza is $1.25, but an entire pie with eight slices is $8.00. He concludes that the law of supply is hogwash.

    Evaluate this conclusion critically; has the law of supply been contradicted? Discuss. Is there another economic principle at stake?

2. A person cites the following example: Prices at convenience stores are much higher than those at large supermarkets because supermarkets can buy in bulk and therefore at less cost. This shows that the law of supply is not true.

    Evaluate the claim critically and discuss. What economic principle does the example really illustrate?

3. The chapter brought up the case of taxing toilet paper. Do you think there is any good that, if the price is raised or lowered, has a constant quantity demanded? If so, how would firms price the good? Why?

4. True or false: Amount sold = Supply.

5. A three minute phone call between New York City and Washington, D.C. costs $1.00, while a three minute call between New York City and Los Angeles costs the same. How come?

6. Distinguish between the following two determinants of supply: expectations regarding future prices and expected long run profitability.

MOCK TEST

1. Why does a supply curve slope up and to the right? Use the concepts of scarcity, productivity, and costs to explain.

2. Invent a story that helps explain how price expectations can affect market supply.

3. Of the following two, which schedule represents supply?

P	Q	P	Q
5	14	5	22
6	16	6	20
7	18	7	18
8	20	8	16
9	22	9	14

   Plot the supply schedule on a graph.

4. What things could conceivably lead to a decrease in supply? List four and briefly explain each. Draw a single graph which depicts a fall in supply, being clear about the price and quantity effects.

5. Examine the following statement critically: Firms are not concerned with costs because they can pass costs on to the consumer.

CHAPTER 6

THE MARKET EQUILIBRIUM PROCESS

INTEGRATING SUPPLY AND DEMAND

When a good suddenly becomes very popular, some people will claim that supply has risen. Others, thinking there won't be enough to satisfy everybody, will declare that supply has gone down. And there will be some who will get it right: popularity marks consumer preferences, so in fact demand is rising.

Still, the potential for confusion should be obvious.

Perhaps more than anything else, economics is a language to describe the myriad events of the economic world. For the language to be enlightening, however, we need a common vocabulary, and every term in that vocabulary must carry a clear and specific meaning. Each word or phrase must denote a particular kind of economic event. And that event should conjure up a single picture in a person's mind.

As the example in the first paragraph illustrates, people without any economic training often use different words to describe the same thing. Here in this chapter we'll develop a framework for avoiding this jumble of jargon. We shall present a scheme which categorizes all market events into one of four types. Each type corresponds to one of four simple phrases. You know them already: rise in demand, fall in demand; rise in supply, fall in supply. By dealing with market forces this way we'll be able to reinforce the vocabulary of supply and demand and simplify the complexities of the real world of evolving markets.

The intersection of supply and demand

The prices and quantities we actually observe in the market are the result of the twin forces of supply and demand. As we saw in Chapters 4 and 5, supply and demand both contain a series of price and quantity combinations.

Now we don't actually observe supply and demand curves in the market. Rather, we see purchases and, to a lesser extent, the forces which generate sales and non-sales. Of course the prime factor making or breaking a sale is price. Hence, it's altogether appropriate that we draw our trusty supply

and demand curves with price and quantity on the axes.

If we combine supply and demand graphically, we create an intersection between the two. The intersection represents a balance, an **equilibrium**, between the (independent) forces of supply and demand. There is an **equilibrium price** and **equilibrium quantity** (or **output**). They correspond to the point of intersection between the two curves. In the market for soda shown in Diagram 6-1 below, the equilibrium price is $9.00 for an entire case; the equilibrium quantity is 1400. The graph can represent the market activity for any period of time, in any specific locale.

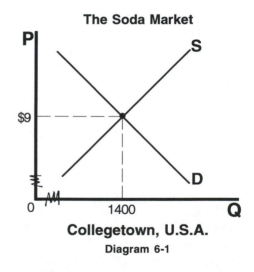

The Soda Market

Collegetown, U.S.A.

Diagram 6-1

The curves themselves come from information provided by the supply and demand schedules appearing in Table 6-1.

Demand		Supply	
P	Q	P	Q
$6	2500	$6	1100
7	2100	7	1200
8	1700	8	1300
9	1400	9	1400
10	1200	10	1500
11	1050	11	1575

Table 6-1

Equilibrium in a market is reached more in a theoretical sense than in a practical one. Economists do not mean to imply that markets are *always* at equilibrium; we aren't suggesting that markets never go haywire. Equilibrium is simply the price and quantity combination that we'd expect to occur when the forces of the market play themselves out. But since the forces are sifting themselves out continually, we can't expect rigid market prices at every turn. Instead, they hover around specific values. In the example about soda, some retailers may be offering a case at $8.95; some might be charging $9.25; still others may be having a sale and selling at $8.50. The point is that when an average price is sought for the market, there would be a kind of settling, a concentration of retailers who offer the good at $9.00.

The analogy of a pendulum is apropos. After being struck, a pendulum will swing back and forth, but as it does it also returns to its center. In time, it is said to come to rest. In fact, however, there are always minute forces imposing themselves on the pendulum so that it never really is fully "at rest." If you should ever go to a science museum where a large pendulum is displayed, you would notice an ever so slight swinging motion. So it is with markets.

Or, to pursue another analogy, the equilibrium of the market is like the equilibrium of the sun and the planets. They are always moving, reacting to forces imposed on them, adjusting, and maintaining their respective orbits. Together, the center holds.

Equilibrium, then, is the end result of Adam Smith's guiding, invisible hand. But the hand guides in much the way a child's hand builds his castle on the shore: there are continual additions, subtractions, finishing touches to be made; and then the tide comes up and washes it away. Tomorrow, another child will build another castle and another high tide will wash it away. There is no final figure.

For all of our emphasis on equilibrium price and quantity, we will probably be no better at *forecasting* the price of cars or *divining* how many will be sold. Our efforts at this stage are much more modest. We want to acquire a solid conception of what *can* happen in any market. On that foundation, progress can be made.

THE FOUR POSSIBLE EVENTS

Market life is not stationery. So the changes between two points in time are of utmost importance to the economist. He or she must classify the various types of changes he or she sees and provide a single phrase for each of them.

Changes in demand

a rise

Let's review the case of a good that becomes more popular. Because this is really a case of changing preference, we should classify it as an example of an increase in demand. How would this appear on a graph in which supply and demand appear together? What are the effects on equilibrium price and output?

A Rise in Demand

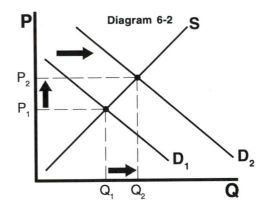

The graph reduces the increase in popularity to its essence: price and quantity both rise. But the conclusion applies even more generally. Whenever it happens and for whatever reason it happens, a rise in demand brings higher prices and greater quantities sold.

Examples abound. A rise in demand is what happens in the Christmas tree market in December, in the bathing suit market in June, in the flower market around Valentine's day. It happens whenever Wall Street speculators hustle to buy stocks they *think* will rise in value. In each case, prices and quantity (i.e., the number of units purchased) rise together.

a fall

And a fall in demand? What would that bring? Naturally, the opposite of an increase in demand: lower prices and lower output as seen below in Diagram 6-3.

A Fall in Demand

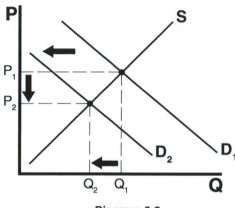

Diagram 6-3

Again, we have lots of examples: winter gloves in the spring; meat over the past 20 years (ever since doctors have advised us to consume less of it); and roses right after Valentine's day (even though flowers are good anytime!).

Changes in supply

a rise, a fall

We saw in the previous chapter that an increase in supply would shift the supply curve to the right, and a decrease in supply would shift the curve to the left. The beauty of the graphs begins right here. Even if we had no instinct for the price and quantity effects flowing from either situation, the graphs lead us to the correct conclusion: if a good's supply rises, its price will fall and the amount sold (quantity demanded) will rise; and if supply drops, price will rise and less will be sold. Observe how Diagrams 6-

4 and 6-5 change the equilibrium position on the graph and indicate the changes in prices and quantities.

A Rise in Supply

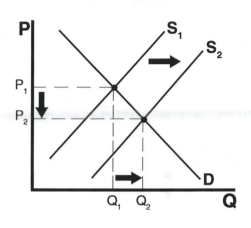

Diagram 6-4

A Fall in Supply

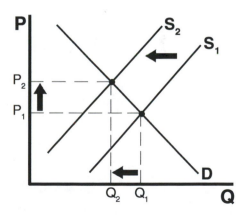

Diagram 6-5

We discussed examples of each case in Chapter 5, though now is a good time to review some classic ones.

In 1978, the U.S. government deregulated the airline industry to allow much more open, unfettered market conditions. The immediate result was the entry of a slew of competitors, usually small ones that tried to steal customers away from the major carriers. Prices fell and the number of tickets purchased by consumers swelled. Diagram 6-4 is completely consistent with this example; it shows the effects of an increased number of sellers.

Regarding a fall in supply, we can see the effects of resource cost changes practically monthly through the interplay of the oil and gasoline markets. If, for some reason, the price of a barrel of oil in the world markets rises--perhaps OPEC wants to limit deliveries again--then a few days later gasoline prices at the local service station will climb a few pennies. That is enough to discourage *some* purchases. That's the essence of Diagram 6-5.

Thus, from the broadest perspective, all market events must fall into four possible categories: demand

can either rise or fall; supply, likewise. In the final analysis, changes in a market's equilibrium position are reducible to one of these four possibilities. Four possibilities exist and only four because there are two sources of change (supply and demand) and two possible directions for change (rise or fall). Diagram 6-6 provides a helpful mnemonic.

The usefulness of this diagram goes far beyond what one might expect from it initially, given its simplicity. There's *nothing* here a person could not have figured out on his own. But, without getting specific pictures in mind for particular events, *and a specific vocabulary attached to those events*, building one's economic understanding becomes impossible. In fact, it's probably best to attach a memorable story to each of the four boxes in Diagram 6-6. That way, you will have a solid basis for interpreting economic events from the real world.

The Four Possible Events

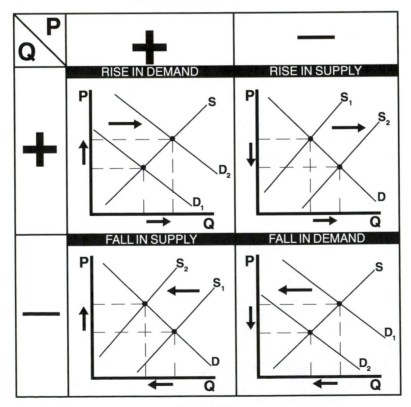

Diagram 6-6

PITFALLS IN INTERPRETATION

We often read in the newspaper the following statements that purport to explain market phenomena: "The price of copper is rising, which indicates rising demand." Or, "Since we had higher sales, we knew that demand was rising."

Unfortunately, there are fundamental problems with such claims. The primary difficulty is a conclusion that is drawn on the basis of limited information. In the first quote we have news about the price of copper. Then, on this basis, the conclusion is drawn that something occurred on the demand side to motivate the price change. To reason this way is equivalent to saying that since somebody is on first base, somebody got a single. Just as the person on first might have gotten there by a walk, higher prices can come about in one of two ways: either from a rising demand *or* a reduction in supply. We can't be sure which applies in this case without information about the market quantities involved. Similarly, regarding the second quote, just because more goods are being sold, that does not mean demand for the good rose; supply could have increased. A rise in supply would have lowered the price, and, via the law of demand, more purchases would have been induced.

So what *can* one say about these quotes? Economically, not much. They could be correct, but they could just as easily be confusing demand and quantity demanded, the number for the curve.

All such confusion can be avoided by relying on Diagram 6-6's arrangement of the four possible events, attaching the four key phrases to each "box" and keeping in mind one simple example of each case.

OUT OF EQUILIBRIUM

There is even confusion regarding the occasional occurrence of an unbalanced market. Usually, the situation is described as one where "supply is greater than demand," or vice-versa. But this is too imprecise. The remark compares apples and oranges. When the words "supply" and "demand" refer to a distinct relations between prices and quantities, it won't make much sense to say one is greater than the other. One can compare an old demand with a later one, or an old supply with a new; but supply and demand denote two different animals.

One *can* compare quantity supplied with quantity demanded, since a certain price specifies each of them. In equilibrium, quantity supplied and quantity demanded equate: the forces of supply and demand strike a coordinated balance. The equilibrium price encourages buyers to purchase what sellers provide to just the right degree.

When the market's balance gets undone, it's because the market price has wandered from its mooring, so to speak. The market experiences either a **shortage** or a **surplus**. A shortage occurs when quantity demanded exceeds quantity supplied; a surplus occurs when quantity supplied exceeds quantity demanded. Either one of these situations must be described with reference to a specific price. We can re-use the schedules developed for the soda market in Collegetown, U.S.A. to illustrate both shortages and surpluses.

Demand		Supply	
P	Q	P	Q
$6	2500	$6	1100
7	2100	7	1200
8	1700	8	1300
9	1400	9	1400
10	1200	10	1500
11	1050	11	1575

Table 6-1

Shortage

Let's suppose the actual price in the soda market one week had been $7/case. At that price consumers would be willing to purchase 2100 cases. But suppliers would feel enough incentive to deliver only 1200 to market. Obviously, at $7 the buyers' quantity demanded exceeds the firms' quantity supplied. Diagram 6-7 illustrates the situation. It highlights the role of the $7 price in creating the market imbalance. Since it's below the $9 equilibrium price it encourages consumers but discourages firms.

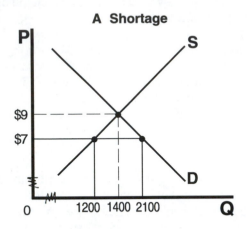

A Shortage

Diagram 6-7

In real life, we get evidence of a shortage when lines build up at the register. Present day Russia is experiencing chronic shortages of consumer goods because governmental regulations often set prices too low (among other reasons). Here in the States, long lines formed at the gas pump during the 1970's OPEC oil embargoes. From the other vantage, store managers will get clues to oncoming shortages when their store's inventory drops precipitously.

Many economists would argue that the ultimate confirmation of a shortage is the existence of an underground market. In such markets, sellers earn premiums by providing commodities not easily available. In less economically developed countries, cigarettes often attain such premium value. Alcohol and foreign currencies also see underground markets develop. In the former Soviet Union, for example, the ruble and dollar could be exchanged at banks at an official, government-established rate. In the streets of Moscow, however, the dollar was more readily had, but for more rubles. Clearly, there was an opportunity cost for waiting in lengthy bank queues!

The basic adjustment the market must undertake to eliminate a shortage is to drive up the price. That simultaneously reduces quantity demanded and

increases quantity supplied. Further adjustments may occur in the long run, especially if firms interpret the situation as indicating a permanent rise in demand.

Surplus

A surplus would see the market's price temporarily above the equilibrium price. Firms would be overly eager to deliver their goods to the market; but at the same time buyers would be deterred by the relatively high price of the product. As a result, there is an excess quantity supplied vis-a-vis quantity demanded.

Still using Table 6-1, suppose the price of soda were $11. Firms would not sell all that they produced. Diagram 6-8 depicts the surplus rather clearly.

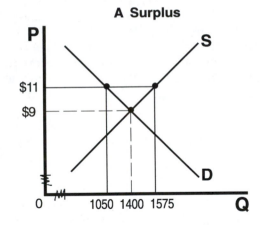

A Surplus

Diagram 6-8

With quantity supplied at 1575 units and quantity demanded at 1050, the surplus would add 525 cases of soda to the inventories of the various stores in the Collegetown soda market. A proprietor would probably observe, "My product is not moving." As time wears on, he or she will acquiesce to the market's pressure to reduce prices. This would increase quantity demanded, cut down excessive inventories, and prod the market back to equilibrium.

The diagrams stress the idea that shortages and surpluses occur only under specific market conditions, namely when non-equilibrium prices prevail. Normally, such conditions don't last. If *market prices remain flexible*, they will coax buyers and sellers to make appropriate adjustments. When all the adjustments have been made, the market re-establishes the ideal balance between supply and demand. At that juncture we observe firms delivering to market an amount of product satisfying consumer desires at the going price; moreover, inventory levels stabilize in number and in terms of managers' expectations for them.

SUMMARY: DIAGRAMS AND WORDS

The lessons from Chapter 3 to this point should help illustrate the various goals economists have as they work. Primarily, economists want to make an account of the forces that exhibit themselves through market prices and output. This will enable them to explain events of the past and to spell out the more *and less* likely possibilities of the future. By systematizing their acquired knowledge about market determinants, economists hope to acquire insight into the underlying patterns by which markets accomplish their design, namely to inform and allocate. Beyond these scientific interests, economists might be able to suggest to society how it can use market mechanisms to achieve desired goals. Economists acquire their greatest value when they can clearly and honestly assess for society the true opportunity costs of its choices and aspirations.

To accomplish these goals, economists must develop a specialized vocabulary, for only precisely defined terms can permit a systematic analysis of past events. So, for instance, defining supply and demand as a price and quantity relation, rather than as mere numbers bought and sold, allows us to think of *all* market phenomena as belonging to one of four categories.

The graphs, meanwhile, attempt to capture the essence of what makes markets move. Is supply up? Then prices are down, and greater quantity is demanded: that's what any good graph would tell us. Graphs aren't meant to confuse. In fact, they should clarify where words get cumbersome. (If they don't there's something wrong with the graph.) These pictures should say 1000 words!

It is hoped that you can now see what the economist sees in the ideal market: movement motivated by free choice, changes upon changes, patterns underlying a confusing array of hustle and bustle; a loosely structured free-for-all, sustaining an order, maintaining a balance; an equilibrium forged by many opposing influences. All this to resolve the problem posed by scarcity.

In the end, understanding market processes is nothing more than common sense.

VOCABULARY

Equilibrium – the market's reconciliation of the forces of supply and demand; the equality struck between quantity supplied and quantity demanded in any given market

Equilibrium price – the price which equates quantity supplied and quantity demanded

Equilibrium quantity – the output level corresponding to the equilibrium price

Shortage – when quantity demanded exceeds quantity supplied at a given price

Surplus – when quantity supplied exceeds quantity demanded at a given price

Substitution effect – the change in the amount of a good purchased as a result of a change in the price of its substitute

Fixed input – a resource whose employment during a single production period remains constant

• •

END-OF-CHAPTER QUESTIONS

1. If a certain market is experiencing a surplus, how does the going market price compare to its equilibrium price?

2. If a certain market is experiencing a shortage, how does the going market price compare to its equilibrium price?

3. Distinguish the idea of shortage from scarcity. Does scarcity mean market shortages everywhere? Are goods scarce or not when the market is in equilibrium?

4. Plot the following schedules. Which is supply and which is demand? Find the market equilibrium. At what price(s) is (are) there a surplus? At what price(s) is (are) there a shortage?

P	Q	P	Q
$10	80	$9	69
9	76	8	72
8	72	6	75
7	68	5	78
6	64	4	81

MOCK TEST

1. (a) Consider the market for TWA flights. Suppose pilots take a 10% pay cut. What will happen in this market as a result? Draw the appropriate graph.

    (b) What would happen in the market for Continental as a result? Draw.

2. Corn syrup is an important ingredient in most soft drinks. Now consider: How would a drought in the growing corn-growing regions of the U.S. affect this market? How would it affect the sugar market? Use graphs to depict the series of changes occurring in key markets after the drought.

3. Suppose a clothing manufacturer, for whatever reason, decides to raise the prices on all of its clothing. What will occur in the market for its competitor's clothing? Draw the appropriate graphs and explain.

4. In France, energy is chiefly supplied by nuclear reactors. If the French president declared that nuclear energy could not be used because of environmental dangers associated with nuclear waste, what would happen to the supply of energy in France?

5. Why does a supply curve slope up and to the right?

6. Is it always the case that when fewer items are sold in the market, it is due to a fall in demand? Explain.

7. Make up a story that illustrates the effects of expectations of future prices on the market supply curve. Illustrate using a graph.

8. Flights between New York City and Houston cost $300.00, but flights between New York City and San Francisco are $250.00. How come?

PART THREE

MACRO-ECONOMICS: CONCEPTS AND STATISTICS

"Economics is not yet a science."

Alfred Eichner

CHAPTER 7

BASIC MACRO CONCEPTS

This part of the text will move beyond the common language of market outcomes and venture into the vernacular of macro-economics. It will serve as a prelude to the material in Part Four about economic theory.

This particular chapter has two aims: first, to provide a context and an approach to macro-economic study; second, to act as a primer on the oft-discussed matters of inflation, recession, growth, unemployment, government deficits, etc. The first aim will help us avoid the error of learning the material for the test and forgetting it thereafter. A studying strategy like that will prove costly because the approach and principles introduced here will serve us for the next ten chapters. In regard to the second aim, we need to acquire a precise command of macro terminology so that we'll be able to get the most from our treatment of economic theory in Part Four and beyond.

EVERYTHING COMES IN PAIRS

One of the most effective methods for understanding basic macro-economic principles is to organize the material (vocabulary, concepts, etc.) into pairs. Because more often than not, macro concepts will complement one another in some fashion. If a student can learn key terms in their proper pairings, he or she will eventually grasp the underlying basis for their grouping.

For instance, one thing we've learned is that, in economics, prices and quantities reign supreme. Those *two* variables comprise the chief data for observation and study. Moreover, the laws of supply and demand get expressed in terms of prices and quantities. Indeed, P's and Q's have been stressed from our initial discussion regarding scarcity and opportunity costs. Only through such constant emphasis do we come to intuit why prices and quantities carry the weight of the science: *buyers' and sellers' behavior always manifests itself in terms of price and quantity results.*

Another example of things coming in pairs: Consider this simple question, "What is a trade?" A trade is an exchange of *two* assets between a buyer

and seller. Buyers generally have a money asset of some sort; sellers offer their merchandise. Hence, transactions between buyers and sellers involve two parties who exchange their respective assets. Anything else is simply a gift.

It should occur to the reader that much of the material in economics can be grouped into pairs: supply and demand, normal and inferior goods, substitutes and complements, etc. This pattern is so pervasive in our study, it's worth echoing: everything comes in pairs.

TWO KINDS OF VARIABLES: STOCK AND FLOW

Suppose we were to fill two ten ounce glasses halfway with water. One glass is intact; the second has a hole in the bottom. The second glass must therefore be continuously re-filled so as to maintain a constant level of five ounces in the glass. Thus, we assume that its rate of leakage exactly equals its rate of intake. Diagram 7-1 depicts the situation.

Consider the following questions: (1) How much water is in the first glass? (2) How much is in the second? (3) How much water is flowing through the first glass? (4) How much is flowing through the second?

Well, *there are five ounces in the first glass and five ounces in the second.* No water *flows* through the first glass. As to how much water is flowing through the second glass, it turns out we need more information: what is the rate of the leak?

Suppose there's a complete turnover of water in the glass every minute. Then we'd say that 150 ounces flowed through the leaking glass during one half hour (5 ozs. per minute x 30 mins.); 300 ounces during an hour (5 ozs. per minute x 60 mins.). Clearly, we'd have to be given some rate of leakage in order to calculate the amount of water which flows through the glass over time.

What does our example show? What does it have to do with macro-economics?

Macro-economic variables come in two kinds: **stock** variables and **flow** variables. The distinction has paramount import in terms of understanding how

Two Glasses of Water

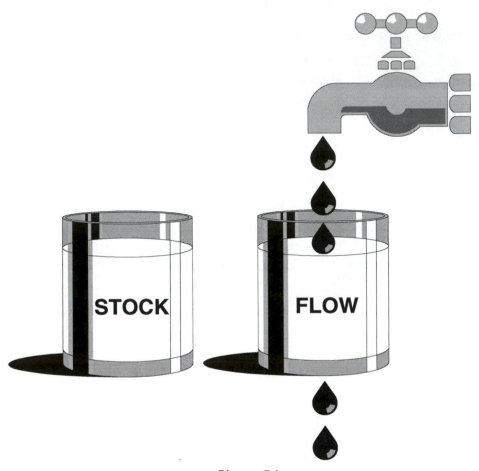

Diagram 7-1

the economy actually functions. The macro–economy cannot be properly analyzed unless one begins to think in terms of flow concepts. For example, the nation's business activity is really *flow* activity. The incomes we earn are really income *flows*. The monies we spend as households are really cash outflows.

But we're getting a tad ahead of ourselves.

Stock and flow variables are themselves distinguished by their measurability with respect to time. A stock variable is one whose value (often a volume, such as 5 ounces of water) gets measured *at some specific moment in time*. A flow variable, on the other hand, is only measurable *over a period of time*. Flow variables therefore require a time-based

usage rate for their calculation (as in 5 ozs. of water *per minute*).

We are familiar with the distinction in everyday life, but unconsciously so. For instance, home electrical use is a flow. The electric company bills us over a month's time according to kilowatt hours used. That measure is obviously a flow measure. But asking someone how much milk is in the refrigerator elicits a response without reference to time: a half-gallon is simply there (or not) at a given moment. The milk in the refrigerator represents a stock concept.

So again, where do we see this distinction at work in macro-economics? Everywhere! Consider what follows.

Wealth and income

Two concepts are primary in assessing a nation's general welfare: first is national **wealth** and second is national **income**. Initially, these terms might strike the reader as being synonymous. But they are, in fact, different; and their difference turns on the distinction between stock and flow.

To know how wealthy a country is we need to know how many goods, or **assets**, it has in its possession. A rich country will have many resources at its disposal and will possess a terrific talent for developing those resources. Its people will lead a comfortable lifestyle (i.e., have many goods). On the other hand, poor countries may have few resources or, more distressingly, often lack the knowledge to realize maximum advantage of the resources they do possess. A nation's wealth, then, represents its *accumulation* of goods from past activity, valued at a specific point in time. Just as we would measure an individual's wealth on any given day by adding up the value of his or her personal assets (minus liabilities), the assets which a nation's populace possesses at a given moment constitutes its wealth. Therefore, wealth is a stock variable.

Given all that, economists are more inclined to measure how well a **domestic economy** performs by studying and calculating its activity flows. One reliable statistic for this purpose is **national income**. This measure assesses the incomes collected by all participants in the economy over a specific period of time, usually a year. When we ask a person how much he or she makes, we expect a response couched in time: $50,000 for the year, $20 per hour, etc. Thus, income is a flow variable. Likewise, a nation's annual dollar earnings represent an economic flow.

Capital and investment

Most economists consider capital to be the fixed assets owned or operated by a firm. To describe it another way, capital includes the man-made plants and equipment used by firms in their production processes to make a profit. If an auto maker uses robots to assemble cars, those robots represent a portion of the firm's capital. If an accounting firm owns three office buildings, those structures count among its capital stock.

Capital is measured in monetary terms. If a firm owns a plant valued at $1,000,000, and the five machines inside the factory are worth $500,000, then that firm's capital stock is worth $1,500,000 *at the time it was appraised*. So capital is a stock variable, one hint to which is the very phrase "capital stock" commonly heard among business people and economists.

An **investment** expenditure is an expense made by a firm for capital equipment. More generally, investment is an *expenditure flow* measuring the dollar value of all payments made to acquire capital over a certain span of time. Investment and capital are therefore companion terms, one of which is flow, the other, stock. As we will see in the next chapter, investment flows are generally measured over a year's time and serve as a useful indicator of a domestic economy's fitness. When firms can confidently project that the final goods made from capital will reap profits, they will feel emboldened to purchase capital, and that's good for the overall flow of commercial activity.

Savings and Saving

These two terms also seem synonymous (and, mistakenly, get used interchangeably) but must be distinguished when we want to describe the functioning macro-economy as it truly behaves. **Savings**, with the s at the end, is a stock variable. It's considered a stock variable because savings refers to a particular kind of asset, money in a bank, whose value is measurable at a point in time. Notice: we have no problem interpreting the remark, "I have $500 in the bank," and it need not be expressed in terms of a rate of time.

Saving – no s at the end – is a monetary flow. To see this, an intuitive approach proves most helpful. Think back to the image of water flowing through a leaky glass. In and out, the water re-filled the glass just sufficiently to maintain a 5 ounce level.

Consider now your bank account, especially your checking account. Each week or two it gets augmented by a paycheck. But only temporarily so. In the interim between paydays, the saving flow will deplete as you pay your bills and meet everyday expenses. Later the account is replenished. Then it's depleted again. Then it's replenished. Then depleted. Then replenished. Depleted. Replenished. Depleted. Replenished.

And when you have finally departed--rest in peace--it'll be depleted for good. Saving, like life, is a flow.

Summary

Macro-economic terms and concepts should first be categorized under the broad taxonomy created by the distinction between stock and flow variables. This is essential for both understanding and analyzing macro-economy activity. Our choice in this text is to view the macro-economy as a flow, i.e., to view it in motion and in time, as it actually operates in the real world. Except for cases where we want to compare and evaluate theories, we will avoid unfruitful discussions of flow activity described with "stock" tools of trade, where time is not of the essence. Such approaches distort true macro-economic relationships.

MACRO-FLOW MODELS

Modern capitalist flow activity can be captured in what we'll call the **macro-flow model**. This model is similar to Quesnay's Tableau (which we saw in chapter ii) in the sense that it (a) is a time-based model of flow-exchanges, (b) indicates very clearly how large social groups play a specific role in economic life, and (c) demonstrates the inter-dependency among the groups via their exchange activity.

But the new model is different in other aspects. We are thinking here of a conglomeration of firms and a collection of households in a nation-state, not of groups of farmers and artisans in a village where landlords hold supremacy. Second, we are thinking here of late 20th century capitalism, not the period of feudal-capitalist transition seen in the 18th century. For we live today in the post-industrial age, not during the advent of the Industrial Revolution, and our models must appropriately reflect the age.

Basic macro-flow model: product and monetary flows

Two large groups participate in market activity: firms and households. These groups have two points of contact: the resource market and the product market. In the resource market, households offer their labor services in exchange for pay. Firms sell their offerings in the product market, for a price, to households. Of course, the household dollars used to purchase goods and services come from earnings in the resource market during that same time period. So the product and resource markets are, as we said, inter-dependent, one complementing the other's existence.

Diagram 7-2 below is our **Basic Macro Flow Model**. The model's real highlights are the paths traversed by the arrows. These paths denote two distinct flows connecting households and firms, a **product flow** and a **monetary flow**. The product flow traces a counter-clockwise route and signifies goods and services rendered through time. The monetary flow runs clockwise, tracing the course of expenditure-income flows through time.

Each section of the monetary flow designates a particular type of monetary flow. The top left denotes all those costs of production which get directly paid to households. That expense, at the same time, represents income (wages and salaries) received by households. On the bottom right, the path for **consumption** spending signifies household expenditures for final goods. From the firm's point of view these same monies are **revenues** from sold products.

lessons from the basic flow model

This simple model reiterates a principle introduced with the Tableau: *one person's cost is another person's income.* Indeed, we take this as *the* core lesson of the basic flow model. When firms write out checks to compensate labor, households at the same time receive income, and every penny spent by households constitutes a penny earned in firm revenue. In economics, a payout must also be a receipt!

This simple cost-income relation can enlighten

The Basic Macro-Flow Model

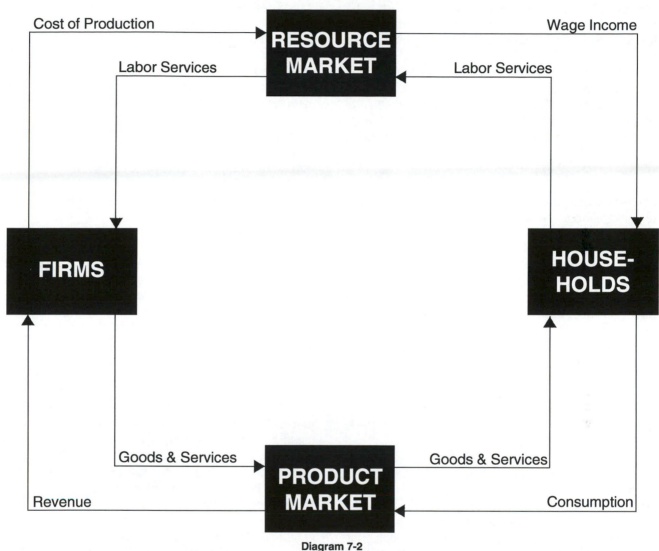

Diagram 7-2

our perspective on any number of events of the macro-economic world. For example, during a **recession**, when business activity slows down, household income tends to decline. But why? According to the flow model, it must be due to some lack of *spending* in the economy. Perhaps firms, wanting to avoid some extra costs, decided to lay off some workers. If so, a dangerous trend could take hold: layoffs diminish household income and, hence, reduce the households' potential for future spending. Since one person's cost is another's income, less consumption spending translates into diminished revenues and profits for firms. Should this negative cycle become dominant, a recession is inevitable.

The macro-flow model also suggests that certain accounting relationships exist between the different types of expenditures. First, the wage costs of firms must *identically* equal the wage earnings of households. Second, the consumption spending of households must also *identically* equal the revenues of the firms. We refer to these relations as **accounting identities**; i.e., they are true by definition. They must be equal. Each of these accounting identities is a specific case of the "one person's cost..." principle.

Are there other accounting identities here? What is the relationship between the top and bottom halves of the diagram? Would total wage income equal total consumption spending? Would revenues equal wage costs? Is it not just the same amount of money going round?

This is, truly, a complicated set of questions. Because while relations certainly exist between the top and bottom halves of the diagram, they do not lead to accounting identities. The key to seeing the *disconnection* between the two flows is to consider household saving. Once households save some part of their income, wage income would not equal consumption. And though consumption would still equal revenue, the wage figures wouldn't.

In other words, given any household saving, no figure in the top half of the diagram would equal any figure in the lower half. They would equal only if, by some fantastic coincidence, every household spent all its income. But this would not represent a general accounting identity; it would be a specific and atypical case.

So again, does the same money flow all the way round? No, most likely not. Be that as it may, each half of the basic macro-flow diagram does contain a certain identity: firms' wage costs must equal household wage incomes, and household consumption must equal firms' revenue. These accounting identities hold regardless of household saving patterns because they represent particular versions of the flow diagram's fundamental lesson: one person's cost is another's income.

Extensions of the flow model

No firm buys plant and equipment for motivations other than profit, and this intention is entirely distinct from that of households. When Joe D'Consumer buys a car, he intends to use that car for transportation,

pure and simple. But if Sue L'Entrepreneur buys cars for her taxi cab business, those cars would be considered capital purchases because the cars are long-lived assets used to garner profit. Similarly, a commercial airline buys a plane for commercial purposes; but a hobbyist-pilot acquires a plane for recreation. Thus, it becomes useful to separate monetary flows by product type, which in turn is determined by the expenditure's intent.

Let's modify our macro-flow diagram by capturing segments of the resource market glossed over in the simpler diagram. To make the diagram more realistic of modern capitalistic practice, we can divide the resource market into two sectors, labor and capital.

The category designating transactions for capital goods is investment spending. In Diagram 7-3 we can see investment represented as a subset of exchanges within the resource market--a flow within a flow. We can as well see that these intra-firm exchanges create a second source of revenue for firms.

bringing in the banks

Modern capitalism, as Marx noted, entails the extension of credit to entrepreneurs for the expansion of capitalist activity and the creation of wealth. This places the banking system front and center in actual contemporary business practice. In order to appreciate the primary role of the banking system in 20th century capitalism, Diagram 7-4 situates the bank in the picture's hub and introduces eight distinct monetary flows to our previous version.

In the real world, the banking system connects all market participants through various saving and loaning mechanisms. Most of us would be familiar, for instance, with the money market accounts and certificates of deposit (CD's) banks make available to customers. Such saving vehicles represent components of the general saving flow. Firms, meanwhile, have accounts where they deposit checks forwarded to them by customers for payment. Firm revenues, therefore, constitute the primary source of the firms' (gross) saving flow. On the credit side, loans occur in the form of mortgages, car loans, etc.; firms also borrow money to buy capital.

The Macro-Flow Model II

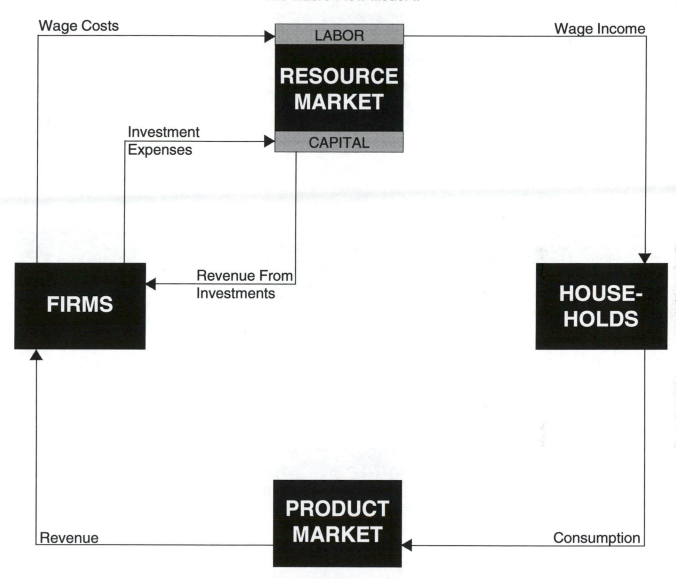

Diagram 7-3

Diagram 7-4 tries to capture all these particular monetary flows at a general level so that saving is flowing into the bank from firms and households; in turn, those dollars help to fund loans to members of both groups. Completing the cycle, banks charge interest, then distribute it to households and firms that have deposits.

the ultimate macro-flow diagram

Diagram 7-5 shows a macro-flow diagram in all its domestic detail. The diagram introduces the government's real and monetary relations to the **private sector**, i.e., to households and firms. Also, the diagram includes financial flows by which households

The Macro-Flow Diagram III, with Banks

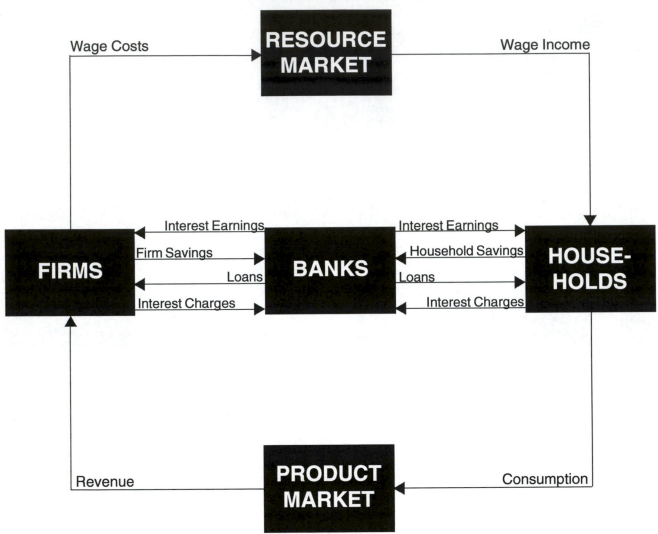

Diagram 7-4

and firms bypass banking intermediaries. When households acquire corporate bonds or **equity** (shares of corporate stock) they become a direct source of funding for new investment.[1] In return, households have the opportunity to receive interest (on bonds) or **dividends** (on equity holdings) should they be issued.

---

[1] To be most precise, households become suppliers of *net* funds only if the financial asset acquired is a new issue. In most cases, household purchases of corporate bonds or equity are actually second-hand purchases and therefore represent a trade of assets between two households, as might occur when two philatelists swap stamps for money well after the stamp is newly purchased.

the flow diagram and economic theory

We have made extensions to the macro–flow diagram for a couple of reasons. First, the words attached to the various individual flows provide the vocabulary for many subsequent discussions; so having in one's mind a picture of there these flows fit in the grand scheme of macro things is particularly helpful. Second, they illuminate relationships between the major macro variables. One of the most crucial relations is that between saving and investment. Some economic

The Ultimate Macro-Flow Diagram

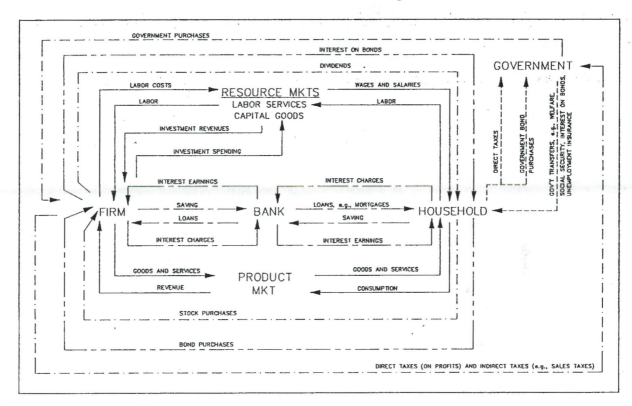

Diagram 7-5

theorists claim that investment is the key to economic growth and that saving is a by-product of investment spending; others will place saving in the lead role, saying that ample saving is a necessary condition for both investment and growth. There is simply no way to understand these claims and counter-claims without knowing initially what certain terms actually stand for. Nor could one evaluate the claims without understanding their precise meaning.

NATIONAL INCOME-DOMESTIC PRODUCT ACCOUNTS

Insofar as the flow models are based on the pairing between product and monetary flows, they stand as a grand overview of the business activity of a domestic economy. But the diagrams in no way serve as measures of that activity. They simply model categories of transactions. In order to record the magnitudes of

spending and income flows generated over time, a complete accounting framework must be developed. Such a framework would unite the double-entry bookkeeping procedures of accounting with the economic principle that one person's cost is another's income. To be more specific, two approaches can be taken when measuring the performance of a domestic economy: (1) via incomes and (2) via expenditures. Yet as every cost is also an income, these two approaches must yield the same monetary figure. That is, the income side and the expenditure side together form accounting identities. The two components of the identities are called the **national income** and **domestic product**.

The incomes approach

We imagine, as earlier, a **two-sector economy** with two main players: households and firms. What are the (final) incomes of each group? Wages and profits, respectively. Wages stand for all the monetary compensation to workers, profits for the difference between revenues and costs to all firms. (We use profits here rather than revenues so as to isolate *final* incomes.) So by definition:

National Income = Wages + Profits

$$(1)\ NI = W + \pi$$

where the Greek letter π stands for profits.

The expenditures approach

The other side of the "ledger" records all final expenditures of households and firms. That would boil down to:

Domestic Product = Consumption + Investment

$$(2)\ DP = C + I$$

The two principle private sector spending flows, consumption and investment, both seen in the previous macro-flow diagrams, will comprise a given nation's domestic product. These expenditure flows correspond to the real product flow of goods and services delivered to households in the product market *and* the real capital exchanges implied by intra-firm transactions for durable plant and equipment. The term itself is the shorter version of the most prevalent of all economic statistics: the **Gross Domestic Product** (GDP). ("Gross" in this context is another word for total--as in gross pay.)

GDP receives so much attention because it stands as a kind of granddaddy total revenue for the entire economy. More technically, GDP measures the monetary value of the aggregate real product flow generated by domestic producing firms, regardless of buyer. As the number one indicator of economic performance, it's the most watched and awaited number in the world. Reliable data for GDP come out quarterly, and the information contained in a given report can directly affect financial markets in New York and abroad.

the basic identity

As we suggested, national income and domestic product must be identically equal because one person's cost is another's income. Written out, we'd show:

Domestic Product = National Income

$$(3)\ C + I = W + \pi$$

More reconciliations and identities

We need to investigate other aspects of the national income side. In particular we have to ask the question, "What happens to wages and profits after they're received as income?" Our pursuit of this question will suggest new accounting identities and reveal hidden relations between saving and investment.

What can be done with income? It is either spent or saved.

This should seem like common sense as far as households are concerned--the macro flow diagrams had illustrated a consumption-saving split. But with firms things are a bit more complex. Since firms by definition do not *consume* final goods, it is more accurate to say that profits are either distributed (to shareholders as dividends) or kept within the firm. Profit income not doled out to shareholders is aptly called **retained earnings**. Getting deposited in banks, these dollars precisely make up firms' collective saving flow, net of production costs and dividend payments. *Hence we can say that firms' profits are either saved or paid out as dividends.*

We can write that out mathematically as follows:

National Income

$$(4)\ W + \pi = (C_{hh} + S_{hh}) + (\text{Dividends + Retained Earnings}),$$

where C_{hh} represents the spending of households and S_{hh} represents the saving of households.

Meanwhile, monies meted as dividends are once again subject to the only two alternatives open to households: consume or save. The mathematics would look this way:

National Income

(4) $W + \pi = (C_{hh} + S_{hh}) + (\text{Dividends} + \text{Retained Earnings})$

(5) $W + \pi = [(C_{hh} + S_{hh}) + \text{Dividends}] + \text{Retained Earnings}$

(6) $W + \pi = (C_{hh} + S_{hh}) + \text{Retained Earnings}$

where C_{hh} represents household spending traceable to wages and dividends and S_{hh} represents household saving from the same sources.

In the final analysis, all incomes either get spent by households (which by definition is consumption) or get deposited in the banking system. That immediately implies that wages and profits must together be equal to household consumption and the combined saving of households and firms. Below we complete the mathematics.

National Income

(6) $W + \pi = (C_{hh} + S_{hh}) + \text{Retained Earnings}$

(7) $W + \pi = (C_{hh} + S_{hh}) + S_f$

(8) $W + \pi = C_{hh} + (S_{hh} + S_f)$

(9) $W + \pi = C + S$

where S_f is the saving of firms. The very last line says in math what could be said in plain English: all income gets either spent or saved.

And since wages and profits are *identically* equal to consumption and saving, more identities follow:

Domestic Product = National Income

(10)	$C + I$	$=$	$W + \pi$
(11)	$C + I$	$=$	$C + S$
(12)	I	$=$	S

Line (12) may be the most important identity in the entire field of macro-economics. The equality serves as a cornerstone for all serious macro theories. And as the following chapter will show, economists use the $I = S$ identity to structure their statistical research of the domestic economy.

• •

Appendix to follow vocabulary and questions...

VOCABULARY

Stock variable – an economic measure independent of time

Flow variable – an economic measure expressible only in terms of time, e.g., per hour, per year, etc.

Wealth – the value of personal or societal possessions

Income – the flow of earnings over time to a person, firm, or institution

Asset – a possession

Domestic economy – refers to the commercial activity occurring within a nation's borders

National income – refers to the income flows of a nation's households and firms from both foreign and domestic sources

Investment – the spending flow of firms for capital equipment

Saving – the difference between an income and spending flow

Savings – refers to the unspent monetary assets in a person's possession

Product flow – the output of goods and services over time; related to the concept of real output and real GDP (chapter viii)

Monetary flow – cash expenditures for goods and services over time; related to the concept of nominal GDP (chapter viii)

Consumption – household spending for goods and services

Revenue – firm income from product sales

Dividend – corporate payment to shareholders from profit income

Equity – the total value of holdings in corporate shares

Recession – a negative trend in domestic product (real GDP) lasting at least six months

Accounting identity – a necessary equality between two economic measures

Private sector – refers to the non-governmental sectors of the economy

Two-sector economy – simplified model economy comprised of just households and firms

Three-sector economy – simplified model economy comprised of households, firms, and the government

Gross Domestic Product – the total value of goods and services produced in a domestic economy in a year's time; the total spending for those goods and services

Retained earnings – undistributed corporate profits

END-OF-CHAPTER QUESTIONS

1. One of the themes of this chapter is that everything comes in pairs. We noted as an example the fact that any exchange requires two persons with two assets. Leon Walras, however, makes this observation: "In every single transaction, there are two buyers and two sellers." In what sense is this claim true? What is Walras thinking?

2. In the realm of human exchange, do you think there is such a thing as a pure gift, where nothing is expected in return?

3. List all the economic pairings you can think of, either from what's been covered in the text till now or others you're familiar with.

4. Evaluate these definitions of stock/flow: "Stock variables don't move or change, but flow variables are always changing and moving."

5. Is the human body a stock or a flow?

6. When someone asks, "How much money do you have in your wallet?" is money in this context a stock or flow?

7. Is there a stock of money in a bank or a flow of money in a bank?

8. Make up a basic macro-flow diagram that includes the foreign sector. What are the monetary flows between the domestic economy and the foreign economies called?

APPENDIX

In the upcoming chapter, we'll be examining a set of national income and product accounts put together by the Bureau of Economic Analysis (BEA). The structure of the accounts, while still based on the $I = S$ identity presented in this chapter, is a bit more complicated because of its inclusion of the foreign and government sectors. In consideration of this difference, we present here a fuller version of the Product and Income Accounts' reconciliation, the very one used in the economic analysis.

COUNTING THE GOVERNMENT

The $I = S$ identity assumed a two-sector economy of households and firms. In a **three-sector economy** which includes the government, a similar, yet new, identity appears. The government's spending, represented by G, shows up on the product side; the government's income from taxes appears as T. Governmental spending and taxation here includes local, state and federal branches.

Domestic Product = National Income

(1a) $C + I + G = W + ; + T$
(2a) $C + I + G = C + S + T$
(3a) $I + G = S + T$

Written this way, business investment spending no longer needs to exactly equal saving; nor is there a stipulation that $G = T$. Yet, to any degree which G and T differ, I and S must offset that divergence: If $G > T$, then $I < S$; if $G < T$, then $I > S$.

The economists who compile the data for the Bureau of Economic Analysis algebraically manipulate line (3a) as follows:

$$\text{(4a)   } I = S + (T - G).$$

Within the parentheses, we have the term for the government's surplus. Sometimes, however, this value is negative—a negative surplus. This would indicate that the three branches of the government have collectively run a deficit for the year.

COUNTING THE FOREIGN SECTOR

The foreign sector entails our domestic economy's transactions with foreign buyers and sellers. On the spending/product side are imports and exports. For statistical purposes, economists combine imports and exports to get **net exports**, which is calculated by subtracting imports from exports and represented by E_n below. On the incomes side, earnings which domestic producers collect in foreign lands *and* earnings which foreign producers gain in the U.S. must each be recorded. Like imports and exports, economists net out these earnings to arrive at **net income transfers**, represented by R.

Domestic Product = National Income

(5a) $C + I + G + E_n = W + ; + T + R$

(6a) $C + I + G + E_n = C + S + T + R$

Grouping the terms together as is done customarily, and subtracting C from both sides, we arrive at a new identity

$$\text{(7a) } I + (E_n - R) = S + (T - G)$$

which contains the new term $(E_n - R)$ called **net foreign investment**. When this is positive, the domestic economy invests in foreign businesses to a degree greater than foreigners invest in U.S. firms. If $(E_n - R)$ is negative, then foreigners' investment in the domestic concerns outweighs U.S. investment in foreign ones.

We shall see that line (7a) perfectly corresponds with the saving and investment tables that appear in Table 5.1 of the BEA data set.

CHAPTER 8

MACRO STATISTICS AND ECONOMIC HISTORY

This chapter develops the concepts and themes of the previous chapter in more concrete ways. To accomplish this task, a new model of a domestic economy will be developed. This model will provide data on output and prices that we will use to calculate Gross Domestic Product. Then, as a follow up, we will turn to data extracted from government Internet sources to get an accurate sense for (a) real world data on output, prices, etc., and (b) U.S. economic history of the 20th century.

First, though, some preliminaries.

MACRO P's AND Q's

Macro, no less than micro, boils down to questions about prices and quantities. Each variable can travel a positive or negative route. This allows for four possible phenomena in the macro realm: **inflation**, **deflation, growth,** and **recession**. The first two involve prices; the latter two involve quantities. Let's see more about how economists evaluate general price and quantity trends.

The general price level

Since the Second World War, statistics bear out an unbroken progression of the general price level in the United States and other developed countries. Year to year, the rate of increase in the general price level has varied; but inflation itself appears as a constant companion. In the U.S. for the past ten years (1993-2003) inflation has been in the 2-3% range annually. During the 1970's, inflation rates were considerably higher, reaching 11% in 1974 and 1979. The last episode of deflation occurred during the 1930's, when the U.S. economy suffered its infamous Great Depression.

Identifying inflationary or deflationary trends requires economists to devise a measure for the average price of goods and services available in the economy. There are several ways to do this, but regardless of method, calculating the extent to which the price level has risen (or fallen) entails using the price level from two years and finding the difference in percentage terms--the same way one would calculate one's own increase (or decrease) in yearly wages.

Output and growth

Even more than price movements, trends in the economy's product flow reveal its underlying vigor. **Real output**, as the product flow is usually called, can be assessed by measuring the gross (or total) spending of all market participants. Thus, the trend in total spending can tell us whether a nation's real output is expanding or shrinking.

But there is one qualification: given any domestic output flow, total spending rises under the conditions of domestic inflation. Such spending growth would be deceptive, however, since the increase is purely price-driven. **Real growth** occurs only when increases in total spending in the economy stem from the increased production of goods and services; in other words, real growth occurs only if the rate of growth in total spending exceeds the economy's rate of inflation.

In order to gain a better feel for the trends in prices and output, and to see exactly how economists quantify these trends, we're going to create a hypothetical economy and follow the movement of prices and quantities through three years' time.

A MODEL ECONOMY

Our model economy will produce only two goods-- just to keep things simple. We will invent prices for both goods and assume that they represent the average price of the given product during the year. At the same time we will devise some quantity figures that represent the total number of units produced and sold through the year.

Our two goods are pizza and beer. The price and output data for these two industries cover a three year period: 2002, 2003, 2004. By multiplying respective prices and quantities, we arrive at the total flow of dollars collected by firms during the year in the respective industries. For example, on Table 8-1 we can see that during 2002, a pizza pie cost $9.00. Beer cost $3.75 per six pack. 725 pizzas were sold. Meanwhile, consumers bought 4800 six-packs. Thus, $6525 in revenues flowed to the pizza industry and $18,000 flowed to the beer brewers.

For both industries, or for the economy as a whole, the aggregate spending of households was $24,525. This figure therefore designates 2002's **nominal GDP**. By "nominal" GDP we mean the gross expenditure flow, based on money-prices which existed in that very year. The $24,525 nominal GDP figure permits us to make a crucial conceptual link: gross domestic product, the aggregate spending of all the major sectors of a domestic economy in a given year, is like a grand-daddy total revenue--the composite of *all* annual industry revenues from final sales. By the same token,

therefore, nominal GDP measures the value of the entire economy's annual production flow, given that year's prices for goods.

Now, the purpose of constructing this make-believe data is to provide us the means to determine the model economy's two most revealing trends: the path of prices (inflation or deflation) and the route of real growth (expansion or recession). For that we must begin to examine the succeeding year's price and quantity results.

		PIZZA	BEER	TOTALS
2002	**NOMINAL**	$9.00 x 725 = $6525	$3.75 x 4800 = $18000	$24,525
	REAL	$10 x 725 = $7250	$4 x 4800 = $19200	$26,450
2003	**NOMINAL**	$10 x 750 = $7500	$4 x 5000 = $20000	$27,500
	REAL	$10 x 750 = $7500	$4 x 5000 = $20000	$27,500
2004	**NOMINAL**	$11 x 775 = $8525	$4.25 x 5100 = $21675	$30,200
	REAL	$10 x 775 = $7750	$4 x 5100 = $20400	$28,150

Table 8-1

In 2003, things changed. Pizza prices rose, as did the cost of a six pack. Each industry also produced and sold more items. On this basis alone we can deduce that (a) the nominal GDP will rise, (b) the economy is in an inflationary phase, and (c) the economy is enjoying real growth.

But to what degree did these changes occur? How significant are they? To address these questions economists must develop statistical means to distinguish price movements from quantity movements and precisely calculate each.

Constant prices and real GDP

The first step in this process requires the selection of a **base year** for prices, which implicitly serves as a standard for comparison against other year's prices. At the same time, the selection of a base year for prices permits the calculation of **real GDP**. Real GDP, like nominal GDP, boils down to a P x Q computation. But with real GDP the prices used in the process must be from the base year. In Table 8-1, 1993's prices have been chosen as the base prices; hence, the 1992, 1993, and 1994 real GDP's all use 1993 prices.

These statistical procedures suggest the following formulas:

$$P_{current\ year} \times Q = \textbf{Nominal GDP}$$

$$P_{base\ year} \times Q = \textbf{Real GDP}$$

If we examine 2003's figures it's obvious that nominal and real GDP are the same. And it should be equally obvious why this is so: we determine 2003's real GDP by employing 2003's prices. The equality between 2003's nominal and real GDP simply confirms that 2003 had been selected as the base year. Thus, we arrive at another fundamental lesson: *nominal and real GDP will be equal in the year selected for base prices*.

Now the trick involved with base prices comes in figuring all the other years' real GDP's. All real GDP calculations on Table 8-1 use the $10 pizza price and $4 beer price from 2003. It's therefore inevitable that the real GDP of 2002 will be *higher* than 2002's

nominal GDP--because 2003's prices are higher than 2002's. It's equally inevitable that 2004's real GDP will be *lower* than 2004's nominal GDP--because the 1993 prices are lower than 2004's.

calculating real growth

And what's the point of all this? We now have the necessary components to determine the rate of real growth, the percentage by which *real* production *really* expanded. This calculation requires us to use real GDP's from two years as this formula indicates:

$$\text{Rate of real growth} = \frac{\text{New real GDP - Old real GDP}}{\text{Old real GDP}} \times 100.$$

For the rate of real growth in 1993 we take:

$$\text{93's real growth} = \frac{27500 - 26450}{26450} = \frac{1050}{26450} \times 100$$

$$= 3.97\%.$$

This rate of growth is slightly better than the average yearly growth rate in the United States since World War II.

At this point we should review what we've done. By using the concepts of base prices and real GDP we were able to isolate the growth in production in the economy. Had we used nominal GDP's ($24525 and $27500), part of the difference would have been due to the influence of higher 2003 prices; i.e., 2003's nominal GDP is greater than 2002's because of higher prices *and* quantities. Using 2003's prices as a base, the real GDP price level remains constant; hence, changes in real GDP exist only because of changes in the real output of firms.

calculating inflation

We can extract still more information. Using Table 8-1's data, a precise measure of the rate of inflation can be reckoned. The inflation calculation is actually a *two-step process* which utilizes both nominal and real GDP values from *two* respective years. The nominal and real figures will generate a single year's **GDP Deflator**. After two GDP Deflators have been found, the percentage difference between them is figured accordingly.

For the GDP deflator,

$$\frac{\text{Nominal GDP}}{\text{Real GDP}} \times 100 = \text{the year's Deflator.}$$

So in 2002,

$$\frac{24525}{26450} \times 100 = 92.72 \, .$$

And in 2003,

$$\frac{27500}{27500} \times 100 = 100 \, .$$

The GDP Deflator should not be interpreted to be the actual price paid for a good. Instead, it should be seen as an average of all prices, akin to a student's GPA. Thus, if from year to year the GDP Deflator rises, then inflation reigns; if from year to year the deflator falls, then deflation rules.

Using the same percentage change formula, it should be easy to see that 2003's inflation rate, the percent to which that year's prices were higher than 2002's, is 7.85%.

$$\frac{\text{New deflator - Old Deflator}}{\text{Old Deflator}} \times 100 = \text{rate of inflation}$$

$$\frac{100 - 92.72}{92.72} \times 100 = 7.85\%$$

To solidify your understanding of the real growth and inflation measurements, practice is essential. In the next section data is presented that should provide ample material for this sort of practice. You are encouraged to use it extensively and creatively. Ask yourself the question about growth during some stretch of time, or inflation during the Reagan years. Other questions will appear at the end of the chapter.

THE "REAL" (HISTORICAL) ECONOMY

Pizza and beer do not an economy make. There are millions of types of commodities produced in the modern economy. And moreover, the mix of things produced changes year to year. Once, car manufacturers produced the Edsel and the Pacer. Today, these cars would be collector's items. Once, students used slide rules for their arithmetic; today calculators are preferred. Once upon a time there were no television sets.

Economists at the Department of Commerce and Bureau of Labor Statistics, to the best of their ability, keep track of these trends. Somewhere, somehow, all these changes get reflected in the data, though perhaps not in such specific terms. The statistics are compiled and presented by the Bureau of Economic Analysis (BEA) at www.bea.gov.

The information from the Bureau yields is set in the framework discussed in the previous chapter. There is the domestic product side recording expenditure flows of households, firms, and government; the national income side traces income flows earned by the same groups. The two sides are then reconciled. In the following pages, we will present the most immediately relevant sections of the Analysis to reinforce the concepts from this and the previous chapter and to acquire some important lessons from the data itself.

Gross Domestic Product, Table 1.1.5

Table 1.1.5 from the Analysis lays out the major divisions of Gross Domestic Product. Recording nominal GDP from 1965 to 2001 in the far left column, the broad categories across the top tell us what the components of GDP are: Consumption, Investment, Net Exports, and Government, as we should expect.

All the numbers on Table 1.1.5 are in nominal terms or **current dollars**. Again, this indicates that the calculations herein used the price level from the respective year. 1965's figures used 1965's prices; 1979's GDP figures, consumption figures, etc. used 1979's prices; and 1989's figures used 1989's prices.

The trend in nominal GDP could not be more clear. By 1995, nominal GDP had reached 7.4 trillion dollars. That was more than 10 times its 1965 figure of 720.1 billion. But what does this growth represent? Since GDP is essentially Price times Quantity, only two things could possibly account for the growth of Nominal GDP: a higher price level or growth in the nation's output of goods and services. In fact, it's been the combination of these that accounts for the 10-fold increase in nominal GDP.

consumption sector

The major categories of consumption spending differentiate three very general types of products purchased by households: durables, non-durables, and services. Durables are, for the purposes of these statistics, those goods that are expected to last at least one year. Thus, car purchases and most household appliances get recorded here. Non-durables last less than a year. Food purchases would be an obvious major component of this column. Services include payments to doctors, lawyers, and others that provide a non-tangible commodity to a consumer.

investment sector

The GDP statistics for the next major kind of spending is critical for understanding what moves capitalist economies. Overall investment is a relatively small percentage of the total spending, yet it serves as an engine for all other activity. If consumption is the end of production, then investment propels all subsequent enterprise. At this point, we can examine the breakdown within the investment sector. (When we proceed to Table 1.1.6, we'll delve deeper into historical examples.)

First, there is fixed investment, which represents all that spending for durable, man-made assets—in a word, capital spending. Here we see the lone exception to the idea that investment is, strictly

speaking, the capital expenditures of firms. For included in this fixed investment category is residential construction spending (for new homes only). This exception was made due to the special nature of the home construction industry itself. Second, in addition to fixed investment, are the **changes in business inventories**. Fixed investment plus changes in business inventories equal total private domestic investment.

"Changes in business inventories" calculates the difference between the value of the present year's total inventory and the value of the previous year's total inventory. This difference must be recorded because changing inventory levels really do reflect changes in the production level—or output level—of the economy. For instance, when business inventory levels expand, the economy has actually increased its total production from the previous year—even if that new production doesn't get sold. Thus, the economy's gross output measure, the GDP, will change due to changes in business inventories, since these changes figure into the investment calculation, and investment is one of the four major components of GDP.

While the preceding comments on inventory can be difficult to grasp, they are mentioned because inventory figures have a unique place among the various statistical categories. Changes in inventory can indicate future trends in capital spending. When the changes are negative, we might expect firms to expand their operations in order to restore inventory levels to the desired level. Conversely, if inventory levels exceed desired levels, indicated by a positive number in this column, firms might choose to cut back on future capital outlays. (They don't want mountains of inventory!) Now, due to population trends and whatnot, some expansion of inventories over the long run would be expected and normal. Thus, we can expect positive numbers in this column for the most part. The actual figures in this column show that in recession years, firms were moving to reduce their inventory levels—but even in that case, there's a limit to such cutbacks and restoring inventory levels to normal is the first stage in the economy's eventual recovery.

net exports

Net exports means exports minus imports. The reasoning here is that exports, a real flow of products to foreign customers is compensated by revenue from those same customers. Hence the sales of those goods by domestic firms should be recorded as a positive. Meanwhile, imports, foreign goods bought by domestic households, imply that domestic funds are flowing out of the domestic economy, thereby negating potential domestic sales. Combined, net exports would indicate whether a nation enjoys a net gain or loss in terms of product sales with the rest of the world.

In the popular press, as well as among economists, the term **foreign trade deficit** means that net exports are negative. But a trade **surplus** indicates net exports are positive. There is controversy surrounding the impact upon the economy of having either a trade surplus or deficit. We saw in chapter ii that most economists discount the benefits of manipulating the terms of trade. But what is more disturbing is the confusion surrounding the very meaning of the term. It *does not* signify that one country owes another, be it a surplus or deficit, for the monetary exchange has already taken place at the time of sale. It is the sale of some good that is being recorded by the import and export columns--no more, no less. Thus, no debt is directly created by any foreign exchange.

government

Government spending is fairly straightforward at this point. It is divided into federal, state and local (county, municipal). The federal spending is broken down into two categories, defense and non-defense (payments for NASA projects and expenditures within the Department of Justice, Interior, etc.).

Real Gross Domestic Product, Table 1.1.6

Table 1.1.6 takes the figures from 1.1.5 and converts them all to 1996 dollars. Thus, the figures on 1.1.6 are *real* figures. All the changes in nominal GDP which occurred between 1965 and 2001 due to changes in the price level have been completely eliminated. 1996's price level has been selected as the base year.

To see the effect of this selection, we should compare three things. First, 1.1.5 and 1.1.6 for 1996. Across the entire row, the 1.1.5 and 1.1.6 figures are identical. (Why?) Second, compare the GDP figures on 1.1.5 and 1.1.6 for any year *prior* to 1996. The 1.1.6 figures will be greater than 1.1.5's. (Why?) Third, compare the GDP figures on 1.1.5 and 1.1.6 for any year *after* 1996. Now 1.1.5's figures are greater. (Why?) (If you're having difficulty here, return to the nominal and real figures for the "model economy" of pizza and beer and compare them for the hypothetical years 2002-2004: Which was the base year? Which had a nominal GDP less than, equal to, and greater than its real GDP?)

consumption trends

How do we use the data of 1.1.5 to learn about the economy? One of the more revealing statistics comes by ascertaining the *relative* size of the economy's different spending sectors--consumption, investment, and government. When followed over a number of years, this allows us to trace long term trends in the economy.

The computation itself is easy. By forming the ratio C/GDP, we get the **relative share** of consumption spending out of GDP for any given year. Multiplying by 100 converts the ratio to a percentage.

1965	(443.8 ÷ 719.1)	x	100	= 61.7%
1970	(648.5 ÷ 1038.5)	x	100	= 62.4%
1975	(1034.4 ÷ 1638.3)	x	100	= 63.1%
1980	(1757.1 ÷ 2789.5)	x	100	= 63%
1985	(2720.3 ÷ 4220.3)	x	100	= 64.5%
1990	(3839.9 ÷ 5803.1)	x	100	= 65.9%
1995	(4975.8 ÷ 397.7)	x	100	= 67.3%
2000	(6739.4 ÷ 9817)	x	100	= 68.6%

The legitimate observation here is that household consumption constitutes roughly 2/3 of all spending activity in the U.S. There has been some increase in the share over time (about 10%), and some economists find the trend disturbing, since it might indicate that the economy is providing less for its future wealth than it might need. Nevertheless, the statistics bear out founding father Adam Smith's insight that consumption is the end of production.

The rough constancy in the proportion of consumption out of GDP belies other changes over the past fifty years. Within the consumption sector the proportion of spending for services out of total consumption has changed dramatically (Services/ Consumption).

1965	1970	1980	1990	2000
$\frac{189.0}{443.8} = .43$	$\frac{291.5}{648.5} = .45$	$\frac{846.9}{1757.1} = .48$	$\frac{2115.9}{3839.9} = .55$	$\frac{3928.8}{6739.4} = .58$

Over the course of three decades, the percentage of spending for services as a share of total consumption increased from 43% to 58%. It is these sorts of changes, usually called **structural changes**, that economists use to formulate hypotheses about economic change. For instance, the growing importance of the service sector might be part of the explanation for the decreasing influence of unions in the U.S. economy of the 1990's. Service sector jobs are not, for several reasons, amenable to union organization. Thus, if the service sector grows relative to others, we might well expect the percentage of workers belonging to a union to fall during such a period. The same trend might help explain why doctors' incomes have grown substantially over this period, while farmers' incomes fell.

investment trends

There is perhaps no more stark lesson in the data than that provided by the investment figures. Using data from earlier years, (consider the period from 1929 to 1933), the worst years of the Great Depression. They tell a great deal. As a percentage of real GDP we have:

1929	1933
$139.2/709.6 \times 100 = 19.6\%$	$22.7/498.5 \times 100 = 4.6\%$

Stop and consider just how significant this fall in investment spending is.

$$\frac{4.6 - 19.6}{19.6} = \frac{-15}{19.6} = -76.5\%$$

Real investment fell by more than 75% of its 1929 level. Were the engine of the car to lose 75% of its power, we couldn't expect the car to perform anywhere near the level it had at full power. Similarly, a significant decline in real GDP is inevitable when investment spending falls so precipitously. We can see that 1929's real GDP fell from 709.6 to 498.5 in 1933, a 29.7% decrease! As a result of the same slowdown, unemployment rates climbed to 25% from a 1929 level of 3.2% (better than what we today regard as indicative of full employment).

Investment as a percentage of real GDP did not fully recover until the latter part of the 1940's. Some partial recovery occurred in the late 30's, only to be disrupted by the war effort between 1942–45. In that case, the fall in investment spending didn't have a detrimental impact on the real GDP trend, as the resources of the nation were efficiently transferred to the government's war effort. Indeed, the war years constitute some of the best performances of the U.S economy to date.

For practice and comparison, readers should take a random selection of years from Table 1.1.5 or 1.1.6 to verify that, typically, the percentage of investment spending to GDP, in real terms, is within a band of 14% to 18%.

government trends

Most likely because of the Depression and the example of World War II, the government's participation in the economy has changed decidedly in this century. In the years prior to the war, government spending as a percentage of real GDP was generally less than 15%, and that was largely state and local governmental spending. (1933's 19.8% share of Gov't/GDP was extremely high by the pre-war standards.)

The potential benefits of governmental spending were discussed theoretically by John Maynard Keynes in the 1930's. He argued that in the absence of normal investment activity, governmental spending could act as a stimulant towards recovery. At the time this was a radical idea insofar as economic theory, since Smith argued that the least possible governmental intrusion produced the greatest possible benefits to society. According to the pre-Keynes economists, laissez-faire policies allowed the market to automatically recover from any general decline, since any general decline in market conditions held, too, the seeds of its own revival. All *bad* things must end.

But Keynes, like the common man himself, grew impatient. Business failures of the 1930's seemed to feed upon one another. By 1939--the statistics bear this out--the country was no better off than in 1929.

As if by experimental design, the war provided evidence of Keynes' claims. The U.S. government had little political choice after Pearl Harbor but to throw itself against the Axis powers. The fateful course had irrevocable economic consequences. The U.S. economy of the 1940's became a war machine.

The impact of the war seemed to hold a lesson about government spending. The demand for resources for the war effort reestablished normal rates of flow activity. That meant normal rates of unemployment, even if the spending wasn't of the private investment sort. From 1940 to 1945 real GNP grew by 75%. Why? From 1940 to 1944 federal governmental spending rose more than tenfold.

The late 1940's were a period of normalization in the percentage of government spending out of GDP (especially Federal spending out of GDP). But the new normal was different than the old normal in the same way the life expectancy of a 20th century human being is different than the life expectancy of a 19th century person. Since the mid-fifties the proportion of real governmental expenditures of real GDP hovered around 20%. Meanwhile the share of *federal*

governmental spending has been more variable with respect to total government spending and real GDP. (The student should verify this by addressing #5 at the End-Of-Chapter Questions section.)

Domestic Product-National Income Reconciliation, Table B-26

In the previous chapter we showed that National Product and National Income were accounting identities. This is logical because in the final analysis one person's cost (expenditure) is another person's income.

In the real world of national income accounting, several complications intrude. One of the main complications is the wearing out, or **depreciation**, of capital equipment used in production. Another is the use of sales taxes by the government. Let's work through Table B-26, from the Economic Report of the President, and see how real world problems get explicitly accounted for. (These tables, incidentally, are in current dollars.)

capital consumption allowances

First there is the distinction between Gross Domestic Product and **Net Domestic Product (NDP)**. Just as a person's net pay (or, take home pay) from his job would have some payment deducted from the gross pay, so too there would be a deduction between GDP and NDP. That deduction is [technically] called the **Capital Consumption Allowance**. You have probably heard it referred to as depreciation or capital replacement costs. What is the justification for subtracting these expenditures?

Ultimately, economists want to have a number that measures as accurately as possible the welfare of the individuals who participate in a domestic economy--and, too, the progress of their welfare from year to year. NDP is actually a better gauge than GDP. But why is this the case?

Consider the following analogy. A family purchases a house for $200,000. If the family were to do literally none of the regular maintenance and upkeep chores that are involved in home ownership, the real value of the home would fall through the years. Wear and tear on the house asset would reduce the real value of the property, ceteris paribus. Now, suppose the normal wear and tear on the home is 5% of the value of the home. This implies that $10,000/year must be spent merely to maintain the home's value at $200,000. But notice: this $10,000 is not contributing a *net* addition to the property value, even though it is a *gross* expenditure for the household. Not until that household made payments of greater than $10,000/year could there be a net increase in the value of the property. And for that family to spend less than $10,000/year would imply a slow but certain depreciation in the asset's value. The concept we're discussing can be simply conveyed by the picture below.

A Depreciating Home

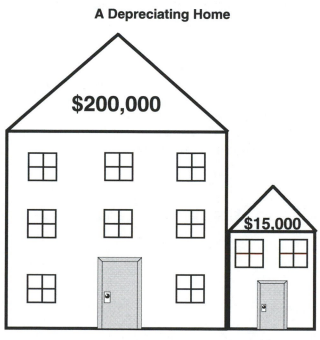

$200,000

$15,000

Diagram 8-1

The property value of $200,000 is preserved only if $10,000/year is spent to replace worn out "parts", keep all hardware in good operating condition, and maintain a respectable appearance to the property by repainting, etc. as required. The property value will *not* rise until a net addition is made. In Diagram 8-1

a den adds $15,000 to the property's value. The year this den is completed, the value of the home will be $215,000, *assuming the normal maintenance costs were incurred*. This implies that in the year the den was built gross expenditures on the property were $25,000, net expenditures, $15,000.

The analogy to a firm's investment spending and the household's expenditures for upkeep and additions is a strong one. The investment spending of firms goes in part to maintaining, repairing, and replacing the depreciating value of capital equipment from normal use. Capital equipment does not last forever; it gets used up--consumed, as it were. But the expenses for real depreciation cannot represent net additions to the capital stock of firms in the economy. Thus, such expenditures cannot represent a real improvement in the welfare of individuals who somehow either directly or indirectly benefit from the use of that economy's capital stock.

Thus, these sort of expenditures should be subtracted from gross expenditures, the GDP. The result is a more accurate portrayal of national well being, the NDP. Moreover, we can say that the distinction carries through to investment generally. So,

Gross Investment - Capital Consumption Allowance = Net Investment

and

GDP - Capital Consumption Allowance = NDP.

indirect business taxes

The second complication has to do with the manner in which the government collects taxes. There are two ways. **Direct** taxes are those collected on household or corporate incomes. **Indirect** taxes, which do not appear explicitly on B-26, are taxes generated from either firms' sales revenues or their property tax liabilities. You are familiar with indirect taxes such as sales or excise taxes. Special taxes placed on imported goods are another type of indirect tax. Whenever the government uses the firm's cash register as a point of tax collection, we have an example of indirect taxes before us. In fact, the only corporate tax which is *not* considered indirect is the government's levy on corporate profit income.

As these indirect taxes are paid out of firms' revenues prior to the calculation of their profits, these revenue collections do not represent any *added value* to the good itself. Rather, the tax, borne by firms and consumers, is simply a *transfer* of funds to the government. The tax should therefore be subtracted in order to arrive at a precise determination of national income.

National income could be approached from the other direction. At this stage the statistics on B-27 bear out that national income has three significant components: **Personal income** (on the far right), which is mostly from wages and rent collections of households; **interest payments** to households and firms; and **profits**.

Reconciling Saving and Investment, Table 5.1

Table 5.1 takes the final accounting identity discussed in the previous chapter (in the appendix) and plugs in real data from the real world. That final identity was based on a four sector economy:

Domestic Product   =   National Income

$$C + I + G + E_n = C + S + T + R$$

and can be manipulated algebraically to read

$$I + (E_n - R) = S + (T - G).$$

Within the parentheses we have net foreign investment $(E_n - R)$ and the government surplus $(T - G)$, which incidentally includes the state and local budgets, not merely the more often discussed federal budget.

Now Table 5.1 puts saving on the left and investment on the right, but this should not create too much confusion. Reading across the top, we see the basic breakdown is Gross Saving and Gross Investment. But Gross Saving is broken down between Gross Private Saving (S, above) and the government surplus or deficit. Meanwhile, Gross Investment is comprised of the domestic variety (I, above) and the net foreign kind, $(E_n - R)$.

Working down the list year by year, Gross Saving, $S + (T - G)$, is equal to Gross Investment, $I + (E_n - R)$, just as anticipated by the accounting identities. There is a small statistical discrepancy--but what's a few billion when we're dealing with what is presently a seven trillion dollar economy?

VOCABULARY

Inflation – a rise in the general price level

Deflation – a decline in the general price level

Real – descriptive term noting that an economic statistic has been adjusted for changes in the general price level

(Real) Growth – any increase in real GDP or in the total output of goods and services in a domestic economy measured in constant dollars

Recession – a decline in real domestic output lasting six months or more, as measured by real GDP

Real output – refers to the aggregate value of a firm's or nation's production, measured in constant dollars (see **real GDP**)

Nominal GDP – the current dollar value of all goods and services produced in a domestic economy within one year

Real GDP – the statistical equivalent of real output, measuring the constant dollar value of all goods and services produced in a domestic economy usually within one year's time

Base year – the year selected to serve as the statistical constant for the general price level when calculating real GDP for any given year

GDP Deflator – a statistical index used to measure the general price level in any given year, and to eventually measure any changes in the general price level

Current dollars – refers to the purchasing power of money within a particular time frame, usually a year

Changes in business inventories – the measured increase or decrease in unsold products of a firm or of the aggregate of all firms in a domestic economy

Net exports – the dollar flow difference between exports and imports

Final sales – the revenue flow to firms generated by end-user purchases of goods and services in a domestic economy within one year; statistically, nominal GDP minus changes in business inventories

Relative share – the fractional or percentage portion of a constituent part vis-a-vis its larger component category; e.g., consumption is approximately a 2/3 share of GDP

Structural change – refers to any substantial evolution wrought upon the performance of a domestic economy from sweeping social forces which themselves are not merely economic, but political, institutional and historical as well

Net Domestic Product – the value of all goods and services produced in a domestic economy within one year after deducting depreciation

Depreciation (capital consumption allowance) – statistically, the estimate of requisite expenditures by firms for the maintenance, renovation and replacement of used capital equipment

Direct tax – any tax levied upon a single economic agent

Indirect tax – any tax, the burden of which is shared between two or more economic agents

Personal income – the cash inflow of a household unit from wages, dividends, interest and transfer payments

END-OF-CHAPTER QUESTIONS

1. Make up your own model economy (or perhaps continue the one provided) to produce a combination of inflation with negative real growth. Verify your results by calculating the GDP deflators and real GDP.

2. During the Depression, when real GDP was falling, the general price level was falling too. Given this fact, which would you expect to fall faster (on a percentage basis), nominal or real GDP?

3. If real growth exists for a given period and the price level is rising at the same time, could nominal GDP fall during these years?

4. If inflation ran at 10% but real output fell by 5%, what would happen to nominal GDP?

5. Trace through the data on real governmental spending from 1930 to 1950 and identify the periods in which there appears to be acceleration in federal spending (as a share of total government spending and GDP). What do you know historically about these times that can help account for the spending increases?

PART FOUR

MACRO-ECONOMIC THEORIES

"For the Classical Theory has.... assumed fluidity [in] money wages; and when there is rigidity, to lay on this rigidity the blame of maladjustment...

.... this theory has nothing to offer, when it is applied to the problem of what... determines employment as a whole."

John Maynard Keynes

CHAPTER 9

MACRO-ECONOMIC THEORY BEFORE KEYNES

The precursors of theoretic debate in economics first appeared in the works of social philosophers, in particular Thomas Hobbes in his Leviathan and John Locke in his Two Treatises of Government. These works grappled with the most fundamental questions about economic man and his wants, a person's relation to others in society, and the concept of property. What is man's work? What things does he have a right to? What things are his by nature and what things are his by consent of his fellow man?

As observers of a changing society, serious thinkers progressed from philosophic inquiries and attempted to set the parameters of economic science. What should the economist try to do? Is he or she an expositor of the problems of scarcity or the problems of money? A disinterested observer of markets or a full-fledged societal guru? What's the chief guiding concern eliminating poverty? Or creating theories to explain the price of tea in China? Because there is no conformity in these matters, it's impossible to have uniformity of opinion.

In the next three chapters, we undertake a thorough and serious discussion of economic theories. The previous two units introduced all that economists have pretty much in common: supply and demand, common assumptions and methods (even styles), common tools and statistical references. But in this section we devote our attention to the differences among economists. For the everyday person is frequently heard to comment that economists rarely agree about economic matters--about, for instance, economic prospects for the upcoming year; whether a certain policy would be beneficial or harmful; whether inflation is more detrimental than unemployment; whether interest rates should be raised or lowered. The task at hand is to understand the real reason for such disparities of opinion.

We must distinguish between two classes of divergent views. First, economists might disagree on the conclusion to be drawn from empirical evidence. As mentioned earlier, the economic world is a hodgepodge of social, political, and purely economic forces. It is rarely clear which set of factors will impose a primary influence in shaping the future. On the other hand, a theoretical disagreement is more

fundamental. This type involves either the method of investigation or the theoretical structure employed. A disagreement on method, for instance, would involve the proper usage of, and reliance on, certain techniques for the collection of data (facts). A disagreement on theoretical structure would be on the order of Copernicus' break from geocentric conceptions of the universe: the vision of what the (economic) universe is and how it operates is called into question.

Thus, the surveyor of economic opinion faces challenging work, because any disagreement he or she might come across could stem from two possible sources: either the *interpretation* of agreed upon facts, or the *theory* that defines facts. It is even possible that the two kinds of disagreement can exist in a single case.

This author believes that if the student can master some understanding of economic debate, he or she will be in a better position to interpret the views of politicians and commentators in the press and contribute positively to that political and social world in which we all partake.

Basically, we will take a look at two major modes of thought in macro-economics. First, we'll consider the economists before Keynes, usually called the **Classical** economists, by concentrating on the ideas expressed by Smith and Jean Baptiste Say. Then we'll study Keynes. In a third chapter, we'll look at other theoretical strains within the discipline.

We place all of the upcoming discussion in an historical context. Like plants that require certain conditions in order to grow, economic theories spring forth within certain historical conditions that make them relevant and meaningful.

SMITH

The changing economic and social structures of 18th century England created the need, as we've said before, of an interpreter and explicator of ideas. Beneath routine daily life lay an uneasy uncertainty about the changes occurring and to what they might lead. Such apprehensions are common in a changing society and economy. Prominent examples exist in our own day in the regions of Eastern Europe and China which have loosed themselves from paternalistic Communistic regimes, only to grope for a new social design that is both vibrant and stable.

In his book The Wealth of Nations, Adam Smith enunciated clearly to his countrymen that, in effect, the developing market network, at once expanding and integrating itself, yet too, irrevocably forging new social relations, was leading the nation to greater prosperity. Smith's explanation of the paradox that self-interest would lead to the greatest social welfare justified a burgeoning entrepreneurial class's pursuit of monetary success. The chaos of self-interested pursuits would weave itself into a coherent, even beautiful, social tapestry. Let's examine Smith's social vision.

Imagine a society of small businessmen, simple craftsmen, and artisans, who, within a single community, provide the basic wants of their community through daily commerce. Suppose this community had heretofore used cotton to provide for most of its clothing wants. But one year it develops a stronger taste for wool clothing. How would the market provide? Relative prices would signal and inform the business community of the changing profit opportunities. Businesses would then allocate resources towards the satisfaction of these newer tastes. For what we essentially see in the cotton market at this time is a fall in demand. This lowers cotton prices and hence diminishes the profits to those providers of cotton. At the same time, the prices for wool clothing rise from the obvious rise in demand. So, the relatively high price of wool clothing indicates to entrepreneurs that relatively higher profits exist there. Thus it is in their own best interest to devote a greater proportion of their limited resources, both financial and capital resources, to that market. At the same time, of course, they have an incentive to exit the cotton clothing market.

Later on a sort of reversal begins. As entrepreneurs continue to devote more resources to wool and less to cotton, the prices undergo a retreat. For in the long run, the supply of wool clothing increases, lowering the price of wool clothing.

Meanwhile, the supply of cotton, reflecting the exit of entrepreneurs and their resources, falls. But this sends the price of cotton clothing back in the direction of its origin. In the end, the prices of the two types of clothing come to a new equilibrium, like a pendulum coming to rest.

This balancing action of prices has a corollary in the physical sciences: for every action there is an equal and opposite reaction. It perhaps should not be expected to hold so precisely in economics as it does in physics, yet the resemblance is so strong that the phrase holds the key intuitive message of equilibrium economics; i.e., the economics of the market as understood by the vast majority of economists since Adam Smith. Again, the forces of the market, expressed in price movements, tend to counter-balance, check, oppose, and limit each other--dynamically--to re-create the balance that existed in the past; in a word, to maintain equilibrium. Each new force seemingly calls forth some other force that brings the former's demise.

Lest it be forgotten, *quantities* of cotton and wool produced (or offered) are more permanently changed. For cotton markets see the fall in demand reenforced by a fall in supply later on. And wool markets see quantity gains reenforced by a rise in supply.

Moreover, resource markets act in concert with events in the two product markets. Wool resource markets can expect rising values for their land, labor, and capital. This is complemented by lower prices for resources used in cotton production. These changing valuations of resources are demand-generated, responding to changes in demand in the product markets. Gradually, cotton resource markets release land, labor, and capital, while the higher prices in wool resource markets call them forth. This re-distribution of resources mirrors the equilibrating motions of the product market as it offsets advances in wool resource prices, and reverses declines in cotton resource prices.

In the end, when the entire set of wool and cotton prices resettles, entrepreneurs receive a signal that no further redistribution of resources would serve their interests. Any relative advantage to the firm in switching to wool ends as prices settle, or, in what amounts to the same thing, when profits return to normal levels.

Thus, Smith envisions a well-coordinated system of independent, yet interrelated, markets providing signals back and forth, to and fro, establishing equilibriums through and through; a system changing and stable like the seasons, like the tides, guided as though by an invisible hand.

Smith thought that free (unfettered) market competition would make the best of all *possible* worlds practically inevitable. Self-interested pursuit would deliver the desired products, raise the quality of products, and bring the greatest accumulations of wealth more efficiently and more fairly than any alternative economic system could hope to achieve. In the final analysis, the interest of society and the interest of entrepreneurs are aligned when individuals can pursue their interests freely. Nearly all economists since then have agreed with him.

In many respects, Smith is a more complex economist than indicated by his explanation of market processes. Because the timing of his work necessitated his being a synthesizer, The Wealth of Nations contains elements of micro and macro, chunks of positive and normative economics, philosophical foundations for both free enterprise *and* Marxian socialism. Thus, no three or four page summary can pretend to do his work justice. What is offered here is simply a synopsis of his insights into the competitive market. The synopsis is offered in context. It is provided so we might begin a much grander story, a story which leads to capitalism's deepest historical crisis, and an alternative vision of the macro-economy.

That grander story begins with the work of another economist.

J.B. SAY

In the early 19th century a famous French economist named Jean Baptiste Say enunciated the fundamental conclusion of Classical macro-economic thinking. Said Say, "Supply creates its own demand." The claim, dubbed **Say's Law,** is the logical extension of virtually

a half-century's discourse on the economics of the marketplace. It takes Smithian insights about particular markets and writes them in the large letters of the macro-economy.

What does Say's Law say? It suggests a couple of things immediately, but it eventually implies a broad sweep of relationships existing between money, credit and the economy *generally*. It is time now to consider both the fundamentals and the nuances of this highly influential economic tenet.

Foremost, Say's Law implies that production in general necessarily creates sufficient income to purchase all output. Is this true?

Recall the basic flow diagram from Chapter 7 and consider the monetary flow starting from the firms' production costs and ending with the firms' revenue. Since the firms' cost flow is identically equal to the income flow of households, and that income could potentially be fully spent to buy a given period's output, then indeed the production of goods does create an income sufficient to buy that output -- or to clear the market. Thus, as an accounting principle, Say's Law is valid.

But there's a problem. The problem is household saving.

While production cost flows and household income flows *must* be equal, it does not follow that household income exactly corresponds to household expenditures (consumption). This is so because households always *save* some portion of their earnings.

As long as households save a portion of their income, demand would apparently be *insufficient* with respect to supply. For firms would have leftover products that they'd place in inventory. And if consumers saved through time, the inventory would grow continuously. This trend would indicate that goods are being produced and supplied, but there's no complementary demand to purchase them.

In this case, the accumulating inventory comes as a result of the dollars households put aside. A *general* surplus develops, since transactions didn't take place that would have cleared the excess inventory (or, cleared the market). Unless there is some process by which these bulging inventories are systematically reduced, it would seem unlikely that supply creates its own demand.[1]

J.B. Say realized this and formulated an explanation. In a properly functioning market, prices *automatically adjust* to clear the market. While markets can temporarily go askew whereby surpluses occur, the adjustment of prices will in the long run correct the imbalance, or disequilibrium. For in a surplus, the **carrying cost** of excessive inventory will provide an incentive for firms to lower prices in order to clear that excess and automatically cause quantity demanded to come in line with quantity supplied.

So, if we consider a case in which we take a given level of household saving and then increase it, it is true that a general glut of products on the market will ensue. But to Say and all classically-influenced economists, that's not the end of the story. Prices will automatically fall too. And this will be sufficient to eventually clear the market.

So far this is all very Smithian: prices adjust, equilibrium is restored, supply and demand adjust to each other. But Say extended his analysis to include the **money market**, or what's usually called the market for **loanable funds**, and tied this to events in the macro-economy.

Say reasoned that if households were to save at increased rates and throw the firms into a temporary tailspin, the problem would fix itself through the adjustments of the **interest rate**, the price of borrowed funds. For when households increase their savings they raise the total amount of funds available for borrowing. This means that in the market for loanable funds, the fund supply rises. Given the demand, interest rates will then decline. But since falling interest rates are inducements to firms to increase their borrowing and investment spending, an

increased *supply* of loanable funds creates its own (investment) *demand* to employ those funds. In the meantime, the higher *supply* of products from the increased investment spending will necessitate gains in employment and wages. Concluded Say, these income gains will create a *demand* sufficient to offset any glut of goods and purchase any additional output.

The import of this law can now be summarized. Say's Law strongly implies that a long run *general* surplus is impossible, so long as prices are flexible. In the macroeconomy, if prices, especially the interest rate, are permitted to fluctuate according to the movements of the supply and demand, the economy will always tend towards its most productive, efficient level: what we'll now call **full employment equilibrium**. The macro-economy is, therefore, self-regulating. It needs no assistance from the government, except perhaps to ensure that prices are flexible. The economy will resolve any and all of its problems in the long run.

A bit more theoretically, supply creates its own demand in the macro-economy because *saving will automatically create investment; any increase in saving will lower the interest rate and thereby call forth new investment in the exact degree of the additional saving.* Money, being useful only when it's spent, will not long stay idle in the banks. No glut of unspent dollars will accumulate. Saved funds get automatically re-directed by the credit market to those willing to spend. The macro-economy works and works well.

Say's Law is the essence of macro-economic theory prior to Keynes' writings during the 1930's. Others, especially Walras, were more technical; some focused their attention on micro-economics. But Say's Law was familiar throughout the world, and known like a mantra.

Graphing the world according to Say

This is a good juncture to introduce Say's macro-economic equilibrium diagrammatically. Some things will change in these upcoming graphs, but the basic format is exactly the same.

_____

[1] Say's Law, if it is to be a viable theory, cannot rest on the idea that households spend every last dollar. It can't be a special-case accounting identity, because that is too limited. It must be able to explain market clearing processes in the macro-economy when households regularly save.

aggregate supply and demand

In the macro–economy, we still have supply and demand tracing a positive and negative slope respectively. But the interpretation is that the supply curve represents the sum total offerings of all the firms that actively participate in the economy. Much as the supply in a given market is the summation of all the firms' individual supply curves (See Chapter 5, # of sellers), the **Aggregate Supply** adds up the various price and quantity combinations for all firms in all markets. Meanwhile, **Aggregate Demand** lists the price and quantity combinations appropriate for the sectors of the economy that purchase the aggregate output: households through their consumption, firms through their investment, government, and net foreign exchange.

Graphically, it looks pretty much the same.

Aggregate Supply and Demand

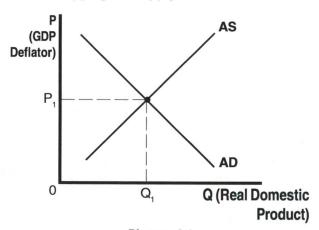

Diagram 9-1

Now the price represented on the vertical axis is not the price of any particular item. Rather, it represents the general price level of all goods offered by firms. We have seen this concept statistically described as the GDP Deflator. Thus, the movements of the GDP price deflator in Diagram 9-1 yield information about whether the economy is experiencing inflation or deflation. The Q on the horizontal axis is not any one specific commodity; it is a compositeof all of them: one part car, one part house, one part tractor, one part health services, one

part bridges and bombs. Its movements correspond to trends in real growth. A retreat left in Q indicates recession; a rightward advance indicates growth.

So, picking up the story, suppose households increased their saving habits. This is depicted below by a fall in Aggregate Demand, since households appear on the demand side via their consumption expenditures. In the short run, inventories would rise and effect a general surplus.

A General Surplus Due to a Fall in Aggregate Demand

Diagram 9-2

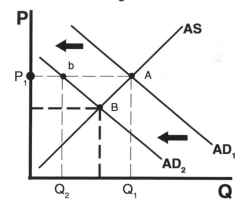

Firms, however, will soon see that the only way to alleviate this surplus is to lower prices. As they do, the Aggregate Supply, in effect, *increases*. (If a firm has a sale on its product, the action is equivalent to a rise in supply, since it is offering more product at each and every possible price.) The surplus dissipates by virtue of a fall in the general price level. Equally important, output, measured by Q, is restored. Diagram 9-3 shows this process.

the money market

Underlying this scenario would be the events in the market for loanable funds. The fundamentals of this market are these: The supply of funds (at least in part) is provided by households via their saving--this, according to Say's version of things. The supply curve slopes positively, since any provider of funds would tend to offer more funds if the interest rate offered is raised. On the demand side, which consists of those

Recovery from a General Surplus

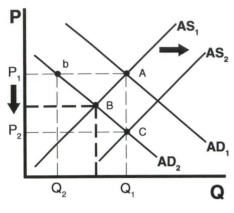

Diagram 9-3

The Effects of Increased Saving

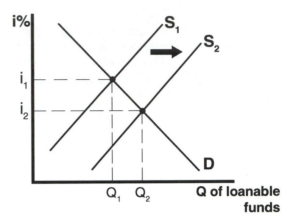

Diagram 9-4

firms which would like to borrow in order to purchase real capital, we have a negative slope, since higher rates charged for borrowing would discourage loaning activity and lower rates would encourage it. So far, this is pretty straightforward. The only difficulty is semantic: the interest rate we speak of here should not be referred to as the price of money (the price of money is exactly the commodity for which money is exchanged), but the price of *loanable funds*, or, more familiarly, the price of **credit**.

When Aggregate Demand falls due to the increased inclination to save, there would also be an increase in loanable fund supply. This rightward shift in fund supply tries to capture a process economists call **capital formation**. Classical economists argue capital formation begins with household saving; that households must be willing to sacrifice consumption, i.e., save dollars, in order to spur investment. This, in turn, paves the way for growth in future consumption as firms become more productive and households pick up interest earnings on their sacrificed assets. In the world according to Say, the saved dollars are funnelled to firms by the banking system when households deposit money to their accounts.[2] The graph below is meant to capture these events in an approximate way.

We can see that a fall in the interest rate prompts an increase in the *quantity demanded* of loanable funds. Presumably, this money will be spent productively to increase the capital stock of firms. This increase in investment spending necessarily generates the income flows which eventually get used to purchase any surplus and any net gains in output.[3]

It is hoped that students recognize this story from two vantage points. First, Say's Law is entirely consistent with the equilibrium process outlined by Smith. Obviously, Say was influenced by Smith. But also, the story we've just been through is similar to one introduced in Chapter 5. The present example is a little more general in that we have a drop in the spending for final goods offset by an increase in investment spending. But the idea of redistribution of funds via the choices of consumers is exactly the same. Also preserved is the idea that society is able to smoothly convert resources from one task to another *while maintaining full employment at all times during this conversion.*

Thus, one of the core underlying intuitions of Say's Law is that *the impositions of scarcity apply as much*

---

[2] This could be done even more directly through a household's purchase of corporate stocks or bonds. Such a purchase is actually saving since households are storing their (accumulated) wealth.

[3] This story need not be modelled exactly as is done here. The shifts in AS and AD are meant to illustrate the thinking behind Say's Law and the self-regulating, self-correcting mechanisms in the macro-economy. The shifts can be handled slightly differently to produce the same basic result, at least in spirit.

to the whole of society as to the individual in society. Why? Because society is faced with a series of trade-offs about the levels of consumption and saving it might select, and these correspond to the levels of consumption and levels of investment they can possibly support. Furthermore, the trade-off exactly coincides with the decision regarding levels of consumption enjoyed today versus levels of consumption enjoyed tomorrow. Say's Law puts the issue directly to society: increasing tomorrow's wealth requires sacrifices in the present. Some of these sacrifices might be acutely felt, but they bring rewards, virtually automatically, in a well-functioning economy. Sacrificed consumption, the very definition of saving,

helps define society's larger effort in capital production. Saving becomes investment, leads to investment, makes investment possible. So with each advance in saving society shifts to a higher capital production gear.

It might be beneficial to step out of the theoretical world for a moment. Students can well appreciate Say's point here if they consider their own positions in life. Students by no means *have* to be in college. In the same time and for the same effort they could be collecting wages. Why go to college and sacrifice potential income and consumption? At least one of the justifications is that the college diploma will help

Say's Law and the Macro-Economy's
Self-adjusting Mechanisms

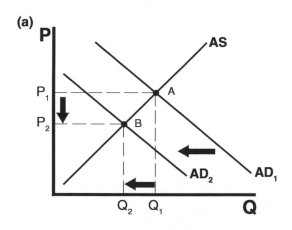

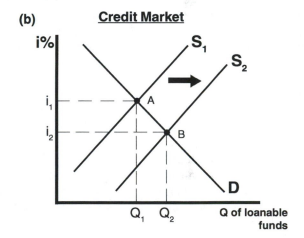

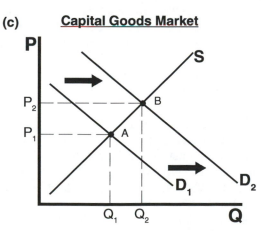

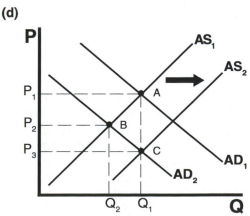

Diagrams 9-5,a-d

provide an even higher standard of living beyond the college years. The sense of sacrificed consumption for even greater consumption tomorrow--as a result of a certain kind of effort *expended* today--is completely analogous to Say's thinking about the economy.

Diagrams 9-5, a-d is a series of graphs which recapitulate Say's macroeconomic picture through the story just examined above. These graphs are meant to cement in the reader's mind the linkages between the key markets in the macro-economy as suggested by Say's Law. We are including a new graph, that of the capital goods market, so that the markets for loanable funds and for capital equipment are neatly tied into the aggregate supply and demand scheme. The single most important thing to see in them is the self-correcting capacity of the macro-economy, its inherent ability to create the conditions for full and efficient use of resources via the adjustment of prices and interest rates. Or as Say says, "Supply creates its own demand."

The Twenties and Thirties in the U.S.A.

We can begin now our consideration of an historical case, a case that begins in full employment equilibrium and ends in full employment equilibrium much as Say explained. But what happened in between was tantamount to revolution. What happened was Say's impossible world: a depression.

Let us begin our history with the 1920's. The roaring twenties they called them: a glorious moment in American history.

Herbert Hoover, elected President in 1928, confidently proclaims that his economic policies will deliver a chicken in every pot and a car in every garage. Nobody doubts him. Wages are attractive and average workers feel like fat cats. Households are buying up equity in the American companies as though they were mere pieces of stationery. They buy "on the margin," a financial arrangement that allows one to buy shares of corporate stock with borrowed funds. Borrowing up to 95% of the cost of the stock is permissible. Speculation, the solemn effort to make a swift buck, sweeps Wall Street. People use

their 95% borrowed stock as collateral! The Dow Jones is rising and everyone wants to catch it. Banks join the fun.

These are the days of The Great Gatsby. Money and wealth are more than society's tool for daily functioning and promise of future security. Money means glamour, romance, and leisure. It is a mere plaything in these rather permissive years. Sexual mores are relaxed. Drugs are prevalent even if, like alcohol, illegal. Gangsters are heroes.

No one foresaw the demise to come shortly following Hoover's inauguration. On October 29, 1929, the century's first stock market crash ripped through Wall Street like some hellacious tempest. Suddenly, the rampant speculation changed into panic selling, eliminating gains in one day that took years to create.

It is difficult for someone not familiar with the financial markets to understand how powerful the forces were that imposed themselves that day. Couldn't these problems be foreseen or were these speculators simply blind to the risks? Wasn't there some kind of escape route? The difficulties can't be appreciated until these events are made a bit more concrete.

The previous seven or eight years of climbing stock values clearly lulled the public into complacency. A lapse in financial prudence is not usually destructive but enduring financial security never rests upon speculative ferver. The financial managers, bankers, and buying public seemed in these years to lose the healthy measure of circumspection that is needed to keep markets stable. The volatility seen on October 29th was only part of a larger instability forming in the years before the Crash.

In the financial markets, where (1) every person's gain is another's loss and (2) every person is out to acquire the highest possible *future* gain, trading implicitly involves two opposing prospects about the future trend of the price of the asset. A person sells a financial asset on the belief that it will be a relative loser (its price will lose relative value). A person buys for the opposite reason: he or she believes its relative value will rise. Thus, trades are possible whenever people *disagree*. Furthermore, so long as the number of optimists and pessimists stand in balance, a stable equilibrium price will appear, one that suits the optimist's need for future gain and the pessimist's need for present profit.

Given this, a crash can't occur in a vacuum. It nearly always will be the result of some exaggerated run-up of values that was supported by a market comprised of 99% optimists and 1% pessimists. Eventually, the lack of balanced perspective "corrects" itself by an equally extreme change of heart. When there are 99% pessimists in the market, the 1% optimists cannot head off the avalanche of selling. The result is devastating.

It can be tempting to think that all an individual need do in this situation is to "keep his head on his shoulders." But it is not realistic that he can do so. This is true not so much because of a human being's proclivity to act with the crowd, though this is certainly part of the problem in an unstable market. The point here is that there's a certain amount of reason in being with the crowd. Perhaps it is easier to understand the up-side of this. If the market is bullish, as they say, a person would forfeit opportunities for gain were he to stay on the sidelines for an extended period. Conversely, when "everybody's selling" and values are plummeting, one should probably sell as soon as possible to minimize the loss in value of one's holdings (portfolio). But of course as each individual considers this and acts upon it, the problem of falling values is exacerbated.

So, literally, fortunes were being lost in an environment wherein even the most level-headed individual was helpless: in the midst of a market free-fall, you're doomed if you do sell, you're doomed if you don't.

So, unprotected from the onslaught, personal fortunes were lost in minutes. Those that could salvage some equity and hold on would recoup, but only after 15 years.

The general sense of insecurity spread into the banking system before too long. And it is here that American capitalism nearly collapsed. Unlike today, banks were not insured by the federal government for their customers' deposits. As the market crash spread panic throughout the country, depositors rushed to their banks to withdraw funds or close their accounts.

Again, these actions should be placed in context. Banks in the early thirties were in serious trouble because of the Crash and its effect on (1) new loans and on (2) existing loans. New loans, the source of the banks' future interest receipts, were curtailed because of the lack of new investment activity. Meanwhile, existing loans were not being repaid as a result of the many steep losses taken, in both the financial and real product markets. Sensing the difficulties that banks were having, and understanding the potential for losses, regular depositors rushed to demand their cash claims against their banks. The run for funds might have been perfectly justified from the individual depositor's point of view, but it was ultimately destructive for the banks. Whenever a bank is in trouble, the worst thing that can occur is to have its depositors close their accounts. Those deposits are the bank's readiest source of cash. And without cash, banks die.

What we saw in the years following the Crash is the price for a sustained loss of trust. In removing all deposits from the banks and hoarding their money, people express the profoundest lack of trust possible. Yet their lack of trust attacks the system, the system which supports their own livelihoods. In capitalism, distrust is death. On the other hand, being reasonably optimistic regarding the future, feeling secure about the financial investments that one has made--these things create the conditions in which a capitalist economy can sustain itself. Today's prudent optimism validates yesterday's. Entrusting a bank with money permits the bank to maximize its flexibility for loan making, which, though risky, is fundamentally necessary in modern free enterprise.

In a final, more technical demonstration of the Crash's impact, we'd do well to reexamine the statistics. Real private domestic investment fell over 75% between 1929 and 1933, the year Roosevelt assumed the presidency. This, too, was symptomatic of the lack of faith in the future. If a firm does not believe that today's investment will be profitable, it will not undertake the project. When this attitude is prevalent in the business community, recessionary trends, or worse, are inevitable. Such pessimism was prevalent from October 29, 1929 onward. And for as long as this attitude held sway, the nation could never gain ground on that prosperity President Hoover kept saying was "just around the corner."

The solution of the Classical economists

What could be done to alleviate the problem? Could the nation respond to this economic threat? Was it permanent?

Here we can begin to see the real effects of economic theory. Whether or not someone feels that the economy should be left to its own devices depends on the economic theory he or she espouses. Why? Because the theory provides the framework for economic analysis and, hence, the basis for assessing what's wrong with the economy. The economist then advises on the basis of the analysis. The Classical economists, having the tradition of 150 years of Smithian analysis of the market behind them, offered the only possible recommendation open to them: do nothing. An automatic recovery process would begin in the credit market. According to their analysis the drop in spending would necessarily imply higher saving in the economy, making new capital funds available. Thus, interest rates would fall and have a correcting influence by stimulating new investment spending. The economy will correct itself.

Classical economists also emphasized the potentially corrective influence of the labor market. During the 30's there was upwards of 25% unemployment. How could such idleness develop if the economy, per Say's Law, always tended to full employment? And how could a labor market in such distress fix itself?

Most economists of that time felt that labor had priced themselves out of the market. Labor could be rehired, these economists said, if only workers were willing to accept a wage that would permit firms to produce goods profitably. Their very idleness served as evidence that labor was desirous of too high a

wage. That is to say, workers were not *competing* for work to a degree sufficient to lower the price of labor. Hence, many went unemployed.

The reasoning here is purely Classical. If price flexibility made markets work, then inflexibility causes a breakdown. The labor market's inflexibility could be found in its rigidly high wages, the true source of the labor surplus. Classical economists argued that workers must reconcile themselves to a reduced wage, or else suffer continued joblessness.

The Classical Conception of the Depression and Unemployment

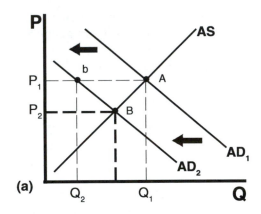

Labor Market

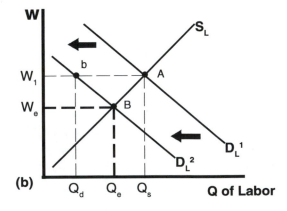

Diagrams 9-6, a-b

Upon accepting lower wages, not only would the labor market return to equilibrium, but a full-fledged, general recovery would follow.

a view with graphs

Let us work through the entire Classical vision.

Given that Aggregate Demand fell due to the dramatic drop in business investment, demand in the labor market would experience a similar decline. For in a less active economy workers become less profitable and hence less demanded by firms.

If we examine Diagram 9-6b, the fall in demand for labor should reduce the wage to W_e. Anyone willing to work at that wage will get a job (up to Q_e). Anyone wanting more takes himself out of the labor market. At point B, the quantity supplied of labor matches the quantity demanded. The labor market would be in equilibrium.

But in the early 1930's the labor market did not seem to be in equilibrium at all. With idle, but apparently willing, workers available, the indications were that a labor surplus existed. This surplus suggested that the 1930's wage was inappropriately high, say at W_1.

How did that come about? Classical economists explained that as the demand for labor fell, workers resisted lower wages. To save expenses, firms laid off workers. In other words, labor collectively tried to

retain its earnings at rates prevailing in the late 1920's (associated with equilibrium point A on Diagram 9-6b). Given the 1930's conditions, such earnings were exorbitant. An over-priced worker, like an over-priced apple, will not be purchased. Rather, a surplus "inventory" will develop. On Diagram 9-6b the surplus can be identified as the difference between Q_d and Q_s at the W_1 wage rate. These persons are willing to work at W_1 but cannot be profitably utilized by firms given the conditions during the Depression.

What can alleviate the surplus? A well functioning labor market would push wages down to the equilibrium set by labor supply and the D^2_L level of labor demand. For this to occur, labor must act competitively in the market.

Eventually everybody would voluntarily accept lower wages in return for a job. How does this play in the market? When workers collectively accept lower wages, the market supply of labor rises. This lowers the equilibrium wage (yet again). And, as Diagram 9-7b shows, the increase in labor supply has even broader implications.

The equilibrium position of the labor market shifts from point B to C. Since workers finally settle for lower wages, the quantity demanded of workers rises. It rises to a level just sufficient to employ at levels seen in 1929. The invisible hand succeeds: supply automatically counter-balances a demand problem.

Equally important, the correcting influence of the

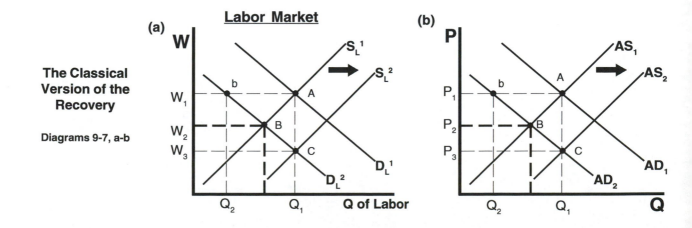

The Classical Version of the Recovery

Diagrams 9-7, a-b

market stretches into the economy generally. Labor's move to accept lower wages effects an increase in Aggregate Supply since labor's lesser wage reduces firms' production per unit costs. With the subsequent shift in Aggregate Supply, real output returns to the 1929 level. The general price level declines. The Depression is over.

For the invisible hand has steered the economy away from the Depression's course--as it always will. And supply has truly created its own demand--as Say had said it would. The Classical vision of the economy is complete.

VOCABULARY

Classical economics – economic theory originating with Adam Smith and continuing through J.B Say; traditional theory which explicated the self-regulating features of the market and argued that governmental incursions into the market were unhelpful

Say's Law – the idea that supply creates its own demand via a series of macro-level price adjustments and interest rate changes; implied that a general depresssion in economic activity was impossible

Carrying cost – the opportunity cost of holding inventory or any bulky asset

Loanable funds (market) – cash available for borrowing through financial institutions (market for such purposes)

Interest rate – the price of borrowed funds

Full employment equilibrium – the full utilization of resources as determined by the supply and demand of those resources

Aggregate Supply – the supply of all final goods and services to firms, households and government as determined by technology and the cost of resources.

Aggregate Demand – the demand for all final goods and services by households, firms, and government

Credit – synonomous with loanable funds (market)

Capital formation – refers to the process of production of capital goods from initial financing to the completion of a given piece of machinery, equipment, or plant

CHAPTER 10

KEYNES' ECONOMICS

"In the long run we're all dead."

Of such utter common sense, great economic theories are born.

John Maynard Keynes, the economic theorist, was himself born in the late 19th century (1883). He was raised in Britain, the son a prominent economist named John Neville Keynes. In this sense, John Maynard was born into a privileged family: educated, well-to-do, with social connections to the most influential in society. He was in want of few things. Now most of human experience would suggest that such a fortunate child would not become the type to upset the proverbial apple cart. But Keynes grew up to do just that in his chosen field.

"...I believe myself to be writing a book on economic theory which will largely revolutionize-- not I suppose at once, but in the course of the next ten years--the way the world thinks about economic problems." So he wrote to his friend, George Bernard Shaw, the renowned, satirical playwright. Keynes' book, The General Theory of Employment, Interest, and Money, was written in response to the American economic experience of the 1930's. Keynes wanted to account for the existence of the very thing classical economists considered impossible: the Great Depression. To be successful he would have to do nothing less than turn inside out a century and a half's worth of economic wisdom.

The matter for Keynes' closest scrutiny would be the nearly sacred tenet that the market had the capacity to automatically correct itself and bring about, in the macro-economic realm, the full employment of society's resources. Nothing could more fundamentally express the import of economic theory prior to Keynes than this idea. To undo it, he would have to play a part not unlike the coolest of card sharks in a grizzly battle of nerves: he would simply call the invisible hand to show itself.

THE CRITIQUE

The labor market

Was labor so in control of its own destiny that it could simply lower its wage and get rehired? Was labor to blame for its own unemployment and the prolonged slowdown in business activity? Ultimately, Keynes said, no.

At least part of the mistake of his predecessors was to believe that what is true for a group of individuals *as individuals* is therefore true for the group itself *as a group*. This belief commits the **fallacy of composition**. Keynes criticized much of economic theory by appealing to this type of fallacy. Keynes maintained that the logic that had been developed by economists to comprehend particular markets would not ultimately be satisfactory for understanding the market.

To understand the fallacy of composition let us consider first a simple example. Suppose a teacher is grading "on a curve." He or she distributes the test and, regardless of the nominal scores of the performances, sorts them relatively. Then, by criteria prescribed before the test (for example, 10% A's, 20% B's, etc.), awards grades to fit the criteria.

Now we can imagine a student asking his teacher prior to the next test, "What can I do to improve my grade?" And the teacher replies, "Study 2 hours more than you planned to."

Now it's true for each individual sitting in that class that were he to study for a couple more hours, he would improve his score. That might translate into a better letter grade for the next test. But it will not translate into a higher letter grade if *every* student studies for two additional hours; i.e., *it cannot possibly be true for the class as a whole*. Since the teacher grades on a curve, when everybody gets a higher grade, there will be no effect in terms of relative results: the same people who were on top with two fewer hours of study will still be on top with two additional hours of study. Those behind will not climb ahead in relative terms; hence their letter grade will remain at the lower end. There's no real or relative change. In the long run...some will pass and some will fail.

Now let's apply the fallacy, as Keynes would, to Classical theory. Take the labor market, for example, and its alleged role as a correcting force in an economy in the throws of a depression. Keynes would point out that if workers as a group took a wage cut (which would necessarily be a monetary wage cut in a monetary economy), it would be impossible for this cut to act as an incentive for increased hiring and thereby initiate a recovery. The self-regulating influence of wages as normally envisioned by economists would not actually be functional in the macro context. Keynes would simply point out that a lower wage, while a boon to an individual's chances of being hired, would not be so when *everybody* lowered their wages proportionally.

Why wouldn't lower wages have a correcting influence? Two themes developed earlier in the text point the way: (1) macro-economic activity is a *flow* of interconnected transactions; and (2) one person's cost is another's income.

Recall the basic macro-flow diagram of Chapter 7. The economy's production costs incurred by the firms are by and large received by households as wages and salaries. These collections primarily determine consumption spending. But consumption spending, in turn, is identically equal to the gross revenues of the firms. Thus, were households to collectively charge, say, 25% less for their labor services, household income would decline by 25%. What then? Assuming that there's no change in the rate of household spending out of income, consumption spending and revenues would fall 25%. There is no way to escape this. For the aggregate wages are, ultimately, the linchpin for which the firms' future revenues are based. Together, firms cannot amass a net gain from falling wages because falling wages imply less revenue later. If aggregate wages had been 4 billion and a 25% cut in wages were enacted generally, wages would become 3 billion and revenues at most would be 3 billion (rather than the 4 billion in the previous period). The *same amount of real-flow activity would exist*. If the economy had been doing well, it still would continue to do well; if it were experiencing a depression, it would remain in one.

Why? Keynes considered Aggregate Supply and Demand to contain interdependencies which made the method of analysis of individual markets (where

it is assumed that supply and demand are independent) ill-suited for macro-economic analysis.

To reenforce Keynes' thinking, we can adopt the tools of Aggregate Supply and Demand analysis. Keynes might begin his analysis by taking the conditions of the depression as given. In Diagram 10-1b, point B (which is the same point B as appears in Diagram 9-7b) represents the price level and real output from 1932. Tracing the thinking of his predecessors, Keynes would assume that workers took a general cut in wages. Yes, production costs would decline and this would shift Aggregate Supply to the right. But the improvement is only apparent. For when households are receiving less income, their consumption spending would necessarily decline. This would suggest a shift leftward in Aggregate Demand. The economy would not end up in the full employment equilibrium of point C but at point D, where the price level is lower (following the nominal wage trend) with a level of real output basically unchanged.

At this point Keynes is venturing into the heretical. For what Keynes' analysis implies is that an equilibrium of the macro-economy can exist below full employment. This is so because the general or aggregate *nominal* wage bill is determined independently from the aggregate level of *real* activity. Furthermore, there is no automatic tendency of the economy to remove itself from its given condition-- certainly not from the labor market--via the adjustment of labors' wages.

In other words, Keynes pursued the implications of the self-adjusting wage story to its logical macro-economic conclusion and found not the elimination of surplus, idle labor but the persistence of **involuntary unemployment**. Before Keynes, economists contended that all unemployment is voluntary.

The credit market

With a breadth of perspective similar to that displayed in his analysis of the labor market, Keynes turned to the market where loanable funds are acquired. The error of Say's Law can also be seen in the context of the fallacy of composition. Ultimately, Keynes will show that while it can be beneficial for

Keynes' Analysis of the Classical Recovery

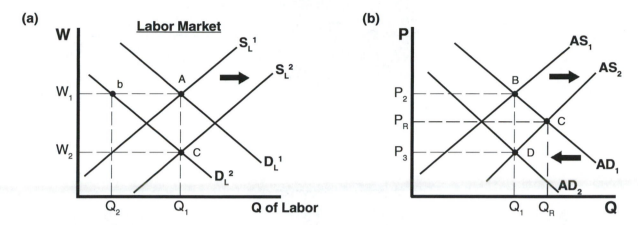

Diagrams 10-1, a-b

an individual (a household) to increase his or her saving, were all individuals to in fact do so, economic outcomes in the aggregate would not be so positive.

The analysis goes like this: with monetary incomes received as wages and salaries, households then decide whether to spend or save.

Suppose household income was $100 in some year and members of the household spent $95 of those earnings. This leaves $5 as household saving. Revenues would be $95. Where will the money flow?

The modern household puts its unspent dollars in the bank. Furthermore, modern firms also deposit their revenues into their own accounts at the bank. Thus, in the firms' accounts there'd be $95. All told, there's $100 in the banking system on the basis of a wage-income flow of $100. Thus, the loaning potential of banks, whose role it is to make loanable funds available, is based on the $100 cash flow.

Keynes continues: but suppose the households had chosen to spend less and save more. Suppose consumption spending had been $90 and saving $10. In this case, firms would have deposited $90 into their accounts, households $10. It is clear that the households increased their saving, but they did so at the expense of business saving. Thus, only a re-

distribution of saving has occurred. Total saving, unaffected by the change in the household decision to save $10 rather than $5, remains at $100. The banking system is therefore supporting activity on the same $100 wage-income flow. And most important, *there's no net change in the available funds in the banking system for loaning purposes as a consequence of increased household saving.*

Diagram 10-2 helps enrich Keynes' view of the of the credit market. It traces the monetary flow between the resource and product markets using $100 as income, $95 as consumption, and $5 as saving.

Keynes' example shows that *in net terms* households cannot affect the supply of loanable funds. If they cannot do this, there can be no change in the interest rate as a result of some change in household saving decisions. If there's no household saving-interest rate connection, then the adjustment mechanism outlined by Say and others *does not exist.* Hence, no automatic increase in business investment comes as a result of household decisions to increase saving. Finally, without the impetus of new investment spending, no recovery in the economy can ensue.

It cannot be over-emphasized how critical this insight is in undermining the logic of Say's Law. Say's

Keynes' View of the Credit Market

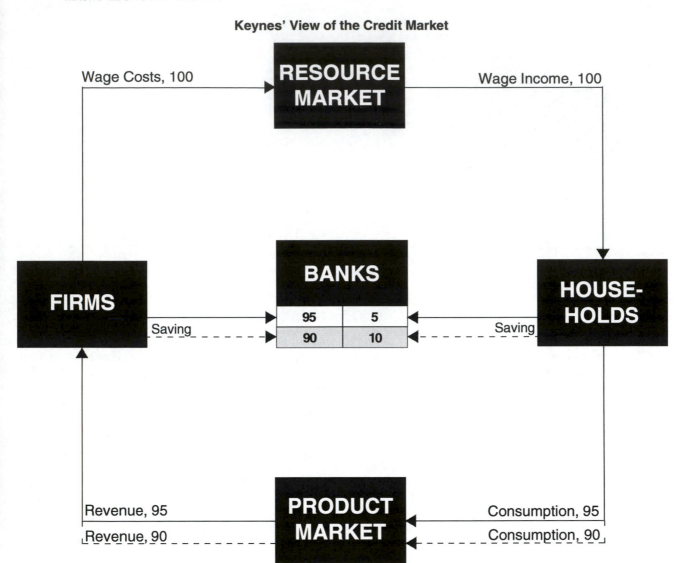

Diagram 10-2

world is that version of economic thinking which holds that household saving (or, monetary sacrifices) *necessarily* creates investment, that the causal link between these two variables runs from saving to investment. This is ultimately one of the things that the phrase "supply creates its own demand" boils down to. When Keynes exposes the inadequacies of classical theory, he upsets some of the main pillars in the edifice of economic theory.

Keynes succeeded in his analysis because he was able to cut through thickets of hoary theory and see the essence of modern capitalism, a system in which money has *real* impact. Money in the modern world creates a separation between what economists call the real sacrifices of households (such as were discussed in the previous chapter in regards to education) and their monetary saving (such as appears in the statistical tables of Chapter 7). Keynes is not saying households should not save. He is saying that household sacrifice in the form of monetary saving is of dubious merit in modern, free enterprise capitalism wherein spending by one person encourages production and spending by others.

The key to recognizing Keynes' insight about the households' inability to contribute to the net supply of loanable funds is to recognize that the real power households have in the saving picture concerns the *distribution* of (national) saving. If a household saves, it necessarily lessens the saving of someone else, namely firms, since firms save out of their revenue flow. If a household spends, its own saving decreases, but this is offset by the increased revenue and saving of the firm (and the saving of those to whom the firm might, in turn, make payments). Otherwise, households are mere onlookers in the financial system. When it comes to loanable funds' creation, they have no positive role.

KEYNES' MODEL

Here then we need to undertake a study of Keynes' enduring contributions to--as opposed to mere criticisms--macro-economic study. The model delineated in this section by no means constitutes the sum of his contributions to the discipline. But it is immediately relevant at this juncture.

Three ideas which Keynes employed in his model to help understand macro-economic processes include the **marginal propensity to consume (mpc)**, the **marginal propensity to save (mps)**, and the **multiplier**. The first two terms describe patterns of household behavior. The multiplier describes the transaction flows following *newly initiated* spending. By newly initiated spending we mean specifically those that represent net changes from the previous period.[1]

We can work through each of these in turn.

mpc

One key to Keynes' model comes in his description of household spending patterns.

"*...men are disposed, as a rule and on the average, to increase their consumption as their income increases, but not by as much as the increase in their income.*"[2]

If households earn an additional income, they will surely consume the better half of it; but they will not spend all of it. We can anticipate households putting aside a monetary saving for any number of purposes: a future purchase, an inheritance for children, pensions, a "rainy day."[3] Thus, when income increases, consumption increases, but by less than income itself. Algebraically this means,

$$\triangle C < \triangle Y \text{ such that } \triangle C \div \triangle Y > 0, \text{ but } \triangle C \div \triangle Y < 1.$$

where $\triangle$ means "change in"; C means total Consumption; Y means total National Income.

The $\triangle C \div \triangle Y$ term is the algebraic equivalent of the mpc. If it were 1, then households would be saving nothing from additional income. Thus, the fact that it is less than 1 indicates some saving occurs.

In plain English, the mpc is the additional consumption that occurs as a result of additional income.[4] The following example will illustrate the concept in the most concrete arithmetic.

Y	C
0	300
1000	1200
2000	2100
3000	3000
4000	3900
5000	4800
6000	5700
7000	6600
8000	7500
9000	8400
10000	9300

Table 10-1

---

[1] We approach the point at which words can't always suitably introduce the concept. The multiplier, especially, is probably better first seen mathematically; then its real world analogues can be pointed out. All this we will develop through the remaining parts of the chapter. After working through it, we will see it has quite specific and familiar real world applications.

[2] J. M. Keynes, The General Theory of Employment, Interest, and Money (New York: Harcourt Brace Jovanovich, 1964), p. 96.

[3] Whether various purposes exist for saving and how various they indeed are is itself a distinct theoretical issue to which Keynes contributed. These issues are discussed in the text's section on money.

[4] The word marginal will always relate a change to a change so as to describe a causal type relation. The effecting variable, the independent one, is set in the denominator's position; the affected or dependent variable goes in the numerator. This is true of a marginal *anything* in economics.

This series of numbers indicates that as National Income increases by 1000, Consumption spending rises by 900. Thus, the marginal propensity to consume in this case is .9. To verify this, take any pair of numbers and find the differences in consumption and income, respectively, arranging the calculation to square with the definition of the mpc. For example,

$$\frac{\triangle C}{\triangle Y} = \frac{1200 - 300}{1000 - 0} = \frac{9300 - 8400}{10000 - 9000} = \frac{900}{1000} = .9$$

Take note of how this example coincides with Keynes' quote above.

The mpc does not vary throughout the entire set of numbers; nor would it were we to extend the columns (extrapolate). Thus, these numbers represent a straight line. This very line is seen in Diagram 10-3, with National Income on the horizontal axis as the independent variable.

To capture the entire scope of household spending patterns we can use this algebraic equation:

$$C = mpc\,(Y) + AC$$

where C represents total Consumption; AC stands for

Autonomous Consumption. This general form of the consumption equation says—in plain English—that the total Consumption of households is of two kinds: (a) that which is induced by Income [mpc (Y)]; (b) that which is independent of Income [AC].

The consumption and income data from Table 10-1 would yield the following equation: $C = .9\,(Y) + 300$. Using the equation, we can ascertain total Consumption at any Income level, be it from the table itself:

C = .9 (3000) + 300	C = .9 (7000) + 300
C = 2700 + 300	C = 6300 + 300
C = 3000	C = 6600

or some level not listed:

C = .9 (4500) + 300	C = .9 (20000) + 300
C = 4050 + 300	C = 18000 + 300
C = 4350	C = 18300

Autonomous Consumption is, algebraically, a constant; it does not change as changes in Income occur. It therefore is the intercept for the vertical axis

The Consumption Line

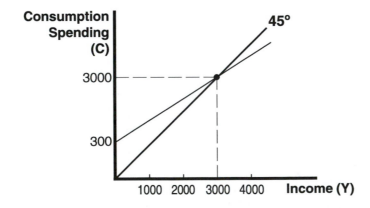

Diagram 10-3

in Diagram 10-3. Economically, Autonomous Consumption is household spending that is not associated with Income. Such spending does occur for any number of reasons. In part it can represent spending out of accumulated saving in a bank, stocks or bonds; it could represent spending from borrowed money. In any case, it is not, strictly speaking, caused by current Income flows. Yet it must be included.

By inserting a 45-degree line which emanates from the origin, the consumption line will intersect the 45-degree line at precisely $3000. This is so because the point (3000, 3000) is a common point for each line. On Diagram 10-4, we can distinguish two areas between the consumption line and the 45-degree line. To the left of Y = 3000 is the region of negative saving, called Dissaving. It corresponds with the table above. To the right of Y = 3000 is the region of positive saving, just as the table describes for us. Geometrically, at any particular Income level, the distance between the 45-degree line and the consumption line will yield the Saving that transpires in the economy at that level of Income.[5]

Y	C	S
0	300	-300
1000	1200	-200
2000	2100	-100
3000	3000	0
4000	3900	100
5000	4800	200
6000	5700	300
7000	6600	400
8000	7500	500
9000	8400	600
10000	9300	700

Table 10-2

---

[5] For those that want to pursue the matter, Saving can be described algebraically: plug in C = mpc(Y) + AC into the equation Y = C + S and then solve for S. The result should be S = mps(Y) - AC.

mps

Of course, National Income is made up of more than just Consumption. As we learned from the chapter on National Income accounting, $Y = C + S$ in a simple two-sector economy. So, algebraically, we can come up with a third column representing Saving, which is the difference between Income and Consumption.

The new Saving column gives us the means to derive the marginal propensity to save. Between any two levels of Income, Saving increased by 100. Thus, the change in Income by $1000 caused a change in Saving of $100. Arranged algebraically,

$$\frac{\triangle S}{\triangle Y} = \frac{-100 - (-200)}{2000 - 1000} = \frac{400 - 300}{7000 - 6000} = \frac{100}{1000} = .1$$

The mps is nothing more than the additional Saving that comes as a result of additional Income. Students should note what occurs at Y = 3000. There $Y = C$ and $S = 0$. At $Y < 3000$, saving was negative; beyond that Saving is positive.

A final observation involves the mpc and mps. Together they must always equal 1. This is so because a household can do only two things with its income: either spend it or save it. This can be proven mathematically.

Since, $Y = C + S$

then, $\triangle Y = \triangle C + \triangle S.$

If we divide both sides of the equation by WY, the equation reduces to:

$1 = \triangle C \div \triangle Y + \triangle S \div \triangle Y$

$1 = mpc + mps$, by definition.

Investment and the multiplier

The final piece of Keynes' puzzle brings in the activity of the firms. The unique activity of the firms is investment. We have seen this in the equation for National Product: $Y = C + I$. Just how to describe the

The Saving Line

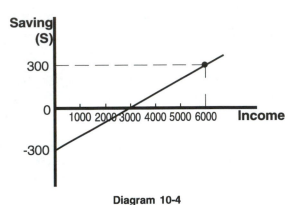

Diagram 10-4

firms' activity in an algebraic equation was a concern to which Keynes gave much thought. The details and intricacies of the matter cannot be explored fully now, but some brief thoughts of Keynes are truly appropriate. Towards the end of a chapter in <u>The General Theory</u> wherein he discusses the determinants of investment, he concludes:

"...human decisions affecting the future ... cannot depend on strict mathematical expectation, since the basis for making such calculations does not exist; and that it is our innate urge to activity which makes the wheels go round ..." [6]

Investment commitments of firms, or any decision involving the use of capital are among those acts which help formulate the future. But, as Keynes might say, the future is something like a tabula rasa—a blank slate—on which we create our stories and our histories. Business investment decisions are therefore only poorly understood when they are expressed as the determinate result of some group of causes. Rather, in the final analysis, they are spontaneous acts of human creativity, the result of "animal spirits." Keynes would point out that much of the crucial business activity needed for a strong economy moved on waves of optimism. Perhaps he appreciated this because he could observe in the States the wave of pessimism among business people which forestalled recovery because it stymied investment.

Thus, Keynes would treat investment as autonomous. In the model it has no link to income; nor will we ascribe it to anything else. It stands alone.

This makes the algebra fairly straightforward. Suppose total Investment, I, is 700. This gives us a means, in combination with the activity of households as captured by the consumption equation, to algebraically describe the whole economy and calculate its **Equilibrium Income**. Below we do just that.

$$
\begin{aligned}
C &= .9(Y) + 300 \\
I &= 700 \\
\hline
C + I &= .9(Y) + 1000
\end{aligned}
$$

Continuing the algebra, we use our economic understanding that $Y = C + I$ to substitute Y for $C + I$. Then, we solve for Y^*, Equilibrium Income.

(1) $C + I = .9(Y) + 1000$

(2) $Y = .9(Y) + 1000$

(3) $Y - .9(Y) = 1000$

(4) $.1Y = 1000$

(5) $Y = 1000/.1$

(6) $Y = 1000 \times 10$

(7) $Y^* = 10,000$

Given the mpc = .9, AC = 300 and I = 700, only one Equilibrium Income exists and that income level is 10000! Diagram 10-7 is the completed picture.

proving the result

How can we verify this? By showing that total Saving equals 700. For in the simple, 2-sector economy of households and firms, I should equal S based on the accounting principles we saw before. The path to total Saving, however, winds down the consumption road:

⁶ Keynes, p. 162-3.

Keynes' Macro-Equilibrium

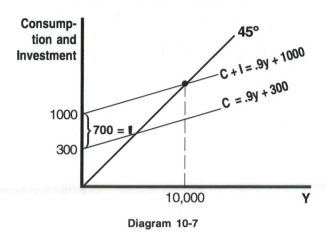

Diagram 10-7

$$C = .9 (10000) + 300$$

$$C = 9000 + 300 = 9300$$

Since, Y - C = S, we get

$$10000 - 9300 = 700 .$$

Thus, we have proven that $S = I$ at the equilibrium Income of 10000. It will always be so at Equilibrium Income.[7]

what the algebra reveals

The steps of the algebra need some review, for it will not be sufficient to obtain an answer and be done with it. The algebra teaches several Keynesian lessons.

First, finding Equilibrium Income requires identifying the mps. This appears in line (4). In any similar problem, the algebra will always first lead to an identification of the mps.

Second, in the final steps, the multiplier emerges. In line (5), the full amount of **Autonomous Spending** (AC and I) is divided by the mps. But that would be

---

[7] In Keynes' model, the equilibrium occurs when household activity coincides with business activity, in terms of *planned* saving and *planned* investment.

equivalent to multiplying 1000 by the reciprocal of the mps, in this case, 10. That's shown in line (6). Mathematically, the multiplier is always the reciprocal of the mps, $1 \div mps$. As should be clear then, the mpc, mps and multiplier are interrelated.

Finally, Keynes' model reduces the determination of equilibrium national income/product to a relationship between Autonomous Spending and the Multiplier. After substituting Y for $(C + I)$ in the second line, the algebraic steps lead to this general equation:

Y = Autonomous Spending x Multiplier.

The algebra cannot vary from this basic pattern.

Since the algebraic steps above led from the mpc to the mps and then the multiplier, it follows that when the mpc changes, the mps and multiplier must change. Moreover, the change in the mpc must ultimately alter Equilibrium Income. Below we change the mpc of the original problem to .8

C	=	.8(Y) + 300
I	=	700

(1)	C + I	=	.8(Y) + 1000
(2)	Y	=	.8(Y) + 1000
(3)	Y - .8(Y)	=	1000
(4)	.2 Y	=	1000
(5)	Y	=	$1000 \div .2$
(6)	Y	=	1000 x 5
(7)	Y*	=	5000

We lowered the mpc. The mps rose to .2. The multiplier fell to 5. The relations between spending habits of households and national income are beginning to come clear. Should households become increasingly thrifty, the pace of expenditure flows necessarily slows, leaving national income lower than previously. The direct implication is that a recession would ensue, unemployment would rise, and the economy would settle into a less vigorous but stable equilibrium. Does the result seem strange? It shouldn't really. The example underscores an old lesson: one person's cost is another's income. If households choose to save a greater share of their income, the unspent dollars represent a lost income flow to firms and, eventually, the workers of the firms.

What more can emerge from this simple example? We can again use the algebra to verify the result and illustrate that the new result is indeed an equilibrium income level.

What do you suppose the effect on total Saving has been? At first glance, one might guess that since the *rate* of household saving had risen from .1 to .2, then *total* Saving increased. (That was the presumption of earlier economists!) But working through the problem we find:

$$C = .8(5000) + 300$$

$$C = 4000 + 300$$

$$C = 4300$$

$$S = 700 \text{ , since } Y - C = 5000 - 4300 = 700 .$$

Total Saving is unaffected by changes in the spending/saving habits of households! This is precisely the same argument Keynes made with respect to issues concerning the credit markets which we reviewed earlier. Now it appears in mathematical form. This should reenforce the idea that households affect the distribution of saving--not the total--when they alter their saving propensities.

REVIEW

We need to tie up some loose ends.

The multiplier is actually a process. It describes a series of spending created from, as Keynes said, spontaneously determined economic activity. In our model of Keynes' system, the spontaneously determined activity is Autonomous Spending in the form of autonomous consumption or investment. The multiplier, meanwhile, is set by the mpc, or the spending/saving habits of households. Another plain lesson from the examples just provided indicates that

lower values for the mpc (higher values for mps), minimize the potential multiplier effects from any autonomous spending. We can take a look at this process in more detail by tracing through the rounds of spending generated by some autonomous expenditure.

	mpc = .9	mpc = .8
Round 1	1000	1000
" 2	900	800
" 3	810	640
" 4	729	512
" 5	656.1	409.6
" 6	590.49	327.68
" 7	531.441	262.144
" 8	478.2969	209.7152
" 9	430.46721	167.77216
" 10	387.420489	134.217728
" 11	348.6784401	107.3741824
" 12	313.81059609	85.89934592
SUM after 12 rounds	7175.70463519	4656.40261632
eventual SUM	10000	5000

It doesn't take long, both mathematically and economically, for a change in the mpc as significant as this to be seen. When each person withholds a greater amount of his or her own income flow for personal saving, less is forwarded to the next person to either spend or save. In a large domestic economy, the effects of individuals' decisions purl throughout, like ripples from a pebble pitched in a pond.

Modeling the Depression

Keynes' insights were inspired by difficulties experienced during the Depression. While we have examined a case in which Equilibrium Income fell by 50% (more or less the amount by which National Product fell between 1929 and 1933) this has not been meant to suggest that the cause of the Depression was a declining mpc. Rather, as we saw previously, the immediate cause was a precipitous drop in Investment, "inspired" by the crash of the stock market. Can we duplicate these results with Keynes' tools?

Suppose originally the mpc = .9; AC = 500; and I = 1500. This will quickly yield:

(1)   C + I   = .9(Y) + 2000

(2)   Y   = .9(Y) + 2000

(3)   .1Y   = 2000

(4)   Y*   = 2000 x 10 = 20000 .

But if Investment fell to 750, then

(1)   Y   = .9(Y) + 1250

(2)   .1Y   = 1250

(3)   Y*   = 1250 x 10 = 12500

This nearly matches the results of events of the early 30's.

In the final analysis, Keynes' model tells us that there are but a few routes out of the Depression: (a) the mpc could be raised so that multiplier effects would become stronger; and (b) Investment could be restored to its previous levels.

Using Government

To pursue a recovery by changing household habits would be unrealistic. Characteristically, households become more conservative in their spending during difficult times. Should they merely foresee bad times, households tend to cut back on their rate of consumption out of income (mpc falls, mps rises).

Even a restoratoin of Investment may be unlikely during periods of economic hardship. In the first place, the entrepreneurs who direct investment would be, with good reason, pessimistic regarding the profitability of new capital spending. Second, as we've seen above, no fall in the interest rate can be forthcoming as a result of an increase in household saving propensities. The mechanisms to which earlier economists appealed don't actually exist in modern capitalism. If the interest rate falls, it would express the pessimism of entrepreneurs, i.e., a fall in demand for liquid capital funds, rather than an increase in supply of those funds due to elevated rates of saving.

To what then can society turn? Keynes suggested the government would be able to offset the fall in **effective demand** (his term) that was responsible for the Depression.

In proposing this, Keynes felt he was offering a fairly conservative solution to an event which seriously threatened the capitalist way of life. Again from The General Theory:

"The State will have to exercise a guiding influence on the propensity to consume partly through its scheme of taxation,partly by fixing the rate of interest ...[But] apart from the necessity of central controls to bring about an adjustment between propensity to consume and the inducement to invest, there is no more reason to socialize economic life than there was before.

"... there will still remain a wide field for the exercise of private initiative and responsibility. Within this field the traditional advantages of individualism will still hold good.

"Whilst ... the enlargement of the functions of government ... would seem ... to be a terrific encroachment on individualism, I defend it, ... as the only practicable means of avoiding the destruction of existing economic forms in their entirety."[8]

So Keynes, a practical man at heart, suggested that the government could put to use its resources to offset the slackened pace of business activity. Such a spontaneous injection of spending into the economy would have similar multiplier effects as autonomous consumption or investment would. We can demonstrate his point mathematically.

Using the same numbers as previously, we can

---

8   Keynes, p. 378-380.

now expand upon the basic C + I equation. We are going to include government spending of 750 as an autonomous fixture in the model. The new equation represents a three–sector economy of households, firms, and government.

(1)   C + I + G = .9(Y) + 500 + 750 + 750

(2)   Y = .9(Y) + 2000

(3)   .1Y = 2000

(4)   Y* = 2000 x 10 = 20000

As before, we can verify that this income level is an equilibrium income by first calculating household saving and seeing that it meets the equilibrium requirement for a three–sector economy, i.e., I + G = S + T. Plugging in,

C = .9 (20000) + 500

C = 18000 + 500

C = 18500

Then,

Y - C = S

20000 - 18500 = 1500

Since T = 0, we do have at Y* = 20000 an equilibrium.

I + G = S + T

750 + 750 = 1500 + 0 .

What the inclusion of government spending shows is that it is possible for the government to combat the ills of a depression by spending. For its spending will have multiplier effects, much as investment spending does. Keynes would argue that it is wasteful and probably futile to sit and wait for business to initiate a recovery. In the long run, we're all dead; in the meantime, we're unemployed. The price, the opportunity cost, of waiting for the promised, automatic revival of activity is too dear. For Keynes, the vision of price–wage adjustments and full employment, which is the essence of classical theory, is nothing but a mirage. If economics is to be a science, it must have an eye to reality.

The following group of exercises are meant to lead the student to a thorough understanding of Keynes's vision of the economy, via the algebraic model introduced here. It is something of a drill. But if attentively done, it can assist you in making the connections between ideas, math, and graphs, connections that are so necessary for a mastery of economics.

■■■

END-OF-CHAPTER QUESTIONS

1. These equations constitute a model for a two-sector economy.

   $$C = .8(Y) + 330$$
   $$I = 640$$

   a. What is its equilibrium income (EQM Y)?
   b. What is its total Consumption at the EQM Y?
   c. What is its total Saving at the EQM Y? mps?
   d. What is the multiplier in this case?
   e. Draw this case appropriately on a 45–degree diagram.

2. In another case, mpc = .75; AC = 100; I = 440.

   a. What is EQM Y?
   b. What is total Consumption?
   c. What is Total Saving? mps?
   d. What is the multiplier?
   e. Draw this case.

3. Suppose that in #2 the mpc had been .9 instead of .75. What would the effects be on EQM Y, mps, multiplier, total consumption, and total saving? On a single graph, show how the change in the mpc would affect the C + I line.

4. The economy of Never–everland is depicted by the graph below. Use it to answer the following questions.

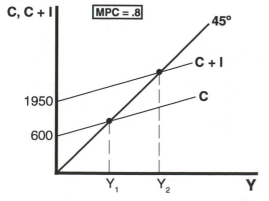

a. What is AC?
b. What is the Consumption equation? C + I equation?
c. What is the level of Investment spending?
d. Calculate EQM Y, total Consumption and saving. What is the multiplier?
e. From the graph, which represents EQM Y, Y_1 or Y_2?
f. What is the significance of Y_1 and what is its value?

5. Again, answer the questions based on the graph below. Assume the mpc = .9.

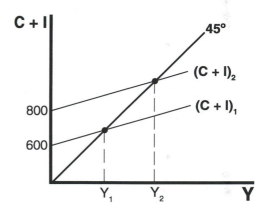

a. What is Y_1? What is Y_2?
b. What possible things could explain the shift in the C + I line?
c. Show that the Multiplier = Y ÷ Autonomous Spending.
d. Show that the Multiplier = $\triangle$Y ÷ $\triangle$Autonomous Spending.

6. Based on the graph below, calculate the $\triangle Y$; what explains this $\triangle Y$? Also, draw a C + I line where mpc = .8 would appear on the graph.

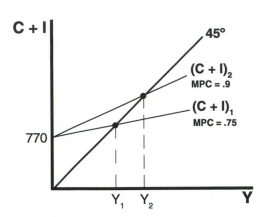

7. Given: AC = 400, mpc = .9; I = 500; G = 300.

   a. Calculate the EQM Y for C + I and for C + I + G; draw each on a single graph, fully labelled.
   b. Based on this model, does government exert a positive or negative influence on the economy?
   c. In what sense can this mathematical model be said to be unrealistic? What other considerations should the model include to make it more realistic?

8. Suppose in #7 I = 700 rather than 500, ceteris paribus. What do the C + I and C + I + G equations become; calculate the new EQM Y's, respectively.

9. Use # 7-8 to do the following:

   a. Calculate total Consumption
      1) # 7 and 8, C + I ;
      2) # 7 and 8, C + I + G.

   b. Total Saving
      1) # 7 and 8, C + I;
      2) # 7 and 8, C + I + G.

10. Based on the graph below, calculate the mpc.

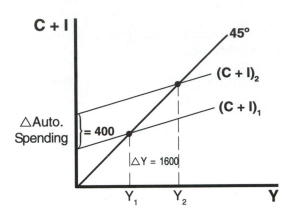

11. Examine the graph below and answer the questions that follow.

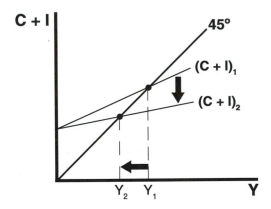

   a. True or false? The change depicted in the graph will create more total saving.

   b. What does explain this change?

12. Use the following data to show that I + G = S + T.

   AC = 200, mpc = .75
   I = 1300
   G = 500

13. Calculate total consumption and total saving for this two-sector economy.

    mpc = .8; I = 4000; Autonomous Spending = 6500

14. If in #13 the mpc were .95, would total consumption change? Total saving? Explain your conclusion in a paragraph.

VOCABULARY

Involuntary unemployment – the condition describing a worker(s) who is willing and able to work at current wages but is unable to secure a job

Marginal propensity to consume – the change in consumption due to a change in income

Marginal propensity to save – the change in saving due to a change in income

Multiplier – a spending and income process which describes the series of expenditures resulting from a single autonomous expenditure

Autonomous consumption – household spending not directly attributable to changes in income

Autonomous spending – any spending by either households, firms, or government not directly attributable to changes in income

Equilibrium income – in Keynes' model the level of national income which equals national product (aggregate expenditures); occurs at that level of income where investment and saving are also equal and inventory levels are stable

Effective demand – Keynes' term for the level of demand sufficient to generate full employment

CHAPTER 11

CHANGES IN THE PRICE LEVEL

Price inflation is among the most closely observed macro phenomena. Along with the unemployment rate, the trend in the general price level gets reported monthly. Articles which make reference to inflation appear more often than that. Consumers, meanwhile, complain about it weekly. And Wall Street gamblers, when they make financial transactions involving stocks and bonds, place indirect bets on it every hour of every day.

The attention is both fortunate and unfortunate. The fortunate part is that its reputation as a source of economic havoc is deserved: domestic economies need a stable price level. Rapid inflation can distort economic processes and planning which require a more stable price environment. Capital spending might be curtailed, if not indefinitely postponed, due to volatile price movements. Budgeting for the state can become an altogether hollow regimen of erasing and re-erasing. *Unfortunately*, inflation comes in different varieties and the popular press is not particularly good at making distinctions between apparently similar events. The result is a mis-education of the voting public, which in turn demands of its political leadership the wrong solution to the wrong problem at the wrong time. The opportunity cost of *that* is a real national disaster.

Inflation is simply a rise in the *general* price level. Its calculation is itself an average, conceptually speaking, which speaks not of any particular good, nor even a particular group of them, but of the preponderance of purchasable goods and services. Deflation is the opposite.

Economists measure the price level in a couple of ways: with deflators as was done in chapter viii or with a market basket approach as is done with the Consumer Price Index (CPI). These two measures usually approximate each other.

In theoretic terms, the factors which determine changes in the average price level are reasonably well understood. Research points to several likely candidates: money, workers' wages, and labor productivity. Still, on any given day one can hear inflation attributed to a veritable brothel-full of she-devils better known as the federal deficit, corporate profits, low unemployment rates, taxes, government regulations, consumer expectations, Congress, liberal Democrats, doctors, lawyers, the religious right, rabid environmentalism, the welfare state, the miliary industrial complex, ethnic groups which are doing well, ethnic groups which are falling behind, sun spots, hemlines, Hollywood, and the moral depravity of the Western world.

Pheeww!!!!!!!!

This chapter attempts to steer the reader away from the confused notions about inflation, to clarify what it really entails, theoretically and practically.

TYPES OF INFLATION

The proper way to begin our discussion of inflation is to categorize the kinds of inflation that we might witness in the macro-economy.

Real inflation

Inflation has stems and roots. The deepest root penetrates to the core principles of economic study: scarcity and opportunity costs. Such fundamental influences on money-prices can be illustrated with something called the **Production Possibility Curve** (PPC). The PPC helps explain the demand-driven, real cost trends which an economy of scarce commodities is prone to. Below is a table and picture.

The PPC

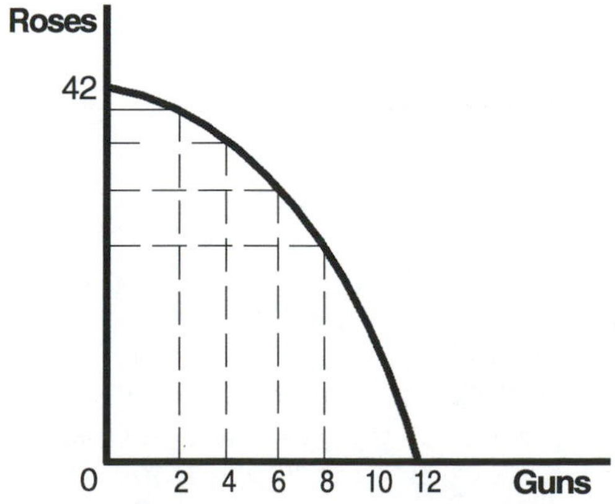

Diagram 11-1

	Guns	Roses
A	0	42
B	2	40
C	4	36
D	6	30
E	8	22
F	10	12
G	12	0

Table 11-1

From the data and Diagram 11-1 we can easily see that for society to choose more and more guns through points A-G, a progressively greater sacrifice of roses must be made: first two, then four, six and so on. If we pretend that a one-hundred dollar bill represented the sacrifice incurred between points A and B, then it's a straight-forward exercise to derive a monetary-based supply curve. This we do in Diagram 11-2.

The Supply and Demand for Guns

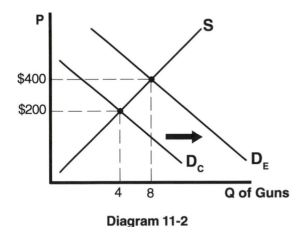

Diagram 11-2

Monetary prices range from $100 to $600 along the gun supply relation. We can interpret the movements along the PPC in Diagram 11-1 as a series of demand shifts on Diagram 11-2. Obviously, the increasing monetary price is a mere veil for the course of real payments made in foregone roses. And why are those real payments increasing? Because the efficiency of production is taking a dive; because the

labor and capital resources being shifted from rose production to gun production are less and less adept at the new task; because gun workers' real wages must increase in order to attract already fully employed labor from the rose industry.

So now that costs and final prices in the gun industry are rising, will the Guns and Roses economy experience inflation?

Not yet--not for sure, anyway. For the higher payments for additional guns is not the entire story here. The structure of the PPC dictates that whenever the demand for guns rises, *society reduce its demand for roses*. The question becomes: in a society of two goods, one whose increased demand lifts prices, the other whose slackened demand brings price relief, will there be inflation?

It depends. If prices are rising in one sector *faster than they are falling in the other*, then that society would more likely confront the purest kind of inflation, one due to the *diminishing efficiency of overall production*. If, on the other hand, prices in the expanding industry are rising *more modestly* than they are declining in the industry where demand is sagging, then that society would probably find itself in a cycle of *deflation*.

This sort of deduction should not be unfamiliar or daunting. Many elements of life present such double-edged processes whose *average* result is dependent on the relative strength of their parts. For example, if we pose for ourselves the problem of population growth, we'd have to take into account two aspects of the process: birth and death. If the number of births is larger than the number of deaths over a stretch of time, then clearly the population grew during that time. Similarly, a baseball *team's* batting average will change in relation to the changes in the batting averages of all the individuals on the team, some of which are rising, some of which are falling.[1]

---

[1] And the relative frequencies of at bats of those who improved vis-a-vis those who didn't. If one batter improved his batting average 10 points and another's fell by ten points, they would have an equal effect of the team's batting average *only if they had the same number of additional at bats through a given period.* Otherwise, the batter who had more *additional* at bats would affect the team's average more substantially.

Can we say anything more precise than what's just been said, i.e., that inflationary or deflationary trends depend on the how swiftly prices are rising in one industry versus how swiftly they are dropping in the other?

The generalities regarding general price momentum come down to these: If society is relatively stronger in the production of one good (say, roses), but experiencing an increase in demand for the other (say, guns), where its talents are weaker, then the net result of the transition in production would more likely be *inflationary*. This is so because the decreasing efficiency of gun production associated with greater gun output would probably outweigh the increasing efficiency of rose production, where only the most appropriate resources would be left to make fewer roses. Since costs run opposite the efficiency path, this is equivalent to saying that, most likely, costs to make guns would rise to a greater extent than costs to make roses would decline; hence, rising prices overall.[2]

In short, real inflationary pressures build whenever society demands more of that good (or *goods*) at which it is relatively less proficient producing. Contrarily, real deflationary forces appear whenever society directs its resources to producing a commodity (or *commodities*) which they can more capably produce.

These conclusions hold under the PPC's standard assumptions that all inputs are fully and efficiently utilized to produce two goods, during a given period of time, and with a given technology.

Nominal inflation

Real inflation belongs to the theoretical realm. After careful, painstaking analysis clear conclusions

can be drawn about factors influencing the price level; and if even greater accuracy is desired, the specific power of the individual influences can be ascertained through economic statistics. But the real world is overwhelmingly messy. None of the tidy assumptions hold in actual life. Real nations produce more than guns and roses. Real economies experience bouts of underemployment. They grow, they evolve, more like an organism than a machine to which an adjunct is affixed. Productive methods change all the time. They have, they do, and they shall--continuously. Such is the nature of capitalism.

Given this, not every inflation (or deflation) observed is the result of *real* factor productivity trends. Indeed it is fair to say that most price trends in modern capitalist economies are driven by nominal or monetary factors. When we say that the price of a car is $15000 and the price of milk is $3.00 a gallon, we speak of money prices. If we recollected that 20 years ago we used to pay half those figures for cars and milk, we would have again spoken with reference to these goods' nominal prices, albeit their old ones.

What are the sources of a nominal inflation? What makes up the remainder of the twisted complex of inflation's roots?

There are two theories on the nature of nominal inflation, an old and new one. The earlier theory, noted as early as 1752 by David Hume, a contemporary of Adam Smith, explains changes in the price level as the result of changes in the supply of money--ceteris paribus.[3] The recent theory postulates that changes in labor's nominal wages account for most price elevations. Each theory has a modern spokesperson. Milton Friedman is the Nobel Prize winning American economist whose research (with Anna Schwartz) into inflation confirmed for him the consistency of the relations between money supply movements and price level's traverse. His influence has been enormous. Sidney Weintraub, 1914-1983, developed his price level theory in 1959[4], and received much notoriety for his anti-inflationary prescriptions, first proposed

---

[2] The author is using "more likely" and "probably" for a reason. The conclusions regarding inflation or deflation are also affected by the composition of output, i.e., the relative size of the industry compared to *total* output. Even in a two good world we need not assume that the composition of output is 50-50. Thus, there are actually two key factors at work in determining the overall *real price* trend: (a) the relative efficiency of production for goods whose demand changes, (b) the size of the sectors involved relative to total output. (The relative size of the industry is analogous to the relative frequency of at-bats mentioned in the previous footnote.)

[3] David Hume, "Of Interest," *Political Discourses*, (1752).
[4] Sidney Weintraub, *A General Theory of the Price Level* (Philadelphia: Chilton Book Co., 1959).

in 1971, at the onset of that decade's stagflation fiasco. Friedman's theory is commonly known as the **Monetarism**; Weintraub developed the **Post Keynesian** approach to inflation.

monetarists and the ye olde cambridge equation

Suppose a helicopter, emptying sackfuls of $20 bills, came buzzing over an otherwise sedate, stable community. What would happen to that area's price level?[5]

Every knee jerk knows that prices have to rise. For after the scurrying throngs fetch those bills they will in turn bid more highly for any goods available. The amount of goods hasn't changed. But the availability of the means of exchange has risen. It is a classic case: too much money chasing too few goods.

The story is a favorite of Milton Friedman's, proffered for expository purposes. The idea has a more rigorous version, captured in the original **Cambridge Equation of Exchange**.

$$PQ \; = \; MV$$

The left hand side expresses the formula for the nominal GDP and thus takes the expenditure view of an economy's domestic output, i.e., price times quantity. The right hand side expresses a second multiplicative relation between the money stock, M, and the velocity, V, of money. Velocity is, at least algebraically, exactly equal to the nominal GDP divided by the nominal money stock. Intuitively, it designates the number of times money "turns over" through some stretch of time so as to generate a value of P*Q in expenditures. Restaurant managers use "turn-over" to describe the rate at which customers come and go, and more specifically, how long it takes for a completely new set of customers to occupy its tables.

Monetarists use "velocity" in much the same way. The analogy works well because the greater the rate of turn-over, the greater the value of the business'

total receipts, which are necessarily equal to total customer spending. And that 's the case with the economy generally: the faster the circulation of dollars, the greater the value of income and spending, each of which is equal to P times Q.

Modern monetarist research indicates that velocity is a stable variable.[6] Thus, we can immediately deduce that it doesn't wield influence over the motions of the price level, since no stationary variable is capable of producing a reaction in others: no cause, no effect.

Meanwhile, for short run purposes, neither would Q, the real stock of goods and services, change. The town which discovered a generous helicopter overhead could not have been undergoing a radical increase in its real output while the helicopter from heaven was hovering. Its attention was elsewhere!

With two perfectly still variables in the Cambridge equation, the link between prices and money becomes mighty direct. If the stock of money is increased, the general price level will go up proportionately. The logic is impeccable.

The assumptions are open to question, but they can be adjusted without destroying the gist of the theory. Notably, real output is not motionless over longer breadths of time. We know historically that capitalist economies grow and retrench, yet the data indicate that, on average, real U.S. GDP grows about 3% per year. This suggests that the money stock could be increased 3% annually and result in a more or less stable price level.

In the real world then, monetarists see inflation as the result of money stock growth which is misaligned with real output growth. Whenever the growth of the money supply exceeds the growth of real output, prices will rise; if real growth exceeds the growth of the money supply, deflation is the result.

[5] Milton Friedman, 7he Optimum Quantity of Money and Other Essays (Chicago: Aldine Publishing Co., 1969) p. 226.

[6] Friedman and David Meiselman, "The Relative Stability of Monetary Velocity and the Investment Multiplier in the United States," in Commission on Money and Credit, *Stabilization Policies* (Englewood Cliffs: Prentice Hall, 1963), p. 171.

Mathematically,

$$WP = WM - WQ.$$

The original Equation of Exchange has minor variants. Some versions put the Q on the right side to form V/Q. Others go a step further and set V/Q equal to k. So elsewhere the student might see these expressions:

$$P = \underline{V}(M)$$
$$Q$$

or

$$P = k(M).$$

Regardless, all the versions boil down to the same thing: The amount of money in circulation determines the price level and changes in the supply of money affect prices generally.

critical thoughts

Monetarism appeals to very basic intuitions we have with respect to matters of scarcity. Whenever a commodity becomes more scarce in relation to another, the price of that commodity rises; conversely, whenever a good becomes less scarce in relation to another, the good's price falls. If the supply of gold increased relative to the supply of silver, then the price of gold would drop, relative to that of silver; whereas the relative price of silver would rise. Prices measure relative availability.

Milton Friedman says inflation is "always and everywhere a monetary phenomenon."[7] What does that mean? It implies that if a helicopter settles overhead and starts dispensing dollar bills, the supply of money would be increasing relative to the supply of goods. Money would become *less* scarce; hence it would have *less* value. Inevitably more dollars would have to be tendered to gain possession of any particular good and the average price level will rise.

A possible difficulty for monetarist theory arises

from problems relating to the measurement of the money supply. It turns out that its measurement is no simple exercise. First of all, we must recognize that many transactions occur by check, and these checks function as money, i.e., acceptable for payment and exchange. Thus, we need to include the amount of checkable deposits at banks and the like. The official measure called **M1** counts currency, checkable deposits, demand deposits and travelers checks. **M2** includes everything in **M1** plus savings deposits, small time deposits and money market accounts at various financial institutions. There is an **M3** and others. The problem then becomes what measure to use in testing the theory. What if different measures provide contrary results about the relation between money and prices?

A second more subtle problem derives from the nature of the association between the two key variables, money and prices. It is possible for a strong relation to be seen, yet not have a true confirmation of the *causal* link between money and prices. Statisticians warn about mistaking *correlation* for *causation*. For example, we might be able to discover a robust statistical association between the population of the United States and the price level. But this would be insufficient to prove that increased populations *cause* higher prices.

Finally, one of the key assumptions of monetarist theory might be inappropriate for the modern capitalist economy. Monetarism assumes an independence between money supply and real output, the variable Q. But modern enterprise relies on an expanding money supply (through the issuance of loans) to initiate, sustain, and increase production. In fact, to curtail the growth of the money supply invites a recession. Hence, money and real output cannot be entirely disconnected.

post keynesian theory

As chapter x mentioned, John Maynard Keynes' General Theory revolutionized economic thinking. The experience of the Depression seemed beyond the ken of theorists trained under the "Classical" school and thus prompted a need for a different account of events.

---

[7] Friedman, "What Price Guideposts," in George Schultz and Robert Aliber, eds., *Guidelines, Informal Controls, and the Market Place* (Chicago: University of Chicago Press, 1966), p. 18.

But to produce an entirely new theoretical apparatus requires on the part of its author a purview beyond the pressing concerns of the day. For it is intrinsic to the nature of effective theory that it provide a foundation for insights into many difficulties, even those not of immediate concern.

In Chapter 19 of The General Theory, Keynes set forth the elements of a new theory of the price level. He explicitly spoke of changes in the money wages of labor as effecting similar changes in nominal prices. The chapter was not a superfluous digression. Though this aspect is too often forgotten, matters of the price level arose naturally from the Depression experience and Classical recommendations for lower wages. To Classical economists, lower wages to labor would inspire a recovery. To Keynes, the *money* wages for which labor bargained helped set nominal prices in the product market. Hence, lower money wages would induce lower *nominal* prices for final goods, but no *real* income advance for individuals or society.

Come 1958, during a mild recession, economists would observe a steady inflation concurrent with the sagging output growth. The double bogey of inflation and recession confounded economists of the 1950's, who had read but forgotten the lessons of The General Theory. In their estimation, inflation indicated an "over-heated" economy; i.e., the result of overly rapid growth.

The Inflation & Growth Relation

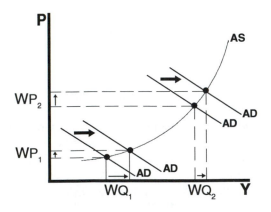

Diagram 11-3

As Diagram 11-3 illustrates, so long as Aggregate Supply (AS) is a positively sloped curve, growth in Aggregate Demand (AD) brings higher output and an ever-accelerating rise in the general price level; on the other hand, constraints on AD growth will check pace of inflation. The preponderant view therefore posited a clear trade-off for society: accept higher inflation as the price of faster growth and lower unemployment, or accept more modest growth--and the extra unemployment that goes with it--as payment due for a more placid price path. (In fact, to this day, this view is still the most frequently-heard account of inflation.)

The scant, but contrary, '58 evidence was nonetheless sufficient to suggest to Sidney Weintraub a new approach to inflation, one based on The General Theory's Chapter 19 and Weintraub's own sense that rising prices reflected a battle over incomes. It confounds plain common sense, he would say, that the price level could remain stable while fireman, doctors, teachers, plumbers, auto workers, longshoremen, lawyers, policemen, et.al. receive nominal gains in wages and salary of 8, 10 and 12 percent. The *nominal* income climbs dictate *nominal* price level advancements of nearly the same degree.

Weintraub formalized his thoughts this way:

$$PQ = k(wN)$$

The formula expresses GDP as a function of the average wage of labor, w, and the number of workers, N. Multiplied together, (wN) represents the entire wage earnings of the households--what Weintraub called the total wage bill.

What is k? Algebraically, it must be (PQ)/(wN), which is the reciprocal of the share of wages from GDP. Since the total wage bill must be less than GDP[8], k's value will be greater than 1. (If, for instance, the total wage bill is half of GDP, k is 2.) But this explains only the technical side. Once again, we need some business parlance to capture the full intuition behind the theory.

---

[8] National Income = W + ; + T + [X-M].

Entrepreneurs and managers who make pricing decisions will speak often of the prices they charge as a "mark up" over their own costs. These mark ups at the retail level might be 50%, 75% or even 100%. If a department store's costs were $10 per unit, and it marks up prices 100%, the customer pays $20. The mark up thus provides to the pricing agent a handy rule of thumb. While retailers think of their mark ups in percentage terms, the equation produces a numeric equivalent that may be applied to the economy generally: if the mark up is fifty percent, k is 1.5; if the mark up is 100%, k is 2. Weintraub referred to his k as the *average* mark up across all industries and dubbed his formula the **wage cost-mark up theorem**.

Why wages? Post Keynesian inflation theory begins by noting that roughly 2/3 of GDP (higher, if NDP is used) is accounted for by wage earnings, (wN). Equally important, that share of earnings, vis-a-vis GDP, is highly stable, more so than the velocity variable of monetarist lore.[9] By mathematical necessity, if the wage share, (wN)/(PQ), is constant, its reciprocal, k, must be too. Therefore, like the velocity variable in Monetarist theory, k fails to have explanatory power with respect to price level changes. But shutting the theoretical door on the mark up opens others. After a few algebraic manipulations, changes in the price level can be tersely accounted for by two variables.

$$P = k \ w \ \frac{N}{Q}$$

$$P = k \ (w/A)$$

What's been done? Dividing by Q on both sides leaves k, w, and N/Q on the right. N/Q is the reciprocal of the **average product of labor**, A, a standard measure of labor's overall efficiency. Fancy footwork yields the rest: $w(N/Q) = w/(Q/N) = (w/A)$.

What do these equations say in plain English? The price level moves on the basis of trends in nominal wages and labor productivity. Wages, via AS, push prices upward. Improvements in productivity

countervail wage pressure through AS growth. Precisely, the tug of war gets expressed:

$$WP = WW - WA .$$

This equation implies that wages and productivity vie for dominion over average price trends. Year in, year out, wages win. Naturally, we have 50 years inflation to show for it.

The remedy? Average annual wage gains must coincide with average yearly gains in labor productivity. Thus, to its Post Keynesian adherents, the wage cost-mark up theorem substantiates the need for an **incomes policy** to ensure price stability. As a group, incomes policies try to minimize nominal increases in wages and salaries. Such policies create, in effect, a social contract between labor and management to keep the incomes squabble within reasonable bounds. Weintraub's own prescription was a **tax-based incomes policy (TIP)**.[10] This would apply tax penalties to corporations which awarded overly gracious pay raises to its work force. Under the threat of penalty, he thought, corporations would be less acquiescent to labor's exorbitant money-wage demands. If the plan succeeded, wage gains would be limited to, say, 5% per year. Since productivity generally climbs 3% per year, inflation could be expected to settle at 2-3% annually.

critical thoughts

The wage cost-mark up theorem constitutes what is probably the best insight into the problem of inflation in 200 years. If a monetarist inflation is always and everywhere a monetary phenomenon, then a Post Keynesian inflation is first and foremost a wage inflation. This suggests that workers wind up competing against themselves when they seek nominally higher wages. Let's see why.

Consider a simple two-sector economy of households and firms. If the aggregate wage bill is a constant portion of the GDP, it follows that the share of capitalist profits is also constant. In modern

---

[9] L.R. Klein and R.F. Kosbud, "Some Econometrics of Growth: Great Ratios of Economics," *Quarterly Journal of Economics* (May 1961).

[10] Henry Wallich and Weintraub, "A Tax-Based Incomes Policy," *Journal of Economic Issues* (June 1971).

capitalist practice these constant shares are well explained by the observation that entrepreneurs price their final goods as a mark up over their own costs. In their minds they are ensuring a revenue flow adequate to meet their businesses' *future* financial commitments. While particular firms and industries might report that their own mark ups vary over time, in the aggregate efforts to secure revenues by raising and lowering prices, i.e., raising or lowering the mark up, don't turn out to be so volatile. Clearly, the competition *between* firms is a micro one. On the other hand, if the vast 2/3 of the GDP pie, labor income, is able to increase its wage claims to any significant degree, then firms will not be able to meet their financial commitments unless they either (a) reduce their own profits or (b) raise final prices and retain the constancy of the mark up.

In other words, Post Keynesian theory sees inflation as a fight for *real* income played on *nominal* turf. The battle occurs on two fronts: (a) among labor groups (plumbers want to keep up with electricians, electricians want to keep up with the auto workers, auto workers want to keep up with plumbers, ...) and (b) between labor and capitalists. As it happens, workers can secure higher real income only through nominal income gains. Yet each subset of labor which wins a desirable wage settlement encourages others to seek the same; meanwhile firms will want to transfer increased nominal wage costs to consumers in order to retain profitability. Thus, by the time workers get a chance to spend, inflation vaporizes the gain they had sought and leaves them in the same position (a) in real terms as compared to the previous period and (b) relative to their peers. The sheer futility

of labor's leapfrogging strategy was pithily described by Weintraub as "...today's attempt to recapture yesterday's losses tomorrow." When everybody tries it, the result is a wage-price spiral.

Too, the theory has held up under scrutiny. If anything, the 70's debacle of stagflation argues in the strongest way that the combination of high money wage gains and lethargic productivity tends to reinforce a price level spree. In turn, incomes policies would seem to be at once a logical and prudent means to prevent incomes-inflation chaos.

Yet most economists resist the idea of implementing a general incomes policy. TIP would, after all, constitute a governmental intervention into the marketplace. Even if inflation were not a mere monetary phenomenon, it is still preferable to let "agents" in the market contest for real income than to let civil authorities pollute it with taxes and regulation. Weintraub himself would respond that the 70's experience demonstrated the costs of letting the incomes shares feud run amok, costs which he believed were entirely avoidable. These costs include not only the unsettled sense consumers and businesses feel in an environment of rapid inflation, but also the waste of capital and labor resources-- read, unemployment--which inevitably follows as the monetary authorities, raised on monetarist milk, lift interest rates, dampen investment, restrain Aggregate Demand, so as to pilot the economy into an inflation-taming recession.

But resistance, like full employment, is natural in a profession where faith supplants reason.

END-OF-CHAPTER QUESTIONS

1. Use the monetarist theory to ascertain the effects on the price level of

    a.   change in velocity, V, ceteris paribus;

    b.   change in real output, Q, ceteris paribus;

    c.   twin changes in V/Q, ceteris paribus; e.g., what if V rose 3% and Q rose 3%?

    Do you think velocity is stable? Is it possible that V and Q are inter-related somehow, either positively or negatively?

2. When Milton Friedman appears before Senate Committees overseeing the economy, what does he say when a Senator asks him about combatting inflation?

3. True or false:

    a.   Nominal wages, in the aggregate, lay like snow over mounds and mounds of real factors to cast its final, inevitable impression. Yet this blanket force can melt away, as it were, under the heat of efficient production.

    b.   In Post Keynesian theory, capitalist's profit shares are implicitly contained in the k variable.

. . . .

VOCABULARY

Average product of labor – a measure of the productivity of labor; Total output/# of workers

Cambridge Equation of Exchange – the heart of the monetarist thoery of inflation; $PQ = MV$, where the left side represents nominal GDP and the right side represents the stock of money multiplied by money's velocity

Incomes policy – policy which aims to control the nominal earnings of large income groups in order to restrain inflation

M1 – measure of the money supply; includes currency, checkable deposits, demand deposits and travelers checks

M2 – a second measure of the money supply; includes **M1** plus savings deposits, small time deposits and money market accounts at various financial institutions

Monetarism – school of economic thought; this school's theory of inflation which ties price advances to increases in the money stock

Post Keynesian – school of economic thought; this school's theory of inflation which relates increases in wages to inflation

Production Possibility Curve – a series of real output combinations feasible by a society under the conditions of full employment

Tax-based incomes policy – type of incomes policy which uses a tax scheme to discourage firms from allowing inflationary wage gains

Wage cost-mark up theorem – the heart of the Post Keynesian theory of inflation; $PQ = k(wN)$, where the left side represents nominal GDP and the right side represents the mark up, k, times the total wage bill, wN (i.e., the average wage times the number of workers)

PART FIVE

MACRO PRACTICE

"We are all Keynesians now."

Richard M. Nixon

CHAPTER 12

FISCAL AND MONETARY POLICY

Since Keynes' seminal work on the mechanisms of the macro-economy, politicians have been much more willing to tinker with the institutional levers of government to effect desirable economic outcomes. For them, the chance to manipulate the economy translates into the ability to grant political spoils, steer votes, and expand their sphere of influence. To have been provided a rationalization -- after having been so long held at bay by the bulwark Keynes called the classical school -- must have seemed to many a statesman like the arrival of some late-reaching orders from high command, orders that said in effect: all rules of engagement have changed.

And well they took the chance. In an ironic twist that Keynes did not live to appreciate, his closing remarks from The General Theory, regarding how politicians become "the slaves of some defunct economist," have, in hindsight, become prophetic. "We are all Keynesians, now," said our 37th President, Richard Nixon, the same one who tried to manipulate too much. To what extent Keynes might have approved of the myriad of measures which governments have adopted since the 1930's to improve society's economic well being, we can never know. Nor is it necessarily important that we know. The fact is that Keynes is alive and well in the posthumous long run: future heads of state will be Keynesians, too, i.e., they will operate the mechanisms of **fiscal** and **monetary** policy for which Keynes' General Theory provides sanction.

Emanating from the '36 tome is a certain new orthodoxy as to how the economy can be coddled into a thriving, noninflationary, full employment entity. Sometimes it is necessary to stimulate; other times, to contract. Sometimes a tilting towards recession must be countered; other times, the inflation dragon must be tamed. Either fiscal or monetary policy might be used in service of these aims. And while these two broad classes of governmental influence fall under the control of autonomous agencies, this chapter's analysis will present the case for viewing the actions of Congress, the President, and the Federal Reserve Bank as inescapably interdependent.

FISCAL POLICY

Fiscal policy refers to the management of government's budget. The budget involves two familiar flow concepts: expenditures and income. Government's gross *purchases* from firms denote its expenditures. The tax revenues of government are its income.

Should the government's tax revenues exceed its purchases in a given year, then the government is running a **surplus**; if the opposite's the case, then it's running a **deficit**. These terms apply regardless of whether we have in mind the federal or state government's budget. Our emphasis here will be on the federal budget, since federal fiscal policy is, naturally, geared toward the macro-economy.

In a nutshell then, fiscal policy entails the decision to run a budget deficit, surplus, or perhaps even a **balanced budget**, where taxes and expenditures are equalized. At the Federal level this decision is made jointly, albeit mostly combatively, by Congress and the President.

Stimulative

When the government decides to run a deficit, the design of the policy is said to be **stimulative**. Stimulative fiscal policy is antirecessionary policy, the justification for which emanates from Keynes' thoughts about the potential effectiveness of government spending to lift a slumping domestic economy out of sub-full employment equilibrium. But inasmuch as the budget is determined by two variables, spending and taxes, then stimulative fiscal policy can be accomplished in either of two ways: by increasing governmental purchases or by reducing tax collections. In short, stimulative fiscal policy entails the use of tax and spending policies to move the budget more to the deficit side. (See Diagram 12-1.)

Contractionary

Contractionary policy is stimulative policy's alter ego. It aims to contain aggregate demand influences that might spark a menacing inflation. Like stimulative policy, the levers for manipulation are spending and

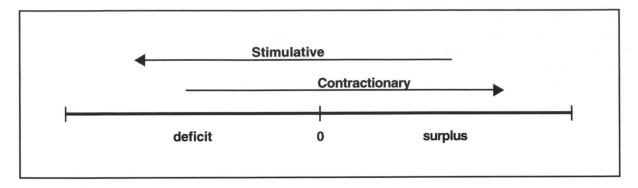

Diagram 12-1

taxes. If federal officials want fiscal policy to run a contractionary course, then either taxes must be raised or governmental spending reduced. This would shift the fiscal budget result more to the surplus side. (See Diagram 12-1.)

In short, deficits are stimulative; surpluses are contractionary. In point of fact, however, the two terms often get used a bit more loosely. In the popular economic press they often refer to the *object* of budgeting goals. Thus, regardless of the current status of the budget, movements *towards* either surplus or deficit will tend to define the nature of the policy: a declining deficit is said to be contractionary--and relatively speaking, it is--while any reduction of a surplus would be stimulative. (See Diagram 12-1.)

MONETARY POLICY

Monetary policy does what it sounds like it might: it employs the Federal Reserve Bank's four tools (Chapter 14) to control the size of the money supply, especially to control monetary growth. By such means, the Fed hopes to modulate real and nominal income growth and temper advances in the general price level.

Even as the Fed has four tools with which to register its influence, the policy decision boils down to a simple dilemma: to accelerate the growth of the money supply or to pull in on the reigns, so to speak.

For the normal course of a growing economy implies that the money supply will grow with an increased population's demand for currency to make transactions and the investment sector's desire for new financing to realize net investment plans. Thus, if *some* monetary growth is normal, the key issue becomes, "How much growth?"

Stimulative

An acceleration in the growth of the money supply is always stimulative. It represents a well-considered attempt to "prime the pump." The logic of stimulative monetary policy turns on the money supply's influence on credit, or **loanable funds**, markets. Net increases in the money supply should increase credit availability, sink interest rates (from the prime rate to credit card rates), spur borrowing and increase, most importantly, the demand for capital goods. From there, the rambling force of the Keynesian multiplier can course through the economy like the Colorado through the Canyon.

Contractionary

Decelerating monetary growth, or action to actually reduce **M-1** or **M-2**, dries up the monetary well. Credit is tighter, loaning reduced, and the aggregate demand tide wanes as investment tributaries dry up.

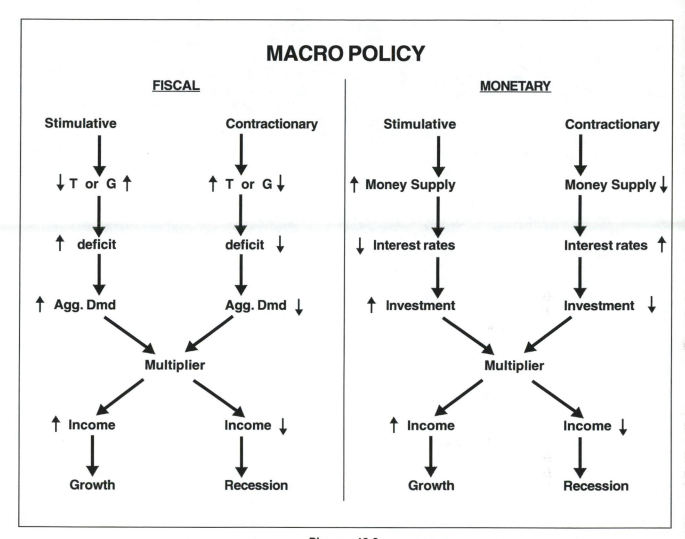

MACRO POLICY

FISCAL	MONETARY

FISCAL

Stimulative	Contractionary
↓ T or G ↑	↑ T or G ↓
↑ deficit	deficit ↓
↑ Agg. Dmd	Agg. Dmd ↓

Multiplier

↑ Income	Income ↓
Growth	Recession

MONETARY

Stimulative	Contractionary
↑ Money Supply	Money Supply ↓
↓ Interest rates	Interest rates ↑
↑ Investment	Investment ↓

Multiplier

↑ Income	Income ↓
Growth	Recession

Diagram 12-2

Why would the Federal Reserve want to do that?

As we saw in the previous chapter, a considerable body of economic theory exists that traces price level problems to the growth of the money supply. We studied this view in the context of Friedman's Monetarism, and the Cambridge equation, $MV = PQ$. The vast majority of Federal Reserve Bank Chairmen have been monetarist by persuasion (even if occasionally they might have acted contrary to the faith during their respective tenures). Given this, the typical Fed head will interpret any upticks in the rate of inflation as evidence that the economy requires a spoonful of monetarist medicine. Of course, this relief is unpleasant. With the resultant decline in activity, the prescription to counter the inflationary flu implies involuntary joblessness.[1]

---

[1] Almost always this labor surplus gets distributed in the most nonegalitarian manner: those least able to sustain an income loss have to ingest the most bitter pill. So, it is this author's strong conviction that the arguments between monetarists and Post-Keynesian views of inflation must be viewed for their moral merit; i.e., in each's ability to deliver society from randomly allocated and avoidable pain. A Weintraubian incomes policy, though now out of vogue, offers hope in this regard since it detaches the price level difficulties from desirable real product trends.

Diagram 12-2 is offered to assist you in organizing the material just presented. It combines lessons from Chapters 10, 11 and 12.

FISCAL AND MONETARY INTERACTION

The foregoing definitions and categories notwithstanding, changes in fiscal policy have inevitable repercussions in the monetary realm. Chiefly, fiscal policy will somehow affect credit markets. Fiscal policy decisions can therefore force the hand of the Federal Reserve to make alterations in monetary policy, not necessarily in sync with its own ends, but to accommodate the Treasury's need for financing some portion of governmental spending. Besides the credit markets, budgetary decisions can upset bond markets, since every dollar of deficit spending must be offset by an equivalently valued bond asset; thus, the Fed is often forced to take action via Open Market Operations whenever Congress and the President decide to use stimulative fiscal policy. The extent to which the Federal Reserve must modify its original plans depends on which method is selected to finance the new expenditures. And as there are several financing methods, political authorities mix them to various degrees to suit their purposes. Thus, the measure of adjustment by the Fed depends on how the politicians mix the financing pot.

Three ways to finance

The mechanics of fiscal and monetary policy interaction begin with the observation that the government has three options when it comes to financing new activity: it can *raise taxes, sell bonds,* or (at the risk of some inaccuracy) *print money.* Somehow, some way, cash must be raised in the present period in order for the government to honor its commitments. This is only part and parcel to accomplishing anything in a capitalist economy.

Let us then begin an extended analysis of the effects of (any net) increase in federal spending. We will suppose that the government has decided to initiate a new project. The President has set a goal to put a person on Mars (and return the same safely) by the year 2010. Billions will be committed to the effort, which has captured the imaginations of poets and

astronomers alike. As with the lunar project, NASA has the charge to accomplish the venture.

Now then, thousands of orders must be placed for the facilities, electronics, computers, materials, et. al. to make the initiative a success. All these orders imply eventual governmental payments to those companies which win the bids to provide the equipment. These firms then pay their workers. The multiplier process ensues. In and of itself, the new spending is stimulative.

The effect of raising taxes

But suppose in order to pay the bills, Washington's powers-that-be decide to *fully* fund the program by raising taxes. What then?

At the most obvious level, this decision levies the household sector with a heavier burden. Although the project is popular, it drains disposable income. With less disposable income, some part of consumption would fall.

Suddenly, the positive multiplier effects seem less clear cut. Surely, raising government expenditures constitutes a stimulant; but that boost is undercut. To what degree? This question requires some technical analysis.

balanced budget multiplier

Let us set up some bearings. Let's say that in some certain year, government spending had been $25 billion; Investment had been $25 billion; autonomous consumption was $10 billion. Thus, total autonomous spending was $60 billion. We'll also assume that the marginal propensity to consume was .9. Given all this, Chapter 10's multiplier analysis suggests that equilibrium income would have been $600 billion, for the calculations would reduce to $60b x 10.

Now suppose the MARS (Man Arrives, Returns Safe) Project were begun and government expenditures rose in that year by $5 billion. We've assumed that taxes would fund the effort completely, so taxes were raised that year by the same amount. Now we can use the multiplier analysis to help us evaluate the net effects.

We would have to introduce the new $5 billion both as a government expenditure and tax obligation of the households. This can be done in the context of the typical C + I + G equation as follows:

$$C + I + G = .9 (Y-T) + 10B + 25B + (25B + 5B)$$

$$C + I + G = .9 (Y-5B) + 65B$$

A couple of things are new. The government side shows the original and new expenditures--just for the sake of clarity. The key new term is **(Y-T)**. T stands for taxes, so we placed a $5 Billion term there. (Y-T) represents the economic term for the **disposable income** of households. It is as though the households earn a gross pay, then the tax is charged in a **lump-sum** payment to the government to meet its expenses. Thus, the underlying consumption equation must be modified in order to reflect the tax burden the households bear. That equation would be written

$$C = mpc (Y-T) + AC$$

whenever the tax is of this lump-sum variety. Now we can pursue the algebra and see the results.

$$Y = [.9 (Y-5B)] + 65B$$

$$Y - [.9 (Y - 5B)] = 65B$$

$$Y - [.9(Y) - .9(5B)] = 65B$$

$$(Y - .9Y) - 4.5B = 65B$$

$$.1 Y = 65B - 4.5B$$

$$Y = (65B - 4.5B) \div .1$$

$$Y = 60.5B \times 10 = 605B$$

The algebra indicates that the multiplier effects of the new spending, financed solely by taxes, would be substantially reduced. To inject $5 billion of spending into the system and have a net increase of national income of only $5 billion means that the strength of the multiplier was reduced from ten to one. Indeed, the **balanced budget multiplier** has a value of one regardless of the mpc's value.

To drive home the point we can examine the consumption sector. Had no tax been collected, the $5 billion governmental stimulus would have created ten times that amount of additional national income through the multiplier process, $50 billion. $45 billion of that would have been *induced* consumption. Yet as our example demonstrates, the $5 billion increase in government spending constitutes the entire increase in national income/product, from $600 to $605 billion. Thus, no additional consumption would be induced from a balanced budget strategy; the lost consumption is that potential $45 billion in spending which *would have been* induced had the full multiplier effects been allowed to work, i.e., had no taxes been collected against the project's expenditures, i.e., had pure deficit financing been used.

That *total* Consumption would be the same both before and after the MARS project can be illustrated with the following algebra.

Before the government initiated the MARS project,

$$C + I + G = .9 (Y) + 60B$$

which led to

$$Y = 60B \times 10$$

$$Y = 600B .$$

So, for consumption, C = mpc(Y) + Autonomous Consumption:

$$C = .9(600B) + 10B$$

$$C = 540B + 10B$$

$$C = 550B. [CHECK: Y - C = 600B - 550B = 50B = (I+G)]$$

After the MARS Project:

$$C = .9(605B - 5B) + 10B$$

$$C = .9(600B) + 10B$$

$$C = 540B + 10B$$

$$C = 550B . [CHECK : Y - C = 605B - 550B = 55B = (I+G)]$$

How should all this be interpreted? *The stimulative effects of governmental spending initiatives will be softened to the extent that taxes are raised in order to finance the effort.* Aggregate demand would rise on the one hand; but the offsetting decline in disposable income would work in the opposite direction. This, then, is the weakest fiscal policy combination.

Critics of Keynes' ideas would surely interpret the matter in another way. Economists of Milton Friedman's persuasion would point out that the share of government spending out of GDP begins to increase as a result of the equivalent increases in G and T. In our example, government spending accounted for $25 billion out of the $600 billion GDP, or 4.17%. After the project and the taxes, the share increases slightly to $30 billion out of $605 billion, or 4.96%. This observation, then, becomes the basis for a set of objections to Keynesian-inspired stimulative policies: the government's claim over the private resources of the economy becomes incrementally greater with each new, usually politically motivated, expenditure.[2]

The increasing share of G/GDP represents an encroachment by political authorities into the lives of private citizens--or, as Friedman would say, the gradual dissolution of citizens' personal freedom.[3] And this is so *even when the deficit is not increased as a result of the spending, i.e.,when balanced budget policies are used.*

The effect of selling bonds

We have seen that raising taxes offsets the strength of any would-be fiscal spending stimulus. Moreover, all the data from the real world tells us that politicians are loath to raise taxes anyway. Their own political interest inclines them to use deficit spending policies, since the surest way to political death is a bevy of levies.

Thus, let's suppose that in order to minimize their own political expenses, the Congress and the President agree to finance the MARS Project by selling bonds. For a $5 billion expense, bonds must be issued sufficient to raise that amount of cash. That way, the firms that sell their goods and services to the government would get their payments. The beauty of the bonds, of course, is that the government would have an extended period to service the debt, rather than having to absorb a $5 billion cost within the given fiscal year. The trade off here, though, is that servicing the debt incurs interest obligations to those that lend to the government via their bond purchases. The total cost of the project, then, is $5 billion plus the interest paid to bondholders. If the rate of interest on this particular issue of bonds were 5%, then eventually the project will really cost $5.25 billion.

Fair trade, one might say. Because if the multiplier effects of the project are allowed to run their course--and one would think they could, since "no new taxes" has been pledged--national income will grow substantially enough to easily cover the $5 billion plus interest. The project should be a *significant* net plus for the domestic economy.

Yet some economic logic dictates that it might not be so easy. With the sale of new bonds the government has to attract buyers with less expensive bonds, just as to induce any new spate of buying the seller must offer his goods at reduced prices. This much is shown in Diagram 12-3 with a simple increase in the supply of bonds.

But at the same time, a crucial interest rate play is made.

interest rate changes

All bonds sell at a discount to their **face value** or **future value**. Otherwise, there would be no interest earning for the holder of the bond. Consider: a $1000 bond payable one year from today would never sell for $1000 *today*, since the bond would have earned no interest. The discounted price is therefore called the **present value** of the bond. And most crucial, the differential between the present and future values of the bond determines its rate of interest.

---

[2] Many of us have heard of, or observed, the lamentable "pork barrel" spending of the government. Even if it is an exaggerated problem--which this author tends to believe--such waste is objectionable in principle. On the other hand, just what waste is needs some careful thought. Seward's Folly, the purchase of Alaska, was not such a folly after all.

[3] See Milton Friedman's <u>Free to Choose</u>.

An Increase in Bond Supply

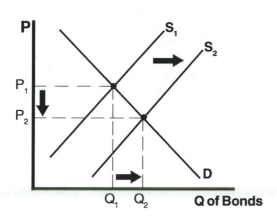

Diagram 12-3

An important formula expresses the relations among these three terms:

$$FV = PV (1 + r),$$

where FV means future value, PV means present value and r stands for the interest rate.

We'll say that prior to the start of MARS the typical $1000, one year term bond was selling at a price of $950. What is the interest rate implied in this relation? We can plug in the numbers and see.

$$\$1000 = \$950 (1 + r)$$

$\dfrac{\$1000}{\$950} = 1 + r$, after dividing both sides by $950

$$1.0526 = 1 + r$$

$$1.0526 - 1 = r$$

$$.0526 = r \; ; \; r = 5.26\%$$

Now, we notice from the diagram that the new issue of bonds would bring a decreased bond price. Let's say that new price was $930, ceteris paribus.

Plugging in,

$$\$1000 = \$930 (1 + r)$$

$$\dfrac{\$1000}{\$930} = 1 + r$$

$$1.0753 = 1 + r$$

$$1.0753 - 1 = r$$

$$.0753 = r \; ; \; r = 7.53\%$$

The lower bond prices have necessarily required the government to offer higher rates of interest. But this is just common sense: the flip side of saying the government must attract bond purchases with lower prices is to say that it must offer those same buyers better interest rates.

But the higher interest rates might diminish capital spending. With investment spending reduced, Aggregate Demand is reduced and so too is national income. In other words, higher interest rates effect a negative multiplier process. And this would offset the gains from the original expenditures.

The conclusion, then, of Keynesian critics is that government deficits **crowd out** private investment by elevating interest rates. As government bond prices fall, then buyers gladly flock to the relative safety of government bonds. Any competing corporate bond-issue will simultaneously feel a reduced demand--a simple substitution effect. Publishers of new bonds will therefore have to raise their interest offers, which necessarily diminishes the profitability of their capital projects. Meanwhile, bank lending rates will climb as credit/cash flows towards the federal government's control and away from the private sector's. To regain lost funds the banks might raise rates for depositors. But that only reenforces the rising rate trend as banks would try to maintain their spread between depositors' and borrowers' rates.

So the bond and credit markets are interlinked and their connection, say the critics, implies the barrenness of alleged fiscal stimuli. What the

Crowding Out

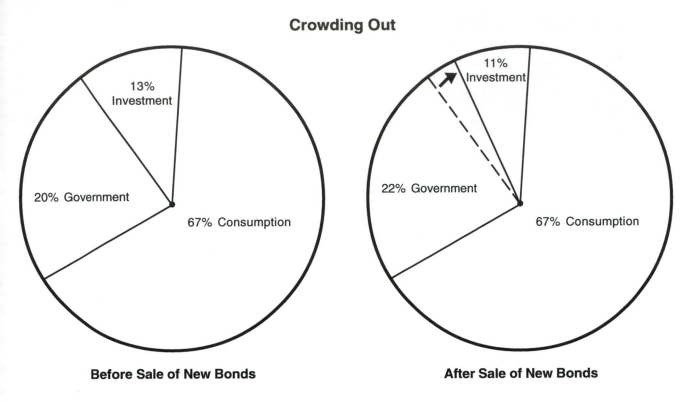

Before Sale of New Bonds　　　　　　　　**After Sale of New Bonds**

Diagram 12-4

government deficits buy in time has no corresponding *real* benefit because bond-financed expenditures boost interest rates and diminish investment *in the very period in which new federal spending occurs.* In the long run, taxes will have to be raised to pay off the bondholders precisely because the new debt crowds out more productive outlets for limited financial capital. The simple pie-chart representing GDP in diagram 12–4 illustrates this point.

The effect of printing money

Well, if the other two things don't work, perhaps we can try a third tack.

Suppose to finance the project the government saw fit to print the necessary cash and make payments with it. The instinctive response to this idea quickly reveals one's monetarist or Keynesian leanings. The Keynesian economist would see an increased money supply leading to lower interest rates and greater

capital spending. National Income advances as the full multiplier effects of the MARS project get realized.

What could be better? What could be worse!?! The growth of the money supply beyond levels warranted by real growth can only devalue the currency. It is the recipe for inflation. No additional real output will come forth from the spending, as the inflationary spell reduces the real incomes and real consumption of households. Inevitably, the private sector is made worse off so that the government can pursue its self-interest, not the interest of individuals. Direct and indirect effects on investment cannot be ruled out: inflation reduces firms' purchasing power, so real investment suffers; any capital project is more dicey in an inflationary environment since a volatile price level makes judgments about the profitability of long run commitments more uncertain; and higher nominal interest rates loom as creditors seek to recover from new borrowers real dollars lost to old ones.

SUMMARY

This chapter introduces the fundamentals of fiscal and monetary policy. We have seen that, although we can separately define the tasks of fiscal and monetary policy, the federal government's spending decisions are bound to affect bond and credit markets.

It is inevitable, therefore, that the monetary authorities of a domestic economy (The Federal Reserve) must take into account the effects of fiscal policy maneuverings as it pursues the management of the nation's money supply. The interaction of fiscal and monetary policy suggests that the strength of any one policy action has limits. For example, increases in the deficit would tend to raise interest rates and crowd out potential investment. Still, it is seldom clear just how much crowding out there will be at any given time.

More specifically, this chapter has tried to outline the contemporary objections to the government's manipulation of economic outcomes. We have gone through these objections in an analytic way, using Keynes' theoretic contributions to the science, so as to strengthen our command of what has become, for better or for worse, the modern economic vocabulary. In the final analysis, we *are* all Keynesians now.

It is hoped that the reader comes to appreciate, too, the fact that today's ideological debates--both political and economic--hark back to the disputes of an earlier generation when Keynes first wrote his "heresies." At their core, they represent a modern redeux of old laissez-faire controversies, ones which go back to Smith and the Mercantilists. No doubt these discussions will get reaired in future discourse, in every developed nation, in every political campaign, in every academic seminar, as long as there is an economic science, and as long as there's a political interest in creating viable domestic economies--which is to say, forever.[4] Thus, economists and politicians are strange and familiar bedfellows, the former providing the intellectual rationale for a fundamental political vision, the latter, an oracle for the grand abstraction. It is impossible to tell whose whore is whose in this profane relation; yet it is certain that an uneducated public prostitutes itself whenever and wherever it ignores economic ideas.

---

[4] Indeed, the level of manipulation has reached the international stage as the "G-7" nations seek to coordinate interest rate policy, trade and currency policy, employment and immigration policy, as well as fiscal policy, all in service of a perceived need for either expansion or contraction.

VOCABULARY

Fiscal policy – the management of the government's budget as determined by its purchases and tax income

Monetary policy – the management of a domestic economy's money supply by the monetary authority

Surplus – condition of the government's budget when tax intake exceeds its spending

Deficit – condition of the government's budget when its spending exceeds its tax intake

Balanced budget – condition of the government's budget when tax revenues and government purchases are equal

Stimulative – describes either fiscal or monetary policy when it aims towards increasing aggregate demand and GDP

Contractionary – describes either fiscal or monetary policy when it aims towards decreasing aggregate demand and GDP, usually to soften inflationary pressures

Loanable funds – money-credit available for borrowing

Disposable income – household income after all taxes are paid

Lump sum tax – a tax levied and paid in the form of a fixed payment, rather than at a rate (say, of income)

Balanced budget multiplier – the Keynesian multiplier derived under the assumption that all government spending be financed under the conditions of a balanced budget

Future (face) value – the promised value of a bond upon full maturity

Present value – the price of a bond at the time of purchase

Crowding out – the diminished investment spending that comes as a result of increased deficits, bond financing and resulting higher interest rates

MOCK TEST

1. List the means by which fiscal policy and monetary policy can be used in order to achieve real growth; i.e., what are the means of stimulative fiscal and monetary policy?

2. What are the three ways a government can finance its activity? What are some of the possible (theoretic) trade-offs that occur when the government must finance its activity?

3. Discuss and illustrate the chain of events that would be considered positive if the money supply were increased. Use graphs to illustrate.

4. A politician proposes a 50-cent/gallon gas tax to be introduced over a five year period. What would be the economic consequences of such a strategy? Is it stimulative, contractionary, or neither? Explain with specifics and with as wide a scope as possible.

5. Discuss and illustrate the chain of events that would be considered negative if the government sold bonds to finance any new spending activity. Use graphs to illustrate.

6. After being elected, George W. Bush engineered significant tax cuts. What would be the economic consequences of such a strategy? Is it stimulative, contractionary, or neither? Explain.

7. After being elected, Bill Clinton proposed raising taxes on wealthy households. What would be the economic consequences of such a strategy? Is it stimulative, contractionary, or neither? Explain.

CHAPTER 13

DEFICITS & DEBTS

In the borough of Manhattan, which locals call "the city," just off the corner of 42nd and Broadway, there's an electronic billboard that keeps up-to-the-minute track of the federal government's monetary indebtedness. This represents the sum of all outstanding bond obligations that the federal government has issued in the past. That is to say, it is a continuous running count of the **gross federal debt** (the **gross debt**, for short). Any out-of-towner, who might have just walked out from the bus terminal located diagonally across the street from the billboard, would gape at the awesome rapidity of the changing units, flashing like subliminal messages on a movie screen.

The eyes search for something more perceptible.

$6,437,754,691,294, *** . **

Then a man stretches out his hand to you.

"No, sorry, I don't have any change right now."

"And God only knows," one muses, "who has a spare four trillion laying around."

****

This anecdote is offered tongue-in-cheek. It illustrates a kind of paranoid fixation regarding big numbers that distorts one's understanding of the figures, not to mention of the debt concept itself.

In this chapter we will try to escape the misunderstanding surrounding government debt. We will rigorously define some key terms and work to gain insight on the nature and uses of debt in a capitalist monetary economy. We will examine historical trends of debt creation and attempt to link macro-economic performance to it. The aim here is to create a more realistic view of what debt is. To preface the chapter briefly, our key point is this: debt is no single thing but, as with all economic concepts, a paired thing. Hence, to say that the gross debt, or any kind of debt, is either all good or all bad constitutes the major fallacy in thinking about debt. (Philosophers call these errors **false dilemmas**; economists might refer to the all-good/all-bad approach to debt as

"single entry bookkeeping.") The fact of the matter is that debt is a risky thing, carrying with it the possibilities of success and failure. It is, therefore, *in itself*, neither good nor bad, unless one feels a certain way about the capitalist means of enterprise itself, i.e., the use of debt. Debt is simply an instrument of the economic system as it currently exists. Beyond this, objections to debt can only be moral ones.[1]

DEFINITIONS

We need to establish with precision what debt is. In the economic sphere, we have in mind **legal obligations** and **legal claims**. One party is obliged to another party to repay a past borrowing. At the same time, the owed party, or **creditor**, holds a claim against the resources of the borrower.[2] Civil authorities will validate what a debtor might owe a creditor if the latter can show something in writing, signed by the debtor, that details the claim. Such documentation comes in several varieties: IOU's, promissory loan notes, bonds of all sorts.

Thus, a debt establishes a binding relation between a borrower and a lender, each of whom has a particular economic motive for entering the relation. The borrower wants a viable, exchangeable asset--money--in order to gather real resources, employ them, and, most importantly, profit from the entire effort.[3] The lender seeks a potentially rewarding outlet for what might otherwise be an idle asset. So the loan is no gift; the lender will claim a share of that bounty that the borrower reaps through his initiative and ingenuity. This demand comes as fair trade for (a) the sacrifice of liquidity implied by the transfer of the asset and (b) the risk of loss. After all, the lender makes a judgment to yield control of the asset to someone who is most likely a stranger. A borrower should owe something in exchange--in principle and interest.

---

[1] And they must ultimately include an objection to the kind of system we live in, if the argument is to be coherent.

[2] Robert Heilbroner and Peter Bernstein. The Debt and the Deficit. W. W. Norton and Company, New York, 1989 p. 31.

[3] We assume here an entrepreneurial motive. Obviously, loans can be issued for other purposes as well, but the relation between the parties is basically the same.

Now the persons involved in this exchange view the entire matter conversely: the debtor acquires an asset (money) *and* a liability (a loan note that says he must re-pay); the lender acquires an asset (the note that says he will be re-paid) *and* a liability (the loss of liquid funds).[4]

As in all trades consummated by two self-interested parties, each feels better off from the deal. Though the lender forfeits control of an asset, he simultaneously gains one that has some potential for appreciation. The borrower's benefit is still more concrete: his intentions could not be fulfilled without the lender's assistance.

Debt is a Stock Variable; Debt is also a Flow

As an economic variable, debt is unique because it can be viewed in either of two ways. Like a firm's inventory, that might be thought of as either a stock or flow, debt can also be seen either way.

a stock

Since at any specific *point* in time a person can calculate the sum of his or her indebtedness, debt is, conceptually speaking, a stock variable. The debt a person carries at any point in time is exactly that amount he obliged himself to repay but has yet to do so, i.e., any unpaid portion. In this view, of one's outstanding debt is the antithesis to one's saving*s*, as savings must be equivalent to the value of all past *accumulations* of (money) assets at any given point in time, i.e., the unconsumed portion of one's income. Debt is, therefore, a negative savings.

a flow

On the other hand, we can view a given debt through entirely different lenses. In a capitalist economy, debt revolves, like business inventory, and can therefore be conceived of as a flow.

How is that? Consider this example. A person uses a credit card to make purchases each month. Suppose she built up a $500 bill on the account in 1995. Thereafter she charged exactly $100 a month on the card and paid off exactly $100 a month on the bill. In this case, the $500 really isn't the same $500 month to month. Even though the credit card debt *at any moment* is $500, some portion of old debt is being paid off and new debt is being assumed. Since the amount paid off equals the amount incurred, the $500 is a revolving debt, turning over completely every fifth month; but of course, the debt's burden is constant.[5]

The example serves for the general case. With respect to the federal government's gross debt, the blinking billboard off Broadway belies a richer perspective. To arrive at the constantly-tripping $4 trillion figure, one must keep track of two things: how much the government is *issuing* in new bonds moment to moment and how much the government is *paying back* moment to moment. It is these *two* things that determine the course and size of the gross federal debt at any given moment.

DEBT AND TIME

An overlooked aspect of economic debt is its relation to the dimension of time. Debts connect the present with the past, since any debt we might have outstanding today was incurred in the past. Debts also link the present with the future, since unpaid debts have to be paid back in the future. Hence, debt connects the past, present, and future.

But in regard to time itself, we can speak of futures and pasts distinct from the future and past we have in our cognizance today. Come tomorrow, neither the past, present, nor future will be the same as it is today.

And so it is with our debts. They are not stationary, but travelling through time with us. And they are turning over, revolving, as they move through time, much the way planets rotate as they trace their orbits.

---

[4] The lender's action can also be viewed as a decision to trade asset types within his or her own *portfolio*. A portfolio is simply the listing of assets which someone holds. For the person who lends, the loan must always entail a portfolio exchange wherein a paper asset loss gets exactly offset by a paper asset acquisition of equal value: the legally binding promissory note in lieu of cash.

[5] The example ignores interest compounding, but the concept is unimpaired.

What is debt? Debt is a time tunnel, a trading funnel, through which money flows and conjoins all capitalist motion.

It's worth a measure of your time to meditate upon the somewhat metaphorical concepts provided here. Only by understanding that debt is kind of a connective fiber that weaves the fabric of modern capitalist life can the common misconceptions regarding debt be escaped. Moreover, the success of our economic future together relies on just this kind of understanding.

GOOD DEBTS AND BAD

Paul Simon, the popular singer, has a line from a song that goes: "You know, a bad day is when I lie in bed and think of things that might have been." Bad debt has precisely the same impact. All the borrower and lender can do is examine the books, stare wistfully over the nonperforming assets, and think of things that might have been.

Since debt is an instrument to provide entrepreneurs with the means to accomplish a project, the vital determinant in assessing the quality of the debt is the quality of the asset: is the asset that debt bore credit-worthy; is it productive? That depends on whether the asset generates a revenue-flow sufficient to cover (1) the flow-costs of the project, (2) pay-back to the creditor, and (3) a reward to the entrepreneur. That this might occur does not so much depend on the engineering quality of the asset--a factory with state-of-the-art technology is no guarantee of success--nor on the intellectual or aesthetic worthiness of the effort--there are plenty of inventors and artists whose contributions went ignored by society. Ultimately, the existence of a palpable market demand makes debt a positive thing, and from the absence of demand comes a debt absent of value.

This conception focuses on debt creation for the purposes of an investment project. That is, it emphasizes *the entrepreneur* in relation to his creditor. But not all debts abide by the same test of market demand.

The government can't be held to a market demand criterion for credit worthiness; for example: it provides only non-profit public services. Nonetheless, governments do have a continuously replenishing revenue stream from which to draw: taxes. Furthermore, a national government has the power to issue its own currency. For these reasons, U.S. government bonds are very secure debts to own and, consequently, post lower rates of interest than their corporate counterparts.[6] In a word, the approximately $6.4 trillion gross debt of the U. S. government represents some of the best legal claims money can buy. So good are they that continuous, second-hand markets operate worldwide for the resale of previous issues; i.e., if someone holds a U.S. Federal Bond he or she can get cash for it rather easily from a willing third party purchaser. Major financial corporations such as Merrill Lynch and Citicorp buy and sell outstanding U.S. obligations all the time. And if worse comes to worst, the government itself would buy back an old issue.

PUBLIC DEFICITS AND PRIVATE LOSSES: APPLES AND ORANGES

Inasmuch as the gross debt is the sum of all previous federal surpluses and deficits, the method of accounting used to calculate and categorize yearly inflows and outflows of the government becomes relevant in comparing its annual performance with that of private firms. We raise this matter here because such comparisons appear frequently in the press and get heralded by politicians who decry the government's place in modern society. The inefficiencies of government notwithstanding, the comparison is utterly specious. It's important to see why.

We need chiefly to examine the very method of cost accounting which the federal government employs. We will find that the federal government's accounting procedures predispose its budgetary bottom line towards a fiscal deficit. But in order to see why

---

[6] Another reason government issues post lower rates than their corporate counterparts is that most federal, state, and municipal securities in the U.S. offer *tax-free* interest so that a government issue can often yield a better return than a corporate security's *after-tax* yield.

this built-in deficit bias exists, we must review the accounting procedures of the capitalist firm first.

A Firm's Procedure

Computing profit might seem a simple thing: intake less the outgo, revenue minus costs. Yet as we discussed in Chapter 8, even the revenues of firms include within them some indirect taxes. Thus seemingly simple things have, to someone unfamiliar, their peculiar complications.

We need to focus on the cost side. A firm has basically two kinds of costs: capital expenditures and **operating expenses**.[7] Capital expenses are the firm's purchases for plant and equipment. From the macro-economic perspective, the grand sum of the business sector's capital expenditures is Gross Domestic Investment--the I in C + I + G. Capital expenditures are analogous to a household's purchase of a new car, refrigerator, or an addition to the house structure in three interrelated aspects: (1) they are usually big ticket items; (2) the firm intends to have the asset remain in service over an extended period of time; (3) the purchases are discontinuous with respect to time.

Operating expenses, on the other hand, refer to the firm's ongoing, continuous, flow costs. For instance, labor's wages are an operating cost. So are electric bills and costs for raw materials.

Operating costs depend closely on the firm's level of production. For example, if a firm has to rev up production to meet improved market conditions, total electrical and energy costs will rise, and the total wage bill of the firm would escalate if overtime pay were necessary. What distinguishes the use of resources that determine operating costs from the employment of a capital asset with its associated expenses is that in the very employment of, say, a worker, the resource is *immediately and fully consumed*: an hour's labor time is expended in one hour; one kilowatt-hour of electricity is spent entirely in one kilowatt-hour; a bag of cement used is a bag of cement gone.

The case is different for a capital resource: its use and expense occur over many periods.

That contrast in the *real* "**consumption**" of a resource is the basis for a crucial accounting distinction used by all profit-oriented firms: the separation of the **current account** and the **capital account**. The former keeps track of a given period's revenue and operating expense flow. The latter writes the expenses for capital as **depreciation allowances** that include only a portion of the original expense at the time of the asset's purchase. If, for example, a firm plunks down $1,000,000 on some piece of machinery for its factory, that firm will *not* write in a $1,000,000 expense for the purposes of calculating that year's cost (and that year's profit, in turn). Instead, it makes an estimate as to how much the machine wears out from use and must therefore be "replaced," as it were, within the year's period. This estimate is translated into monetary terms and recorded as the **depreciation expense**. With the commonly employed straight-line method of capital accounting, firms gauge how long a $1,000,000 machine would last them--say, ten years--and write in the proportionate expense in the ledger--$1,000,000/10 years is $100,000: that's what gets recorded and *only that much affects the bottom line profit assessment*. $900,000 of the $1,000,000 expense will be assigned to the next nine year's costs and thereby determine, in part, the next nine years' accounting profits!

An understanding of accounting methodology reveals an important truth about capitalism itself: the profit of the firm in actual practice is nothing but an accounting slight of hand. This does not render standard business accounting techniques bogus, however. In fact, depreciation adjustments make the profit figures more credible. Why? For one thing, were there no depreciation, firms' profit results would be highly volatile due to the irregularity of capital purchases. Because of these sorts of irregularities, profit results would be less meaningful. For example, in a year of improved sales a company might decide to make a major investment outlay. Without depreciation, the certain mathematical loss would hide the upswing that motivated the capital purchase. Obviously, not separating capital expenditures from operating costs would skew the "bottom line" towards

---

[7] Later in the text (chapter xxii) we will come to know these as Fixed and Variable costs.

the negative.

And something would be askew in that style of accounting. After all, to spread capital costs over the duration of their useful life reflects the genuine reality as to how fixed capital gets used. Thus, a capital expense account provides an objective gauge of the firm's absolute and relative performance. Such a reliable measure is precisely what capitalist economies need to allow the market's competitive process to become workable and beneficial.

The Federal Government's Method

Since the orientation of the federal government is nonprofit, there is no overwhelming reason to have a capital account, that is, to have adjustments for depreciation. Consequently, the federal government records its outflows strictly on a current account basis. *If the Defense Department buys a military plane that it intends to have service it for ten years, it records the entire cost of the plane in the year the purchase was made.* No adjustment, no depreciation, no profit; quite the contrary, there's a bookkeeping bias towards deficit.

Since the methods of accounting differ between governmental institutions and business firms, the comparisons of one to the other are usually spurious. When it is argued that the government, were it a firm, would be out of business because of all the deficits it runs, the only proper response can be to point out that the government is not a business, and that's precisely why its budget tends to show deficits. The secret supposition of the argument, that deficits of the government are like the losses of a firm (and surpluses like profits), is entirely without merit. It is to compare apples with oranges.

other measures of the debt

But there's more to it. A second lesson from Eisner and others is that *there is no single way to calculate the government's deficits or debt.* Rather, there are various measures and adjustments possible when trying to define the relation between the income and expenditures of the government. Let us briefly examine some other debt concepts.

So far we have restricted our view to *federal* deficits and debts. A broader measure would include adjustments for the budgets of the fifty states and all the local governments. Taken together, states and municipalities usually run surpluses. Thus, the **gross national debt**, and the annualized **gross national deficit**, both of which combine federal, state, and local results, would be less than the gross federal debt and deficit respectively. The GDP statistics seen in the Economic Report of the President use this gross *national* deficit figure when reconciling Saving with Investment in the yearly accounts. (See Chapter 8, towards the end.)

A second possible adjustment involves considerations for inflation. Given that many of the securities sold by all levels of government are long term (3–30 years) issues, the difference between the nominal payment and real payment owed becomes considerable. Such is true in any kind of long term loan. Consider a mortgage. In most cases a household will make monthly fixed payments for twenty to thirty years. But as one's nominal earnings rise, the burden of the mortgage is less. Even if one's income rises only by the rate of inflation, the monthly payments get easier to bear. The same is true with government debt. Since we pay back old bonds in current dollars, the real debt we carry is less cumbersome than the nominal figures suggest.

Finally, the gross debt of the federal government contains a number of IOU's *not* held by the public like the typical bond. Instead these government securities are held internally by the federal government, which is to say that the government owes itself. While these IOU's count towards the gross federal debt, they represent no *net* burden to taxpayers. An explanation of this fact requires an analogy.

Suppose someone had kept a personal budget and in that budget were a category for food expenditures and a category for transportation. For several years food expenses were less than projected, but the transportation bills went beyond budget estimates. In order to meet the deficit in transportation, the person borrowed money from the food "surplus." Then on a slip of paper the person wrote a personal IOU to his own food account.

Such an IOU amounts to nothing. It can't be considered a real asset because when the time comes for payback the person would be taking money out of his own wallet to pay himself! It is neither real asset nor a real debt, since there's no *net* return on the IOU.

The federal government's gross debt includes trillions worth of IOU's of this type. The Social Security Trust Fund holds approximately $1.3 trillion of this type. The Fund has built up over the past decade a huge "surplus," like the food account above. The accumulation exists simply because on the federal ledgers, Social Security tax receipts have outweighed Social Security payments. The excess cash is then "invested" in government bonds. Of course ,the other way to look at this is to note that the other components of the federal budget have overspent and so have had to "borrow" from the Social Security Trust Fund to meet their current payments. Either way one looks at it, the government has borrowed from itself and hence owes itself--which is to say it owes nothing in net terms from these IOU's.

Thus we arrive at the concept of the **net federal debt**. Technically, it's the gross federal debt less the value of all securities held by federal agencies and trusts. As of 2003, the net federal debt was approximately $3 trillion. The net federal debt more simply is that portion of the gross debt owed to the public.

The fact that some of the gross debt is held by the federal government itself means that the burden of the debt on taxpayers is less than meets the eye. For when one branch of the federal government borrows from another there is, again, no *net* obligation to the citizenry.

A BRIEF HISTORY OF THE GROSS FEDERAL DEBT

Now seems the appropriate time to ask the 6 trillion question: how did gross federal debt get that big? For one thing, it took over 200 years to accomplish. This gross debt is the accumulation of all annual gross federal surpluses and deficits since this government's founding in 1787. Had there been a surplus in a given year, then the gross debt would diminish by the amount of the surplus. Were there a deficit, the debt figure would enlarge. As the 6 trillion figure suggests, there were more years of deficit than surplus.

The period from 1930 to 1945 is remarkable in that it contains within it two of the most dramatic political/economic events of the century: the Great Depression and World War II. The magnitude of these events as measured by the historic norms established over 200 years has only one equal in U.S. history, namely the Civil War period ending with Lincoln's assassination.

In 1930 Herbert Hoover was still President, still promising, despite the havoc wreaked by the stock market crash of October 1929, that prosperity was just around the corner. Convinced as he was, he made no attempt at stimulus, and the federal budget showed a surplus for the year. 1931 and 1932, Hoover's last full years in office, showed slight deficits. By 1934 Franklin Roosevelt took a different route, and the deficits of 1934 and 1936 doubled as a percentage of GDP compared to 1933's result. But even Roosevelt's record for stimulus was modest given the scale and duration of the Depression. From 1937 to 1941 federal deficits were again but a few percentage points of the GDP.[8] Then, big changes came.

With its entrance into World War II American defense spending exploded. In 1942, the federal deficit absorbed 20% of GDP. This percentage climbed in 1943, peaked in 1944 at 25%, and fell just shy of 20% in 1945. In 1946, the war over, the federal government reported a surplus. How did the U.S. finance the war? Bonds: almost $150 billions worth of them.[9] The opportunity cost of those bonds was the consumption households traded off during those four years in patriotic support of the war effort. That household sacrifice freed real resources, which the government then called forth to engage the Axis Powers.

So great was the increase in deficit spending that after the War the value of the gross debt was greater

---

[8] Albert Sommers, with Lucie R. Blau. The U.S. Economy Demystified. Lexington Books, D.C. Heath and Company. Lexington, Mass. 1988. p. 5.
[9] Ibid., p. 5.

than a single year's GDP (271 vs. 211.6). This means, in effect, had the entire national income in 1946 been devoted solely to paying off the national debt, there would've still been obligations outstanding on January 1, 1947. Was that terrible? Irresponsible? Reckless? All things considered, it would have been more irresponsible not to fight the war, for the opportunity cost to the world would have been far higher than $150 billion.

Since the federal government's deficits after the war were a very modest percentage of those years' GDP's, the ratio of the gross debt to the GDP dropped from peaks in 1946-47 of greater than 1.1/1 to approximately .34/1 during the mid-1970's. Interestingly, the *nominal values* of the gross debt never fell to any great degree thereafter. By 1955, the gross debt was greater than it had been in 1946; by 1975-80 the figures were two and three times higher than the figures from the 1940's. Yet the nominal GDP values from 1946-1980 grew even faster than the nominal debt values, so the ratio of gross debt to GDP declined.

In the 1980's the gross debt grew faster than GDP. This rise came from the bond financing associated with the Star Wars program of the Reagan administration.[10] That and the recession[11] of the early 1990's pushed the ratio of gross debt to GDP to above the 6/10 mark for the first time since days of the Korean War. The end result: an approximately $4 trillion debt against the backdrop of a $6 trillion–plus annual GDP. Now, it would take till August to pay off the debt.

ARE GOVERNMENT DEFICITS GOOD OR BAD?

Madame Marie Curie, a Nobel Prize-winning chemist of the early 20th century has said, "Nothing in life is to be feared. It is only to be understood." She

---

[10] For a more interesting interpretation of the build up of the gross debt during the Reagan years, see Heilbroner and Bernstein, The Debt and the Deficit, Chapter 2. They argue that the combination of the 70s inflation and the early 80s recession made the doubling of the debt inevitable.

[11] Recessions tend to lift the deficit for reasons both direct and indirect. Directly, tax revenues fall since household and firm incomes decline; indirectly, government outlays increase in the form of unemployment insurance, welfare, etc.

was not referring to the gross federal debt, but this bit of wisdom has been the guiding principle of the present chapter nonetheless. The dilemmas posed by that debt are serious and compelling, but not overwhelming, not oppressive, and not intractable (unless we allow them to be). $6 trillion worth of bonds is nothing to dread, lament, or decry, no more than it's something to blithely celebrate, laud, or nonchalantly dismiss. It is what it is.

Now then: does deficit spending, and the subsequent increases in gross debt, have a positive or negative influence on economic outcomes?

In the case of the 1940's the answer is clear-cut. World War II and its associated huge gross deficits actually brought the U.S. economy out of the Depression. Certainly the unemployment data would suggest this: In 1940, 14.6% of the labor force were still looking but unable to find gainful employment. In 1944, that figure read 1.2%.

Did the war effort inevitably lead the country into financial ruin? Hardly. The next 30 years rank as the stablest in U.S. economic history. There were recessions, to be sure. But in context, the generation that won WW II, and its offspring, enjoyed a trifecta of economic statistical positives: moderate inflation, low unemployment (the worst rate of unemployment didn't come until the mid-seventies), and a healthy growth in productivity and income.

But these observations represent a mere cursory view of the special case of the second world war. Let's look at the data more carefully.

Eisner's Work

Robert Eisner has examined the relations between the government deficit and GDP in his 1986 book How Real is the Federal Deficit? The research has been updated via several scholarly articles since 1986. In these research endeavors, Eisner simply wanted to ascertain whether changes in the federal deficit would be positively (or negatively) related to changes in GDP.

Notice this investigation implicitly treats the federal deficit as the *cause* of movements in the GDP.

In the real world, this is not purely or perfectly the case. Economists well recognize that during recessions, when unemployment is relatively high, outlays of the government climb due to increases in unemployment insurance payments and the like. The increased outlays lift the deficit higher than it otherwise would be were the economy operating at full employment. More crucially, these higher outlays during recessions are *an effect* of a negative growth in GDP and such are contrary to the assumption of research that posits the condition of the budget as a causal factor. Therefore, in conducting research, it is necessary to remove an influence on the deficit figure that is obviously a symptom of GDP changes, rather than a cause.

The adjustment is called a **full employment deficit**. It indicates what the gross federal deficit would be if there were approximately full employment through time.[12]

Thereafter, the results are fairly straightforward. Eisner finds a fairly strong positive correlation between fluctuations in the full-employment deficit and changes in the GDP: if the full employment deficit rises, GDP tends to rise; when that deficit lowers, the economy tends to sag. It seems, as Keynes said long ago, deficits can help. Perhaps this is why Reagan's economy of the 80s was so successful.

What Are the Real Dangers of Deficits and Debts?

Certain indicators can help identify legitimate problems with the government's debt levels. One key variable has been mentioned: the ratio of gross debt to GDP. A second, probably more important, indicator is the size of interest payments relative to the debt.

Generally speaking, it is a good rule for the nation that the *growth* of its debt should be aligned with the *growth* of its GDP. This would result in a stable ratio of gross debt to GDP. Of course, the 1940's saw a tremendous leap in the proportion of debt to GDP with no terrible consequence. On the other hand, the near-doubling of the ratio in the 1980's prompts some concern.

A second statistic involving the debt can point to more disturbing trends in the government's use of debt: the percentage of the gross debt dedicated to interest payments.

This percentage should be kept stable and at minimal levels. For the interest payments on bonds represent a **transfer payment** from taxpayers to bondholders. Even if these two groups of people are one and the same (i.e., foreigners hold no bonds), a dangerous line is crossed whenever a significant portion the debt is being used simply to transfer wealth. Be it public or private debt, *when debt is used solely to transfer assets, as opposed to creating them, no multiplier effects from that portion of the debt-financing will be forthcoming, since no resources are being put into employment.*

In the 1980's, for example, billions of private, commercial debt went to finance the takeover attempts of major U.S. corporations. Speculators, looking to make large capital gains on stock and bond trades, would borrow heftily, betting that their *anticipated* capital gains could pay off their indebtedness later on. The difficulty here is the opportunity cost of the debt. That financing could have been more constructively utilized were it placed in the financing of a new building, machine, or some other piece of real capital. *Instead, speculators exposed themselves to an increased risk of declining paper asset values (stock prices, bond values, etc.) precisely because no productive, revenue-bearing assets were being created with that debt.*

The analogy to the government debt is this: as a greater portion of the debt is used to pay interest, the less there is available for effective, job-creating, job-sustaining, multiplier-effect-inducing public projects. Instead, more current taxpayer dollars are *transferred* to some other group of government creditors. That is a strange moral recipe, because it will almost certainly redistribute wealth from average income-earning taxpayers to bondholders, most of whom are fairly well-to-do.

[12] Eisner also makes price level adjustments on the deficit figure in the manner described in the section on other measures of the debt and deficit.

VOCABULARY

Gross federal debt (gross debt) – the sum of all outstanding obligations of the federal government; equivalent to the net sum of all annual surpluses and deficits of the federal government from the time of its founding

False dilemma – a mistake in reasoning that assumes that the possibilities from a choice of two must be exclusively one or the other, and not a third possibility by which the two choices might be compatible; for example, someone says, " ... either you love me and will marry me or you don't love me at all." Rational lovers know that it is possible to love someone and choose not to marry.

Creditor - the lender in a loan agreement; one who issues credit

Operating expenses – a firm or government enterprise's adjustable and continuous costs required for the production and delivery of a good or service; also called variable costs, these are solely non-fixed costs that vary with the level of production; e.g.: labor, electric, material costs

Consumption – in this chapter the usage and wearing out of a firm's capital stock

Current account - method of accounting used for recording an enterprise's operating expenses

Capital account - method of accounting used for tracking an enterprise's depletion of capital stock; employs any one of several styles of depreciation

Depreciation allowance - an accounting cost credit for the unused portion of capital stock

Depreciation expense - an accounting cost mark-down for the repair, maintenance, and/or replacement of worn-out capital stock

Gross national debt - the gross federal debt plus or minus the debt or credits of state and local governments

Net federal debt - the gross federal debt less its own internally held IOU's

Full employment budget - calculation of the difference between federal tax collections and spending under the assumption that the economy is operating at full employment

Transfer payments - a group of outlays by any branch of government whereby taxpayers' tax dollars are redistributed to other citizens, taxpayers, etc., within the same fiscal year; e.g.: social security payments, welfare, Medicare and Medicaid

PART SIX

MONEY AND BANKING

"Money is a time machine."

Paul Davidson

CHAPTER 14

THE EVOLUTION OF THE FRACTIONAL RESERVE BANKING SYSTEM

You are hereby invited to reach into your wallet or purse, pull out a dollar bill AND ACTUALLY READ IT. Read all the fine print; notice where it was issued (if it is an older bill), what series it belongs to, the serial number, etc.

The twelve branches of the U.S. Federal Reserve Bank have the specific charge of furnishing **Federal Reserve Notes** to the economy as needed. It does this in conjunction with the U.S. Treasury Department, although, strictly speaking, the Federal Reserve Bank is independent of the Treasury. The most important words on the bill are these: "This note is legal tender for all debts, public and private."

Perhaps the meaning is vague. That's understandable; some older bills were much more explanatory. "This note is legal tender for all debts, public and private, *and is redeemable in lawful money at The United States Treasury, or at any Federal Reserve Bank.*" These are the words from U.S. silver certificates. They imply that if a person demanded "lawful money" in exchange for the "legal tender" in his or her possession, the U.S. government would so honor the demand. Surrounding the portrait on the silver certificate is a statement that sounds as if the U.S. government had issued a bond or a check: "The United States of America *will pay to the bearer on demand...X...dollars*" That X amount of dollars would presumably be in "lawful money," and in the case of a silver certificate, silver itself.

Is the same true today? Can we redeem a series 2003 note for "lawful money"? What is legal tender? Is our dollar really like a bond or a check? How is it different? How does this whole money thing work?

The monetary system used in the contemporary world took centuries to develop. To the extent that the financial system expanded, it released a latent entrepreneurial energy. Enterprise flourished. Banks made profit and gradually developed innovations to allow their customers still greater flexibility with cash. Banks made more profit. In its modern form, the banking industry represents the triumph of the capitalist means of production, to use a Marxian turn of phrase.

This entire unit takes the reader through the evolution of the banking system (in this chapter, in a light sort of way) and the principles behind its methods. Later chapters will detail how the U.S. monetary system works and how the Federal Reserve Bank's Monetary Policy is used to manipulate macro-economic performance. We begin by taking a trip to Italy.

A STORY

Once upon a time, this would be about 1475 AD or so, there was an explorer named Marco Polo. Marco Polo was rich and had spare time. So he entertained himself with travelling adventures, mostly to the Orient. He was quite renown in his native province of Venice, as he treated the inhabitants with tales of exotic, distant lands upon his every return.

Of course in those days to travel to the Orient meant going by foot through Asia. Such voyages could last years and required more than a little planning. The trips created a very practical problem too. Where would he keep his stash of gold, the coinage that served as money in this, the age of the Renaissance?

Marco and Pietro

One day while Marco was paddling his way through Venice, he saw the local goldsmith, Pietro DiPo'oro, paddling the other direction to work. An idea struck Marco, and he quickly reversed direction, catching Pietro as he stopped to exit the gondola.

"Pietro, I need a favor."

"Marco, Marco! How can a little guy like me help a big guy like you?"

"Well, I'm going to take a little trip to visit my friends in the East. But I have no place to store my gold."

"Ah, si, si. I can store your gold, Marco, in my vault and keep it there till you get back. How long are you going to be away?"

"Two years."

Marco was about to climb back onto his gondola, but another thought intruded.

"Ah, but Pietro, Pietro. How are you going to remember two years from now how much I gave you?"

"Don't worry, Marco. I remember."

"Pietro, this is all my gold. I worry. I WORRY."

More discussion ensued. Heretofore, anytime friends entrusted friends with money, they just "remembered." (What are friends for, Marco?) Maybe they were all good friends; maybe they never left for a very long time. Whatever, Marco was not about to back down on this one.

Pietro finally agreed to give Marco, upon receipt of the gold, a paper record which documented that Pietro received it, would hold it, and *give it back to Marco upon his demand*. Marco liked this idea because it protected the gold, assured its return, and still gave him flexibility: he didn't have to be back in exactly two years—he could be early or late and still claim it. Marco could even decide to leave it with Pietro, and it would still be his gold.

Incidentally, Pietro did one more thing. He grabbed another piece of paper and folded it in half. Inside one fold at the top he wrote, "I have" and on the other he wrote, "I owe" Beneath each phrase he wrote,"+500 gold pieces."

moral #1

This little episode tells of the beginning of the modern banking system and its use of paper assets to serve as financial claims and trusts. Equally notable is the way Pietro records the transaction. The critical moment occurs when the deal is struck.

By accepting the gold from Marco and providing a paper record account to him, Pietro founds the world's first bank. He is no longer a mere goldsmith, and the gold he accepted from Marco is not his. The gold belongs to the bank, as distinct from the person of Pietro, who shall oversee the bank's operations. Marco, meantime, has acquired the world's first **demand deposit,** and the paper he holds will be the requisite proof he needs to claim his gold when he returns.

Pietro's little piece of folded paper represents the world's first T-Account. The T-Account is an accounting tool used by financial people to record transactions. On the left hand side, where Pietro wrote, "I have," Pietro recorded the assets now in possession of "The Bank of Pietro." On the opposite side, "I owe," Pietro recorded the liabilities of the bank. Table 14-1 shows a modern equivalent of Pietro's scribblings.

Assets	Liabilities
+ 500 gold coins	+ 500 Demand Deposit, Marco
500	500

Table 14-1

Five centuries later, use of the T-Account remains standard banking procedure. Indeed, the entire science of accounting is based on the T-account's structure. Naturally, its enduring applicability testifies not just to its own advantages but also to the lasting indebtedness we bear to Pietro's cleverness.

The trick involved the double entry: whatever gets added to (or subtracted from) one side must be added to (or subtracted from) the other. This implies that under Pietro's method the sum of all assets must be equal to the sum of all liabilities. We might say that the *net* assets of the bank are zero. (500–500=0) We now call Pietro's procedure **double entry bookkeeping**.

Marco, incidentally, also has forfeited and gained *necessarily* equivalent things. He sacrificed five hundred gold pieces in exchange for a paper *claim* against the Bank of Pietro. The claim promised, upon presentation of the paper, the return of his 500 gold pieces.

But we mustn't get ahead of ourselves: there's plenty left to tell.

Marco and friends

An old friend of Marco, Giuseppe Ioima, arrived in Venice a few days after Marco had left for the Orient.

This friend had been the recipient of several favors from Marco during the years Marco lived in Florence, and now he was travelling from there to see Marco and repay his longstanding debt. Marco himself had considered these favors acts of charity, but Giuseppe had always intended to repay. He ran into Pietro during the evening.

"Excuse me, Signor. I'm looking for Marco Polo, the great explorer. Do you know where he might be?"

"Oh, I'm so sorry. Marco Polo just left on a new expedition to the Orient. I don't think he'll be back for two years. Can I help you?"

"Maybe, signor. I knew Marco when we were both young men. At the time, he lent me some money. Now, I want to re-pay him. But, if I don't find him, I don't know what to do. In two years, I may be dead."

"Signor, I can help you. I have a vault in the village. Marco has left some money there. I can take your money and put it with his money and then he'll get his due. And you-a ... you can rest in peace."

"Oh no, I'm not from Pisa; I'm from Firenze."

"Peace, signor. Rest in peace."

"Oh!"

Giuseppe and Pietro embarked for the village. While at Pietro's shop a third man interrupted.

"Pietro! Where is Marco Polo?" He bought sundries from me for his trip. He said he'd pay me back. When is he going to pay me?"

"Salvatore, Marco won't come back for two years."

"Two years!! I might die before then!"

"That's what I said," interjected Giuseppe.

"Don't worry anybody: I've got an idea," said Pietro.

Pietro's brainstorm involves Marco's two friends in the bank he had just formed. He suggests to each party that they contribute to his new banking service, and in return he will issue them demand deposits of equal value. He explains that once they have accounts on record at The Bank of Pietro he can make transactions on their behalf without the second party's presence. So, after each person makes his initial deposit, Pietro can record a payment to Marco from Giuseppe and a payment to Salvatore from Marco. The T-accounts below show these steps in order.

Original Contributions of Giuseppe and Salvatore

Assets	Liabilities
+ 500 gold coins	+ 500 Demand Deposit, Marco
+ 250 gold coins	+ 250 Demand Deposit, Giuseppe
+ 250 gold coins	+ 250 Demand Deposit, Salvatore
1000	1000

Table 14-2

. . . .

Giuseppe pays Marco

Assets	Liabilities
+ 1000 gold coins	+ 700 Demand Deposit, Marco
	+ 50 Demand Deposit, Giuseppe
	+ 250 Demand Deposit, Salvatore
1000	1000

Table 14-3

. . . .

Marco pays Salvatore

Assets	Liabilities
+ 1000 gold coins	+ 450 Demand Deposit, Marco
	+ 50 Demand Deposit, Giuseppe
	+ 500 Demand Deposit, Salvatore
1000	1000

Table 14-4

Pietro accepts Giuseppe's request to pay Marco by crediting Marco's account and deducting from Giussepe's (Table 14-3). He then accepts the IOU (in Marco's own handwriting) which Salvatore received and adjusts the two accounts accordingly (Table 14-4). These latter two transactions do not affect the asset side of the T-account, since no *net* adjustments take place over and above the new deposits they made. Pietro simply consolidates their contributions on that side for his own purposes.

moral #2

These transactions highlight the primary functions of the banking industry through the Renaissance era.[1] All transactions at that time were hand-recorded and usually required a formal declaration to be consummated.[2] Such bookkeeping chores might seem cumbersome to contemporary computer-friendly earthlings, but they should be considered an important advance. Rather than having to carry and count coinage and meet one's trading partner face-to-face, payments could be made by simple debits and credits to accounts--facelessly, by pen and paper. This would make payment swifter and safer, assuming the bank was forthright. Moreover, the technique is a precursor of the modern checking system, where the bank acts as a "clearing agent" for payments in a nearly all-encompassing exchange network. While the use of checks didn't begin until somewhat later,[3] there is no conceptual difference between the bookkeeping technique above, representing the procedures of the 1400's, and the modern method of recording checking transactions for the payment of bills owed.

Pietro, Luigi, and tortelini

Now about the same time, in the southern part of Italy, in a town called Naples, a culinary renaissance was going on--yes, it was an exciting time to be eating. Some relatives of Marco Polo had developed a new twist on a Chinese noodle recipe which Marco had shared with them through correspondence. The meal was popular among Neapolitans, but the recipe was a secret among the family. They called it tortelini.

The dish drew such rave reviews that the father of the family, Luigi, was sure he could open a restaurant and be successful. But these Polos were poor and had no hope of starting a business. Wife Maria seemed nonetheless prepared for any contingency: "Mangia, mangia," she proclaimed to anyone who walked by their kitchen window.

Now, the spirit of adventure must have run through the family. Each year during Lent, Luigi Polo went off to Rome to have his confession heard on Good Friday. He had always wanted to have his confession heard by the Pope, but in fifteen years of trying he hadn't timed it quite right. Still he kept trying. Some years he'd go by boat; others he walked. Regardless, he'd always arrive on Good Friday.

When Marco had reached halfway to China, it was Ash Wednesday, and Luigi began his annual pilgrimage. Back in Venice, Pietro, the goldsmith, was about to embark on a trip to Rome of his own. He had promised to perform some holy business for the Pope. (Pietro's brother took care of the vault for the time being.)

Good Friday came and found Pietro examining the gold in St. Peter's Basilica--the Pope wanted an estimate. As he wandered through the aisles he saw a man walking, weeping, wailing in terrible grief. It was Luigi.

"Poor man, what's wrong?", said Pietro

"Il Papa just heard my confession, and he said that the devil has given me these thoughts. He said I'm just jealous of my brother Marco and his money."

"Il Papa? Why'd he say that?"

"Cause I want to start my restaurant with the recipe from Marco. Il Papa, I thought he'd understand. He knows Marco. He heard his confession the first time they met.

"He knows Marco is rich," Luigi continued. "He knows I'm poor. But I know I can be rich too. I just need

[1] Charles F. Dunbar, "The Bank of Venice" from The Quarterly Journal of Economics, April 1892, p. 310-312.
[2] Ibid., p. 321.
[3] Ibid.

some money to begin my restaurant."

The eyebrow lifted. "Who is this Marco?"

"My brother, Marco Polo. I am Luigi Polo, locally famous maker of tortelini." Luigi began to tell Pietro all about his dreams for the restaurant.

"Folks will call their order in; I'll respond, 'Ten minutes.'"

Pietro liked the idea. He pulled out his satchel and showed Luigi the paper where he had recorded his dealing with Marco. He said to Luigi,

"Eh, signor, I want you to look at this."

"Pietro, Pietro! You know my brother?"

"Not only do I know your brother, I owe your brother."

Pietro offered Luigi a chance to use the money that Marco had entrusted to Pietro's fledgling bank.

"I'll prepare a note. You sign. I sign. Then, I give you a pad of paper with the stamp of The Bank of Pietro. When you need to pay somebody, you write his name and how much on the top of the paper, then you sign it on the bottom. Tear the paper out, and give to him. If he wants his gold, I'll give it to him. Everything will be taken care of."

"But, Pietro, why will they accept paper from the pad?"

"If they ask, you tell them, I make Il Papa's ring."

So began the expression: it's as good as gold.

moral #3

Pietro's deal with Luigi is the world's first commercial bank loan. Via the loan the bank acquires an asset and liability, but of a different sort than before. Pietro's first asset was hard currency and was accepted from outside the institution; the new loan-asset is a paper line entry and is generated from within. The amended T-Account, Table 14-5, illustrates the distinction.

We've assumed that the loan to Luigi has a value of 1000. The previous rules apply here, so we record 1000 on the asset side and 1000 on the liability side. The loan is an asset because Luigi's promise to repay represents something owed to the bank; we record an equally valued liability, because Pietro has committed the bank to making 1000 gold coins available on demand. It is crucial to recognize that the creation of the loan has *increased* the bank's assets on the left side. (Net assets are still zero.) This indicates that in fact *no gold coinage has left the bank*. Hence, the loan neither signifies nor implies an exodus of currency. The loan is simply a paper asset, a line entry.[4]

The World's First Bank Loan

Assets	Liabilities
+ 1000 gold coins	+ 450 Demand Deposit, Marco
	+ 50 Demand Deposit, Giuseppe
	+ 500 Demand Deposit, Salvatore
+ 1000 loan to Luigi	+ 1000 Demand Deposit, Luigi
2000	2000

Table 14-5

The T-account also illustrates a corollary to the rule that whatever is added to one side must be added to the other. Pietro's loan makes explicit the idea that *every loan creates a demand deposit of equal value*. Indeed, in Pietro's system of accounting, every newly acquired asset, regardless of the type, creates an equally offsetting liability somewhere in the financial network.

That an asset must also be a debt can seem counter-intuitive to those unfamiliar with banking practices. Yet, consider Luigi's position: he possesses a new asset *and* new liability as a result of the loan. He owns potential claims against the bank in the form of a demand deposit; but the loan is something he

---

[4] A familiar analogue in modern life to this sort of entry is a person's credit card. Holders of credit cards possess a credit line which empowers them with potential claims, but which claims are only occasionally exhausted in full. The credit card company is in the same position as Pietro; the holder of the card is like Luigi. (This similarity is limited in that the credit card is essentially a means of deferring payment and not actually an issuance of credit.)

must repay, too. That granted, the bank's record of the transaction must be the reverse. After all, Luigi and the bank are at opposite ends of the deal.

The loan is represented legally by the **promissory note** each party signed. The note is, therefore, a binding contract. The agreement would have stipulated all terms, including the amount, the repayment procedure, fees, etc.[5]

The pad of paper with the bank stamp is the world's first checkbook. As Pietro explained, all Luigi need do is write out the amount of money to be paid and the payee's name. Then, with check in hand, the payee will have a legitimate claim against The Bank of Pietro. That payee could cash the check or deposit it into an account of his own at The Bank of Pietro.[6] This final possibility appears on Table 14-6's T-account, where Luigi pays Tony for work Tony performed.

Luigi Pays Tony

Assets	Liabilities
+ 1000 gold coins	+ 450 Demand Deposit, Marco
	+ 50 Demand Deposit, Giuseppe
	+ 500 Demand Deposit, Salvatore
+ 1000 loan to Luigi	+ 600 Demand Deposit, Luigi
	+ 400 Demand Deposit, Tony
2000	2000

Table 14-6

Checks are bank notes. At first glance they are not terribly different than a simple IOU, inasmuch as the signer guarantees payment, although he or she hasn't the currency in hand. In turn, a signed check is backed by another IOU, i.e., a bank's liability to the person writing the check. But if a check is accepted, then it's not just any old IOU. It is really money, since

money is anything generally accepted as payment for goods or services rendered.

Pietro, therefore, has killed several birds with his double entry bookkeeping stone. First, he's funneled financing to someone who can use it. Second, he's devised an alternate means of payment. Third, he's actually created money—he's created paper money on the strength of the hard assets his bank has on hand.

So Pietro's meeting with Luigi inspired him to recast the bank's role from guardian to intermediary, from money-terminus to money-hub. His agreement with Luigi is the basic blueprint for a complex network of financial transfers. These transfers turn a stagnant money pool into "circulating capital." Were it not for Pietro's ingenuity, Marco's stash would be no more powerful than a pauper's pittance.

MONEY RESERVES AND MONEY MAKING

And what is the net result of Pietro's inspiration? To borrow a term from an earlier lesson, the velocity of activity surges. The issuance of credit induces commerce that would otherwise not occur. This is surely the case with Luigi, whose restaurant would not have opened without financial assistance from Pietro. Truly, the banker plays front and center on the stage that is free enterprise.

How much money can be created? By necessity, a bank's loaning capacity limits its money-making prowess. In the final analysis, the loaning constraint depends on (a) the amount of idle currency the bank possesses and (b) the propensity of depositors to demand hard currency. These two factors are interrelated, for if depositors tend to make frequent and substantial withdrawals from their accounts, then the bank, in order to honor these claims, will have to set aside a large store of hard currency *that could not then be used for loaning purposes.* Such a provision is called the bank's **money reserve** or **reserve requirement.**

Obviously, the modern banking system could not have evolved as it did unless individual banks were able to precisely assess three things: (1) what portion

---

[5] For the time being we must put aside the matter of interest.

[6] The system eventually permitted the deposit of checks from one bank to another. This required a central network for interbank payments, or what has become known as a clearing house. Civil authorities eventually took on this role.

of their currency should be set aside to honor customers' withdrawals, (2) what portion is able to support a loan, and (3) the maximum loaning capacity they have. Our next section will be devoted to examining how banks determine these values and how, generally, they manage their assets, liabilities, currency and T-accounts.

Fractional reserves

The story about Pietro, Giuseppe, and Luigi is not literally true of course, but neither is it a blatant falsehood. The modern banking system evolved out of the commercial life of the Venetians, who had trading partners throughout the world. Several factors coalesced during the Italian Renaissance (1450–1600, roughly) to bring about the modern **fractional reserve banking system,** including the improved ability to travel, which permitted ever-expanding opportunities for commerce and the era's merchant trade boom, the complementary need to improve the efficiency and convenience of trade, and--though this factor is often forgotten--the advancing intellectual skills of the populace, especially the acquisition of arithmetic skills.[7]

As commerce developed, bankers began to notice patterns in their customers' use of money. Those who had deposits were content to leave them be, issuing directions to make payments, writing checks and what have you, but not cashing in a large percentage of their claims at any given time. Moreover, deposits to accounts were, roughly speaking, as frequent as withdrawals. Consequently, even if there were a *net* outflow, it was quite small in comparison to the total liabilities. Of course the bankers' aim is to create a net inflow of deposits, since more hard currency would allow them to make more loans.

Furthermore, the banks gained advantages as the confidence in the banking system grew. As more and more depositors received checks from friends or business patrons, the inclination to simply deposit the check in one's own account without actually "cashing" it in for hard currency increased. Thus, check writing amounted to a bypass of hard currency exchange and hence a reduced demand for the bank's **monetary base**, the amount of genuine hard currency the bank had on hand. Later on, banks would issue their own paper notes, which were backed by a metal asset. People then began to exchange those notes. The evolving patterns of money usage, i.e., *the infrequency with which people required the hard currency*, suggested that the unit-demand for hard currency would constitute only a fraction of the monetary base the bank had on reserve to honor liabilities. Gradually, bankers realized that their depositors' inclination *not* to exhaust all claims, and to avoid currency when convenient, presented them with opportunities to advance loans in values many times greater than the well defined currency base.

Still, there's a limit.

The banker has two conflicting motivations. He or she would like to expand the money supply by making loans, because the bank will receive interest payments in return. On the other hand, each loan can be expected to increase the demand for currency, of which the bank has a limited amount. The pertinent question boils down to this: to what extent can the bank create loans such that on any given day the bank can still honor all requests for (net) money withdrawals?[8]

Using Pietro's latest T-account, let's experiment with some numbers.

Suppose Pietro decides that in the event depositors want to monetize (cash in) their claims, the bank should maintain a hard money reserve of 50% against each demand deposit. Thus, taking Table 14-6's T-account as current, Pietro figures that 225 needs to be held against Marco's demand deposit, 25

---

[7] Prior to the Renaissance, Europeans used the Roman numeral system. This system is not amenable to the needs of banking given its cumbersome way with large numbers, its clumsy form for even the most routine addition and subtraction, and, perhaps most important, the absence of naught. Recall that banks must be able to net out their assets at any moment to zero. But one can only come to zero if one has a zero in mind and script. When the Romans needed zero, they drew a blank. For a fascinating account of the arithmetical foundations of capitalist trade, see Frank J. Swetz, Capitalism and Arithmetic, The New Math of the 15th Century, Open Court, La Salle, Illinois, 1987.

[8] Also of concern is that the daily *outflow* be balanced with a daily *inflow* of deposits such that a reserve exists for tomorrow.

against Giuseppe's, 250 against Salvatore's, 300 against Luigi's, and 200 against Tony's. That's 1000 in all: Pietro should maintain a reserve of 1000 gold coins in order to meet any potential claims. That, of course, is exactly the amount of currency the bank has. Hence, were the bank to make another loan, it could not continue to meet the 50% reserve stipulation, for even a small loan of 100 would boost liabilities to 2100 against which the same 1000 is reserved. So, Pietro would conclude that his bank with 2000 in liabilities and 1000 in reserve can make no more loans: his bank is **fully loaned up**.

Our approach to the matter can be more general; that is, it's not actually necessary for a banker to calculate, say, 50% of each deposit. The precise amounts for the money reserve and loaning capacity can be verified with a formula that consolidates all deposits.[9] The formula introduces terms which are essential in discussing the condition of a bank. These terms are:

1) **Excess** or **Free Reserve** (ER), which designates the amount of money available to a bank beyond its requisite money reserve. These provide the basis for continued loaning. In Pietro's case, there are none.

2) **Monetary Base** (MB), the total value of hard currency the bank has at its disposal. For Pietro's bank this is 1000.

3) **Reserve Ratio** (RR), expressed as a percentage or fraction, this is the portion of currency which must be held against a bank's liabilities, or its usual equivalent, Total Demand Deposits (TDD).

Pietro chose 1/2 or 50% for his bank.

The formula is:

$$ER \ = \ MB \ - \ (\ RR \times TDD\ ) \ .$$

When a bank is fully loaned up, it has no free reserves to draw on to create a new loan. By plugging in the appropriate figures in the case of Pietro's bank we should arrive at a result suggesting as much.

$$ER \ = \ 1000 - (1/2 \times 2000)$$

$$ER \ = \ 1000 - (1000)$$

$$ER \ = \ 0$$

lowering the reserve ratio

A 50% reserve ratio is actually quite conservative. Figures of 25% and below are typical. Let us investigate the effects of a smaller reserve ratio.

If the RR is 25%, Pietro would find he has positive excess reserves, and were the RR 10%, the ER figure would be even greater.

ER = 1000 - (1/4 x 2000)	ER = 1000 - (1/10 x 2000)
ER = 1000 - (500)	ER = 1000 - (200)
ER = 500	ER = 800

An immediate relation comes to mind. The smaller the reserve ratio, the smaller the money reserve need be, and the greater the excess reserves are for loaning purposes. Thus, the bank with the lower reserve ratio will possess considerably more loaning power on an identical monetary base. We see systematic evidence of this in the few calculations we've performed. Given a monetary base of 1000, and the descending RR's of 50%, 25% and 10%, excess reserves ballooned from 0 to 500 to 800. Ultimately the pattern suggests that the lower the RR, the greater the **loaning potential** or **loaning capacity** of a bank.

Bankers will always want to immediately convert "barren" money reserves into interest-bearing assets. For the moment let's work with the 25% figure for RR and ascertain how much the bank will be able to support, in loans and liabilities, once the ER have been brought down to zero. The result might surprise you.

---

[9] It makes no difference to Pietro who comes in to claim his or her money. Indeed, it is unlikely that everyone would come in and withdraw exactly 50%. Some may withdraw everything, others nothing. So to Pietro, and to the modern banker, the expected *average* (net) outflow with respect to the *whole* of liabilities is paramount in ascertaining the proper reserve requirement.

The formula leads the way. Since we assume the case where the bank is fully loaned up, we can plug in zero for ER in the equation and then solve for TDD.

$$0 = 1000 - (1/4 \times TDD)$$
$$1/4 \times TDD = 1000$$
$$TDD = 1000/(1/4)$$
$$TDD = 1000 \times 4$$
$$TDD = 4000$$

When the RR is 25%, Pietro's highest supportable total demand deposits is 4000, i.e., 4000 in liabilities, quadruple the monetary base. This immediately implies that the bank has a *full* loaning potential of 3000, assuming the 25% RR. Table 14-7 illustrates.

As he has already made a loan for 1000 to Luigi, the *remaining* loaning potential is 2000. Pietro is free to make one loan for 2000 and bring his bank into a fully loaned up condition with one stroke of the pen. The bank would be properly covered because it has 1000 gold coins, or 25% of the 4000 required.

Assets	Liabilities
+ 1000 gold coins	+ 450 Demand Deposit, Marco
	+ 50 Demand Deposit, Giuseppe
	+ 500 Demand Deposit, Salvatore
+ 1000 loan to Luigi	+ 600 Demand Deposit, Luigi
	+ 400 Demand Deposit, Tony
+ 2000 } new loans	+ 2000 } new Demand Deposits
4000	4000

Table 14-7

Now if the RR were actually 10%, considerably more loaning potential would exist. Again the formula:

$$0 = 1000 - (1/10 \times TDD)$$
$$1/10 \times TDD = 1000$$
$$TDD = 1000/(1/10)$$
$$TDD = 1000 \times 10$$
$$TDD = 10,000$$

Pietro could thus create up to 9000 in loans to make his bank fully loaned up. Table 14-8 shows this possibility.

Assets	Liabilities
+ 1000 gold coins	+ 450 Demand Deposit, Marco
	+ 50 Demand Deposit, Giuseppe
	+ 500 Demand Deposit, Salvatore
+ 1000 loan to Luigi	+ 600 Demand Deposit, Luigi
	+ 400 Demand Deposit, Tony
+ 8000 } new loans	+ 8000 } new Demand Deposits
10,000	10,000

Table 14-8

the money multiplier

In the calculations of each TDD above, the algebra led to a straightforward relation between the monetary base, reserve ratio, and the TDD. In its standard form we would have:

$$MB/(RR) = TDD$$

$$MB \times MM = TDD$$

where MB is the monetary base and MM is the money multiplier. (Students should perform this derivation as an exercise.)

This is the mathematical account of how the fractional reserve system works. The base supply of money is divided by a fraction, which in turn is like multiplying by the fraction's reciprocal. By definition, the money multiplier is the inverse of the reserve ratio (just as the Keynesian multiplier of chapter x is the inverse of the marginal propensity to save). Thus, the power of banks to expand the money supply is a geometric one. It becomes easy to see why banks would prefer low RR's, which allow maximum interest earnings, to high ones.

Obviously once the RR is known, bankers can swiftly ascertain the TDD its institution can support from any given monetary base (or addition to that base) and how much in loans it should create in order to become fully loaned up. Even in the uppermost reaches of high finance, this fundamental relation holds. As Tables 14-7 and 8 verify, the **full loaning potential** must be the difference between the TDD of the bank when it's fully loaned up and the monetary base (4000-1000; 10000-1000), whereas the **remaining loaning potential** of a bank subtracts current TDD (liabilities) from the TDD when fully loaned up (4000-2000; 10000-2000).

It may seem remarkable that mere pen and paper accounting techniques like the T-account can render such a profound influence on economic activity and structure. That a relatively small amount of money is sufficient to safeguard newly-formed loans probably strikes some readers as being terribly risky. It might, finally, seem miraculous that one unit of currency can support ten times that amount in liabilities, as when the RR is 10%. But, as Albert Einstein said in regard to fundamental questions concerning space and time, "The incomprehensible thing is that it is all comprehensible."

Summary

Fractional reserve banking is not Einstein's theory of relativity, mind you, but the system is not without its subtleties. Practice devoted to its mastery will reveal the strength and resiliency of a uniquely human invention, centuries old. The essentials deserve a summation.

The foregoing paragraphs reveal how fractional reserve banking evolved and presently operates. Though we studied make-believe examples set in a distant time and place, where gold was the currency of choice, the fundamentals of contemporary banking, where cash is king, are no different: A banker's job is to make money, i.e., *create* money. He or she accomplishes this by the simultaneous issuance of loans and demand deposits. Banks are able to make loans because *depositors, individually and collectively, tend not to exploit all legitimate claims to money assets at any one time.* This way, the bank can create many

more claims upon a given monetary base than the value of the base itself. The system is stable so long as the bank has sufficient hard assets to honor the demand for them. The system is efficient because idle monies get steered to claimants who would circulate the funds. The effect, however, is not just to create a *claims-flow* from standing assets, but to design an economic universe where matters of money most definitely matter for the creation of real output.

Even in regard to the specifics of the T-account procedures, the differences between the old and the new are of the most minor sort. Cash replaces gold as the monetary base; and the modern bank has a wider array of assets which it might hold, government bonds being the most prevalent. Everything else is the same. The exercises at the end of this chapter will use T-accounts with cash as the monetary base and make this final point vivid.

THE POWER OF CASH

Let us take one giant step into the modern world. The main adjustment is the use of cash, paper money, as the means of exchange and the monetary base. First, we should consider how cash became the exchange medium of choice. Then we'll look at how that change liberated economic activity and the banking system well beyond what was possible through the bank's clearing functions and the introduction of a loanable funds network.

Barely a fortnight passed before 15th century bankers became cognizant of the potential of paper money. While checkable deposits greatly simplified payments and encouraged people to maintain accounts at financial institutions, bank notes offered the ability to transact business with someone who held a claim for immediate gold (or silver) payment. Banks would issue paper assets which included a (legally binding) promise to no specific payee, but to "the bearer." Paper could then be traded for goods, as gold was earlier, but unlike checks, which specified a payee.

We use cash this way today, of course, and we don't think twice about it. Long ago, however, paper money was novel. We need to try to put ourselves in the position of a person of the 1400 and 1500's, a person to whom cash was dubious and foreign, while familiar metallic coinage represented sturdiness and certainty.

A concrete example might get the point across. We in the States use the U.S. dollar universally. If we returned from a voyage to a foreign country with some spare foreign bills we'd be out of luck trying to purchase goods with those bills here. Even if we argued that the currency is exchangeable for dollars we'd get no sympathy. It is simply too time-consuming for any of us to traipse to those few and far-between financial institutions which happily handle currency conversions. (They are located, incidentally, almost exclusively in the downtown sections of big cities and at major airports.)

As the modern U.S. dollar does today, gold and silver had always commanded a special sort of respect. Gold does not rust; silver glistens; each is highly malleable and can be pressed to slivering thinness; silver happens to be the best metallic conductor of heat. Each was accepted as currency for those valued qualities and because those qualities were thought of as intrinsic. In other words, silver and gold were seen as having a value of an enduring and universal nature. Hence, each brought universal acceptance.

To introduce cash in a world where metals had always served as the means of exchange would be akin to convincing Yankees to use pounds, pesos and pesetas.[10]

But once people discovered that the banks really would exchange the paper money for hard assets, suspicion subsided and the advantages of cash came to be valued in their own right. Trading paper bank notes was found to be many times more convenient than having to lug metal or write checks for every occasion. What initially had to be explained--the paper says that the bank owes me, but if I give it to you, then the bank will owe you--became second nature. Gradually, the adoption of paper money lifted a veil of ignorance regarding the nature of value itself:

things possess worth because people *say* so, and if respected, civil, authorities vouch that word, so be it.

The introduction of bank cash brought about a second boon to market activity. This spurt occurred not merely because cash reduced the opportunity cost of exchange to a minimum, but also from the swelling confidence in the notes themselves. In the incipient days of paper-monetary exchange, every cash transaction would represent a distinct inducement to reuse cash, since the more it was used, the more it was seen *in use* i.e., as something having value. In the early days, every additional paper-for-goods transaction quelled another skeptic's fear.

When people start exchanging bank notes for goods, yet another revolution waits in the offing. This revolution concerns the *quality* of commercial practice, the aims and orientation of business activity itself, rather than the pace of activity. With greater spending, income, and wealth supporting ever-burgeoning trades and crafts, *paper money makes possible a commercial life based on the satisfaction of wants*, rather than on the provision of needs. Wants are expansive; human needs are defined. To orient an economy around either implies vastly different economic systems and incentives. An economy which requires hard assets for exchange will develop little wealth beyond that which is sufficient to meet some basic needs. This is so because the availability of the hard assets used in exchange is itself strictly limited. In order to create affluence, society must invent a readily expandable money supply and create institutions, such as banks and firms, whose *raison d'etre* is the pursuit of money. As we might all attest, many a capitalist entrepreneur will throw out all notions of nobility--perhaps even integrity--and focus solely on winning profits for the business. And this perfectly complements the role of the converted consumer, who seeks not to ensure survival, but to satisfy insatiable desires.

Finally, greater reliance on cash transactions strengthens the relations between banks, borrowers, and depositors because, even though more and more transactions would occur outside the system's immediate purview, those independent exchanges would still be tethered to the fledgling financial

---

[10] The currencies of The United Kingdom, Mexico, and Spain, respectively.

network. That's because a tacit faith in the banks' promise to legitimate every paper claim imbues each monetary exchange. Hence, either directly or indirectly, banks underwrite all activity. Indeed, effective banking operates like a good drummer in a band: the less noticed the better. During the 16th through 19th centuries, a solid confidence in private bank notes implied fewer trips to exchange notes for hard assets, which in turn gave banks maximum room to maneuver assets and to forward loans.

A loss of confidence

The true power of cash, then, begins with the promise. Ultimately, the banking system will go only as far as its customer's trust and confidence in the promise allow it. Let us consider a case when that confidence got disturbed.

Consider a somewhat developed monetary economy, one using bank notes for the vast majority of private transactions. The notes are printed by several banks independently. By and large the bank notes are backed by gold or silver, and all of them say that the respective banks will exchange the note for gold or silver, according to the amount stated on the bill, upon demand. Such was commercial life through the 18th and 19th centuries in the U.S. and Europe.

Suppose an entrepreneur receives payment from a customer in the form of a bank note, say from The Bank of Much Bullion. The next day the entrepreneur enters a branch of Much Bullion so he can exchange some of their notes for gold. Ordinarily, this request should pose no difficulty. But this day the bank refuses. The entrepreneur gets incensed and says he's entitled to the gold. The bank manager apologizes profusely, even agreeing that the gold is due him, but, dropping his voice to a whisper, explains that giving him gold is impossible because the latest shipment was stolen en route to delivery.

The entrepreneur still argues. "I have to buy leather for my shop tomorrow morning. It is being shipped from Spain and payment must be in gold. They don't accept bank notes from our country." The banker asks the entrepreneur if he deals regularly with

any other bank. "The Bank of Good Standing," he replies.

"Well, they should be willing to accept our notes-- they know our situation. Why don't you go there?"

The entrepreneur does so and finds that The Bank of Good Standing has gold but will not exchange notes from The Bank of Much Bullion. The entrepreneur, stuck with Bullion notes, exchanges notes he has from other banks, including some from Good Standing, and requests a short term loan to help him with his tomorrow's payment.

End of story? Not really. Bullion's failure to honor its own note spells trouble for the entire network of banks. As more holders of notes from Bullion lose trust in the notes, word will spread to depositors of the bank, who will then--in a word--panic! They'll run to the nearest Bullion branch and seek to withdraw their deposits. Bullion may honor some of their requests and renege on others, or it might choose to satisfy all of them partially. It might close its doors for a couple of days "to get its books in order." In short, the bank manager has to do anything he can to stave off a rapid depletion of the bank's reserves.

In the final analysis, Bullion can't honor all claims at once because the nature of fractional reserve banking makes that impossible: Bullion has issued far more claims against itself, in notes, loans, and regular deposits, than it ever would have in gold or silver reserves. To make matters worse, depositors at such banks as The Bank of Good Standing might try to close *their* accounts when they hear of the news about Bullion. Their fears could be entirely without foundation: their banks might be in good order. But no matter, a loss of trust can spread like a forest fire jumping across an asphalt roadway.

While the reaction of customers to the bank's failure to honor some notes is understandable--no one wants to lose their assets--it only exacerbates Bullion's and the entire banking system's difficulties to rush to withdraw. As with Bullion, it's impossible for the entire network of banks to honor all its liabilities at once. The fractional reserve banking system is built on the assumption that depositors will *not* do that. The entire banking system is now imploding.

VOCABULARY

Federal reserve notes – paper notes of the U.S. Federal Reserve Bank, i.e. dollar bills

Demand Deposit – any legal cash claim of a depositor at a bank

Double Entry Bookkeeping – method of accounting by which financial institutions, using T-accounts, record assets and liabilities in an offsetting manner

Promissory note – a legally binding note signed by the borrower by which he promises to repay under the specific terms of the contract

Money reserve – any available liquid currency held by a financial institution

Reserve requirement – the specific minimum amount of cash which must be held by a financial institution against its liabilities

Fractional reserve banking system – the method of modern banking by which financial institutions are required to keep only a fraction of currency against liabilities

Monetary base – the amount of currency a financial institution has currently available for the issuance of loans

Fully loaned up – the condition of a financial institution when excess reserves are zero, i.e. no more loans can be legally issued

Excess reserves (free) – available currency of a financial institution over and above its reserve requirement

Reserve ratio – the percentage of currency a financial institution must hold against all liabilities

Loaning potential (capacity) – the dollar amount of loans a financial institution can feasibly support, given a specific reserve ratio

Full loaning potential – the legally allowable dollar amount of loans supportable by a financial institution, given a monetary base and reserve ratio

Remaining loaning potential – whatever legally allowable dollar amount of loans is possible after some loans have been previously issued

END-OF-CHAPTER QUESTIONS

1. How does a capitalist economy depend on the Fractional Reserve Banking System?

2. A bank holds original cash assets of a value of $24000; the reserve ratio is 25%. Use a T-account to show (a) the total demand deposits supportable by this bank when fully loaned up, (b) the full loaning capacity of the bank. Repeat the exercise at a 20% and 10% reserve ratio.

3. Use the following T-accounts to answer the questions below. For each of the banks, the reserve ratio is 1/5.

Larry's Bank		Curly's Bank		Moe's Bank	
A	L	A	L	A	L
8000 cash	8400 DD	1200 cash	1200 DD	1900 cash	1900 DD
400 bonds					
33600 loans	33600 DD	6300 loans	6300 DD	5600 loans	5600 DD
42000	42000	7500	7500	7500	7500

a. Calculate the excess reserves of each bank.

b. Calculate the remaining loaning power of any bank with positive excess reserves.

c. Assess the condition of Larry's bank. What could he do to quickly bring his bank in order? Adjust his T-account accordingly and explain these adjustments briefly.

CHAPTER 15

THE FEDERAL RESERVE BANK OF THE UNITED STATES

THE NEED FOR A STABLE CURRENCY

Governments gradually assumed responsibility in the monetary sphere by establishing national (or provincial) banks. One motivating factor in forming these banks involved the rather undependable supply of precious metals: shortages and surpluses were frequent in some countries, and such irregularities in availability played havoc with normal commerce. The value of the metal asset would change quickly and holders could not feel secure with respect to the value of their metallic wealth.

In the late 1600's Great Britain founded The Bank of England, technically a private bank, which was granted the power to issue paper money. By the issuance of paper money, redeemable for metal and backed by the government's promise, England circumvented the problems inherent in a volatile money supply. The Bank of England eventually became Britain's "central bank," and by the 19th century all the major trading nations, save the newly-formed United States, had a central bank modelled after that of Great Britain's.[1]

But the American colonists had some ingenuity of their own. In Massachusetts, at about the same time of the formation of The Bank of England, an unsuccessful military siege on Quebec prompted the colony to issue paper bills of credit (promissory notes), as they had no spoils from a victory to distribute to soldiers and townspeople, and precious metals were highly scarce. Thus began a rather American pattern of state-managed banking. Both before and following the Revolution, states assumed responsibility for the issuance of paper currency either directly or via charter to private banks.[2]

At the Federal level, Alexander Hamilton, whom President Washington appointed Secretary of the Treasury in his first administration, argued successfully on behalf of a federal bank for the new United States (though the Constitution forbade the Federal government from issuing federal bills of credit)[3]. This first U.S. central bank was eventually closed; a second one was opened but that closed, too, in 1836. In the early part of the 19th century the U.S. Treasury issued some interest bearing notes that got limited circulation as currency.[4]

By the Civil War, as many as 8000 private, state-chartered, banks were circulating notes.[5] Not surprisingly, counterfeiting abounded. If a person were to write a check with the stamp of an unknown bank, or present bills from the same, prudence dictated a healthy skepticism on the receiver's part. Out-of-state notes were sometimes not redeemable for gold or silver; instead they were traded for in-state banking currency at discounts from their face value.[6] Obviously, in the already-mobile United States, routine market activity could become chaotic. The pressure to centralize banking grew.

In 1861, the U.S. Government began to issue a new series of demand notes (after overturning the Constitutional restriction). Initially, these were redeemable in coin at designated subtreasuries of the government.[7] Then in 1862 the Congress issued $150 million in "United States notes" which were declared **legal tender** for all public debts, save import duties and interest on public debt (U.S. and state bonds).[8] This action represented a significant step in establishing currency stability in the States. A second step, perhaps just as crucial, entailed the Federal government's new arrangement to charter "national banks," while forbidding the state-chartered banks from issuing notes as they had done since the nation's first days.[9]

Summary

Why did U.S. monetary history move towards centralization? Why didn't private management and private notes suffice?

---

[1] D.H. Friedman and C.J. Parnow, "The Story of Money," Federal Reserve Bank Publication, Federal Reserve Bank of New York, 1977, pp. 13-14.
[2] "Coins and Currency." Federal Reserve Bank Publication, Federal Reserve Bank of New York, 1985, pp. 5-7.
[3] Ibid., p. 7.

[4] Ibid.
[5] Ibid.
[6] Friedman and Parnow, p. 14.
[7] Coins and Currency, p. 7-8.
[8] ibid., p. 8.
[9] Friedman and Parnow, p. 15.

The evolution of the banking system, both in the States and around the world, reveals a checkered course. Besides the problems associated with the supply of precious metals, there was also the matter of trust. Frequently undermining public confidence in banks, charlatans, shysters, and crooked sneaks rambled through the nascent financial network. They counterfeited. They embezzled funds. They left liabilities grossly underprotected. They set up shop, stole, then skipped town. Panics were common.

Way way back, government officials entered the fray to restrict the shenanigans. In Venice, public legislators curtailed the banking business to accounts for payment purposes only, i.e., limiting the issuance of credit.[10] Bankers would in effect be little more than recorders and safekeepers. Other regulations specified hours of operation and the presence of the payer in order to approve payment.[11] These restrictions appeared so as to avoid the loss of entrusted depositor wealth. At the same time they curtailed commerce.

Yet the commercial demands of the mercantilist age created irresistible incentives to finagle credit to both sides of the financial fence, bankers and borrowers. The undeniable advantages of expansive credit, meanwhile, pressured public officials to manage a system of fractional reserves differently. Gradually, nations started their own banks.

Of course, laissez faire skeptics might say that those in political authority had their own self-interest at heart. Clever politicians would soon stumble upon the unique tricks one can perform with pen, paper, and T-account.

But it had become urgently clear to all that greater stability in the paper currency was needed to sustain a vibrant economy. And a centralized authority was thought to be able to offer that. Even the rather simple task of clearing payment among various private banks necessitated a central clearing house, a central bank.[12]

THE FEDERAL RESERVE BANK OF THE UNITED STATES

The current Federal Reserve Bank of the United States was founded by Act of Congress in 1913. The stated purpose was to provide an "elastic money supply."[13] The various recessions, booms, and panics between 1865 and 1900 demonstrated a need to furnish more regularity in the money creation process. Centralizing "member" (commercial) banks under a "monopoly" bank ("the Fed") afforded supervision and relatively greater control over the money supply.

the Federal Reserve has several specific roles to play in its daily operations. The Fed must act as the government's bank, in effect underwriting loans of the Federal government and "making good" on U.S. Treasury's checks. It is the central clearing house for all commercial bank checks and hence, indirectly, for all checks written by depositors of member banks. The Reserve Bank also sells government securities on behalf of the Treasury. In a fairly recent addendum to its responsibilities, the Fed acts as an ombudsman for the community, a task which recalls the early days of Venetian banking. In this role it enforces truth in lending practices, prohibits discrimination in lending and resolves disputes between commercial banks and their customers. In addition, the Fed assumes a few supervisory tasks: it must ensure that commercial banks abide by the rules that the Fed itself establishes, and (since 1932) it oversees the Federal system of deposit insurance, which protects depositors in case of bank failure. The Fed makes emergency loans to member banks facing a cash crunch. Last, but hardly least, it manages the nation's money supply.[14]

THE FED AND THE ECONOMY

Our immediate task is to examine the various means the Fed has at its disposal to manipulate the money supply. This founding role of the Bank draws the most controversy because a person's economic

---

[10] Charles F. Dunbar, "The Bank of Venice," The Quarterly Journal of Economics, April 1892, pp. 310-316.

[11] ibid., p. 313, 321.

[12] When John Doe writes a check to his local utility, cash will have to be transferred from his bank to the utility's bank.

[13] "Coins and Currency," p. 13.

[14] Lawrence Murdoch, Jr., "The Hats the Federal Reserve Wears," Federal Reserve Bank Publication, Federal Reserve Bank of Philadelphia, April 86, p. 3.

persuasion usually determines his or her view of the Reserve's actions. But to boil the matter down, money's effects traverse the credit and capital markets to, ultimately, P and Q. We will look briefly at the theoretical ideas regarding money's effects and later at the specifics of how the Fed operates to impart its will.

From money to prices

Those economists who subscribe to classical and monetarist views of money (the common denominator of which is to emphasize money's role as a means of exchange) believe that when the money supply is expanded its eventual impact goes to the price level. The story is explained in various degrees of complexity. Some use the metaphorical helicopter on high (Friedman); many claim a direct relation between money and prices as captured by the Old Cambridge Equation of Exchange--but with a time lag of uncertain duration inserted; others appeal to the **inelasticity** of the **long run** Aggregate Supply curve (a vertical AS curve) which in essence argues on behalf of a natural, full employment rate of output as the aggregate norm. It is not far fetched to think that these different expositions are in fact interchangeable versions of a single parable.

From money to output

More Keynesian-influenced economists maintain that expansion of the money supply will bring lower interest rates, which leads to higher investment spending as firms will be induced to borrow at reduced rates. Greater capital spending has multiplier effects so that Aggregate Demand will rise directly due to higher levels of investment and indirectly due to additional induced consumption. Any rightward shift in AD raises output and, *then*, depending on the elasticity of supply, the price level might evince inflationary pressures. Within this group, controversy continues regarding secondary price effects, with distinctive opinions turning on interpretations of Keynes' General Theory and his views on money.

Summary

Each of these views relate monetary expansion

to demand phenomena. It is fair to say that classical/monetarist views hold that money has its impact on retail demand rather more swiftly than Keynesians are willing to concede, perhaps because they tend to believe that markets are more efficient, and move toward full employment more readily, than the Keynesians. Also pertinent are the underlying views about the demand for money itself. For his part, Keynes stressed that agents regularly hold money as a hedge against "rainy days" (i.e., held without a commitment to spend later); furthermore, it comes into existence as a tool of credit. These two things loosen the tie between money and prices, Keynes thought.

THE FED'S INSTRUMENTS OF CONTROL

The Federal Reserve, in accordance with its various charges from Congress, can control the money supply in four distinct ways. Regardless of the means chosen, the Federal Reserve's policy makers have only two alternatives: either to raise the money supply or lower it. Sometimes by merely altering *the rate of growth of the money supply*, the Fed can influence the course of interest rates, investment, GDP, and prices. But that is a more subtle trick, and for our purposes we will confine ourselves to more basic strategy.

The monetary policy of the Fed can either be stimulative or contractionary. If its aim is to induce new activity in the economy, as it would be during a recession, the Fed will raise the money supply in order to stimulate real growth. If the Reserve wants to curtail spending, usually to combat inflation, it will decrease the money supply. Depleting the banking system of reserves might in fact subdue escalating inflationary trends, but it does so precisely because the action is contractionary. A lower money supply, ceteris paribus, will raise interest rates, diminish investment expenditures, and thus have negative multiplier effects. Real output and employment will decline.

Reserve ratio: the Fed as regulatory agent

The Chairman of the Federal Reserve Bank, in

conjunction with the Fed's six other Board of Governors, together have the specific power to change the proportion of liquid cash assets that must be held against the liabilities of member banks. At will they can decide to raise or lower (any of several) critical reserve ratio(s) which apply to different sorts of accounts.[15]

They rarely do. The ratio is the most powerful tool the Fed has to influence the money supply. As we saw in the previous chapter, a switch from a 10% to 25% reserve ratio would cut the money multiplier from 10 to 4, with a similar loss in loaning capacity. So dramatic a change would never be desirable, as banks require a stable set of rules in order to conduct their daily operations and be confident of the success of their long term loans.

But, for the record, if the Fed should raise the reserve ratio, then commercial banks would most likely find themselves over-extended and in need of money reserves. The certain scramble for cash would raise all interest rates and set in motion a contractionary spiral. On the other hand, to reduce the ratio would immediately increase every member bank's excess reserves and in a flash apply downward pressure on interest rates. The aim of such actions would obviously be to resuscitate a flagging economy.

Open Market Operations

One instrument of Federal Reserve policy is primary among others, both in terms of frequency employed and pervasive influence. That key manipulative tool is **Open Market Operations**: the buying and selling of U.S. government securities. Let us first examine the motivation behind a commercial bank's desire to hold a government IOU.

For banks with idle reserves, a U.S. bond (Treasury Bills, Treasury Notes, Ginnie Mae, and others) represents a prudent alternative to forwarding a loan to a less dependable customer. The U.S. government

hasn't missed a payment since the Fed has been in operation. And while the interest rate would not be as high as those earned from loans, the certainty of payment and the ease of conversion to cash (i.e., its liquidity) offsets the opportunity cost of foregone interest. Indeed, most any bank will try to balance the competing "interests" of making the highest possible earnings from loans and maintaining a store of highly liquid non-cash assets (i.e., government securities). By maintaining a ready store of bonds a bank can acquire cash quickly to meet any emergency or to take advantage of even better lending opportunities.

Once we consider that banks would actually be desirous of the security and flexibility which government bonds offer, it's a short step to the formation of a market for their regular exchange.

The Federal Reserve conducts its Open Market Operations via its New York Reserve Branch. The Federal Reserve Board of Governors and five of the Regional Reserve Bank Presidents collectively set the policy for trading a slew of securities, worth, all told, trillions of dollars.[16]

If the Fed wants to contract the money supply, it can absorb the excess reserves of the commercial banks by encouraging the purchase of bonds at relatively attractive interest rates (i.e., selling them cheaply). The banks will in turn have to write checks to the Fed in the amount of the bond purchase. When the check clears, the purchasing bank has less cash reserves. Thus, the money supply has shrunk. On a grand scale, this contractionary maneuver will raise interest rates across the board and suppress borrowing throughout the domestic economy.[17]

The Fed is also free to buy back bonds it previously sold, but haven't come to full maturity. When it does so, the Fed writes a check to the member bank selling the bond. That bank then cashes in the Fed's check--at the Fed, no less! the Fed honors its word by

---

[15] Reserve Ratios do vary by the type of account. For example, regular demand deposits and NOW checking accounts have higher ratios than small or large time deposits. The various demands for liquidity from the respective accounts explains the differences.

[16] "The Federal Reserve System, Purposes and Functions," written and published by The Board of Governors of the Federal Reserve System, Washington, D.C., 1984, p. 5; p. 27.
[17] ibid., p. 35.
[18] ibid.

crediting the bank with increased cash reserves in the amount of the sale.[18] Suddenly, the commercial sector has new excess reserves. Interest rates should slide, spurring investment--and, if all goes well, ditto for the entire economy.

The Discount Rate: the Fed as loaner of last resort

As mentioned earlier the Fed has the authority to make loans to all member banks. In this charge, it has the specific duty to act, in any emergency, as a *guarantor of liquid funds for all member banks*. When a bank finds itself in acute trouble it can approach the Fed for a emergency loan at its **Discount Window**, the term used for the Fed's loaning operation. While the Fed has discretion to let a bad bank fail, it must avoid precipitating the havoc that might ensue from a bank failure. This is particularly a concern with larger banks, for in the financial sector, not only is it true that "the bigger they are, the harder the fall," but also when a big one falls, the others teeter.

But emergency liquid funds aren't free. The Fed charges interest on these loans, a fee which is called the **Discount Rate**. The rate is discounted compared to other available rates, from other sources, which commercial banks might have open to them.

The policy issue enters with the setting of the rate. A lower Discount Rate signals to commercial banks that the Fed is in a more "generous" mood with respect to making credit available. If the member banks can borrow more cheaply, then the margin between the Discount Rate and rate of interest they charge for loans increases--an obvious encouragement for credit and capital expansion. Of course, the Fed can move oppositely and raise the Discount rate, thereby diminishing banks' margin of profit and inhibiting credit expansion.

Originally, the responsibility for pegging the Discount Rate fell the to Board of Directors of each of the twelve regional banks belonging to the Federal Reserve system. When Congress first formed the Federal Reserve, it foresaw that different regions of the country would have different regional considerations for setting this rate. But with the technological advances in electronics,

communications, and computers, regional factors became negligible compared to those operating at the broad, national level. So today the Governors and the twelve regional banks' directors reach decisions regarding the rate by consensus, with the Board of Directors making recommendations to the Board of Governors, who in turn approve or reject their suggestion.[19] Thus, at nearly all times the twelve branches of the Fed operate under a single Discount Rate.

The Federal Funds Rate: Overseeing money flows

Banks have a second source of liquid funds for those occasions they require cash in short order: their "neighbor" bank. That is, banks are free to lend and borrow amongst themselves. Such trading (i.e., within the structure of The U.S. Federal Reserve System) originated in the 1920's and has long been recognized as a well-functioning market in its own right. It's called the **Federal Funds Market**, a name which is a tad misleading in that the trading itself is strictly between commercial banks, not between the Fed and commercial banks. But since member banks of the Federal Reserve System typically maintain cash reserves at the Fed, and since it is the Fed that verifies the availability of such reserves, it is therefore the Fed that approves and records all interbank loaning--and thus the name.

These are no "small change" dealings in the Fed Funds Market. Regulations dictate that borrowing of cash reserves be in denominations of $1,000,000 or more. The bulk of Fed Funds consists of, literally speaking, overnight borrowings: the loan will be re-paid the next morning. The rate at which these funds may be borrowed is called the **Federal Funds Rate**.

Though the Federal Reserve did not establish the market of its own accord, banking practice and monetary policy have evolved in such a way as to make the Fed Funds Rate an essential part of monetary policy. The rate acts as both a barometer of Fed policy and as a management tool for the targeting of money supply growth and interest rates. When it desires, the Fed can repurchase outstanding government

---

[19] ibid., p. 63.

securities of various kinds held by commercial banks. By purchasing the old IOU's with cash, the Fed increases the money supply in the commercial banking sector and therefore loosens the reins on available credit. The resulting lower interest rates should stimulate capital spending.

Thus, it is the changes in commercial banks' **portfolios**, i.e., their T-accounts, which are part and parcel of changes in the Federal Funds Rate. On the asset side of the typical T-account, bond assets get reduced and cash (hence, idle) reserves climb. (See question #3c at the end of the previous chapter.) The increased excess reserves that banks find themselves flush with act as a temporary surplus quantity of loanable funds. The descent of the Fed Funds Rate is inevitable, ceteris paribus; stimulative monetary

policy is in the works. Diagram 15–1 illustrates.

Obviously, the Fed can select the contrary route. It can sell government bonds and thereby drain cash reserves of the commercial banks. This would induce a brief shortage of credit and raise the Fed Funds Rate. Commercial lending rates would move in "sympathy" with the Funds Rate and likely lead to reduced investment.

Targeting the rate can be tricky, for the Fed does not control every variable in the market. But its policy hand is visible enough, incantations to laissez faire gods notwithstanding. The Fed Funds rate, it turns out, is the policy tool most relied upon by the current Chairman of the Fed, Alan Greenspan.

Stimulative Use of Fed Funds Market

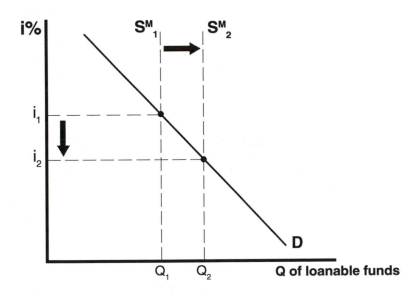

Diagram 15-1

VOCABULARY

Legal tender – money that can be used in payment for any debt and by law must be accepted for such payment; the legally recognized means of dispensing with a debt

Inelasticity – a technical term describing the lack of responsiveness of one variable to another, as in, for example, a lack of response of output to changes in price

Long run – a period of time longer than one production cycle

Open Market Operations: the market for the buying and selling of U.S. government securities between the Fed and some of the largest member banks; one of the Fed's main instruments for the manipulation of monetary policy

Discount Window – the procedure available to member banks of the Federal Reserve to acquire emergency liquid funds from the Fed itself

Discount Rate – the rate at which the Fed makes emergency funds available through the Discount Window; one of the Fed's main instruments for the manipulation of monetary policy

Federal Funds Market – refers to the interbank loaning system used by banks within the Federal Reserve system; loans are for overnight purposes in denominations of $1,000,000 or more

Federal Funds Rate – the rate of interest available through the Federal Funds Market; one of the Fed's main instruments for the manipulation of monetary policy, the rate is influenced indirectly by changing the amount of liquid reserves in the commercial banking system

Portfolio – a listing of a person's, firm's, or financial institution's assets; in a bank's case, a T-account can be said to contain its portfolio

TABLE B–26 Relation of gross domestic product, gross national product, net national product, and national income, 1959–2003

[Billions of dollars; quarterly data at seasonally adjusted annual rates]

Year	Gross domestic product	Plus: Income receipts from rest of the world	Less: Income payments to rest of the world	Equals: Gross national product	Less: Consumption of fixed capital			Equals: Net national product	Less: Statistical discrepancy	Equals: National income
					Total	Private	Government			
1959	506.6	4.3	1.5	509.3	53.0	38.6	14.5	456.3	0.5	455.8
1960	526.4	4.9	1.8	529.5	55.6	40.5	15.0	473.9	-0.9	474.9
1961	544.7	5.3	1.8	548.2	57.2	41.6	15.6	491.0	-0.6	491.6
1962	585.6	5.9	1.8	589.7	59.3	42.8	16.5	530.5	0.4	530.1
1963	617.7	6.5	2.1	622.2	62.4	44.9	17.5	559.8	-0.8	560.6
1964	663.6	7.2	2.3	668.5	65.0	46.9	18.1	603.5	0.8	602.7
1965	719.1	7.9	2.6	724.4	69.4	50.5	18.9	655.0	1.6	653.4
1966	787.8	8.1	3.0	792.9	75.6	55.5	20.1	717.3	6.3	711.0
1967	832.6	8.7	3.3	838.0	81.5	59.9	21.6	756.5	4.6	751.9
1968	910.0	10.1	4.0	916.1	88.4	65.2	23.1	827.7	4.6	823.2
1969	984.6	11.8	5.7	990.7	97.9	73.1	24.8	892.8	3.2	889.7
1970	1,038.5	12.8	6.4	1,044.9	106.7	80.0	26.7	938.2	7.3	930.9
1971	1,127.1	14.0	6.4	1,134.7	115.0	86.7	28.3	1,019.7	11.6	1,008.1
1972	1,238.3	16.3	7.7	1,246.8	126.5	97.1	29.5	1,120.3	9.1	1,111.2
1973	1,382.7	23.5	10.9	1,395.3	139.3	107.9	31.4	1,256.0	8.6	1,247.4
1974	1,500.0	29.8	14.3	1,515.5	162.5	126.6	35.9	1,353.0	10.9	1,342.1
1975	1,638.3	28.0	15.0	1,651.3	187.7	147.8	40.0	1,463.6	17.7	1,445.9
1976	1,825.3	32.4	15.5	1,842.1	205.2	162.5	42.6	1,637.0	25.1	1,611.8
1977	2,030.9	37.2	16.9	2,051.2	230.0	184.3	45.7	1,821.2	22.3	1,798.9
1978	2,294.7	46.3	24.7	2,316.3	262.3	212.8	49.5	2,054.0	26.6	2,027.4
1979	2,563.3	68.3	36.4	2,595.3	300.1	245.7	54.5	2,295.1	46.0	2,249.1
1980	2,789.5	79.1	44.9	2,823.7	343.0	281.1	61.8	2,480.7	41.4	2,439.3
1981	3,128.4	92.0	59.1	3,161.4	388.1	317.9	70.1	2,773.3	30.9	2,742.4
1982	3,255.0	101.0	64.5	3,291.5	426.9	349.8	77.1	2,864.6	0.3	2,864.3
1983	3,536.7	101.9	64.8	3,573.8	443.8	362.1	81.7	3,130.0	45.7	3,084.2
1984	3,933.2	121.9	85.6	3,969.5	472.6	385.6	87.0	3,496.9	14.6	3,482.3
1985	4,220.3	112.4	85.9	4,246.8	506.7	414.0	92.7	3,740.1	16.7	3,723.4
1986	4,462.8	111.4	93.6	4,480.6	531.3	431.8	99.5	3,949.3	47.0	3,902.3
1987	4,739.5	123.2	105.3	4,757.4	561.9	455.3	106.7	4,195.4	21.7	4,173.7
1988	5,103.8	152.1	128.5	5,127.4	597.6	483.5	114.1	4,529.8	-19.5	4,549.4

TABLE B–26 Relation of gross domestic product, gross national product, net national product, and national income, 1959–2003

[Billions of dollars; quarterly data at seasonally adjusted annual rates]

Year	Gross domestic product	Plus: Income receipts from rest of the world	Less: Income payments to rest of the world	Equals: Gross national product	Less: Consumption of fixed capital			Equals: Net national product	Less: Statistical discrepancy	Equals: National income
					Total	Private	Government			
1989	5,484.4	177.7	151.5	5,510.6	644.3	522.1	122.2	4,866.3	39.7	4,826.6
1990	5,803.1	189.1	154.3	5,837.9	682.5	551.6	130.9	5,155.4	66.2	5,089.1
1991	5,995.9	168.9	138.5	6,026.3	725.9	586.9	139.1	5,300.4	72.5	5,227.9
1992	6,337.7	152.7	123.0	6,367.4	751.9	607.3	144.6	5,615.5	102.7	5,512.8
1993	6,657.4	156.2	124.3	6,689.3	776.4	624.7	151.8	5,912.9	139.5	5,773.4
1994	7,072.2	186.4	160.2	7,098.4	833.7	675.1	158.6	6,264.7	142.5	6,122.3
1995	7,397.7	233.9	198.1	7,433.4	878.4	713.4	165.0	6,555.1	101.2	6,453.9
1996	7,816.9	248.7	213.7	7,851.9	918.1	748.8	169.3	6,933.8	93.7	6,840.1
1997	8,304.3	286.7	253.7	8,337.3	974.4	800.3	174.1	7,362.8	70.7	7,292.2
1998	8,747.0	287.1	265.8	8,768.3	1,030.2	851.2	179.0	7,738.2	-14.6	7,752.8
1999	9,268.4	320.8	287.0	9,302.2	1,101.3	914.3	187.0	8,200.9	-35.7	8,236.7
2000	9,817.0	382.7	343.7	9,855.9	1,187.8	990.8	197.0	8,668.1	-127.2	8,795.2
2001	10,100.8	319.0	283.8	10,135.9	1,266.9	1,061.0	205.9	8,869.0	-112.2	8,981.2
2002	10,480.8	299.1	277.6	10,502.3	1,288.6	1,077.8	210.8	9,213.7	-77.2	9,290.8

Source: Department of Commerce, Bureau of Economic Analysis.

Table 1.1.5. Gross Domestic Product
Annual data from 1965 To 2003
[Billions of dollars]

Line		1965	1966	1967	1968	1969	1970	1971
1	**Gross domestic product**	**719.1**	**787.8**	**832.6**	**910.0**	**984.6**	**1,038.5**	**1,127.1**
2	**Personal consumption expenditures**	**443.8**	**480.9**	**507.8**	**558.0**	**605.2**	**648.5**	**701.9**
3	Durable goods	63.3	68.3	70.4	80.8	85.9	85.0	96.9
4	Nondurable goods	191.5	208.7	217.1	235.7	253.1	272.0	285.5
5	Services	189.0	203.8	220.3	241.6	266.1	291.5	319.5
6	**Gross private domestic investment**	**118.2**	**131.3**	**128.6**	**141.2**	**156.4**	**152.4**	**178.2**
7	Fixed investment	109.0	117.7	118.7	132.1	147.3	150.4	169.9
8	Nonresidential	74.8	85.4	86.4	93.4	104.7	109.0	114.1
9	Structures	28.3	31.3	31.5	33.6	37.7	40.3	42.7
10	Equipment and software	46.5	54.0	54.9	59.9	67.0	68.7	71.5
11	Residential	34.2	32.3	32.4	38.7	42.6	41.4	55.8
12	Change in private inventories	9.2	13.6	9.9	9.1	9.2	2.0	8.3
13	**Net exports of goods and services**	**5.6**	**3.9**	**3.6**	**1.4**	**1.4**	**4.0**	**0.6**
14	Exports	37.1	40.9	43.5	47.9	51.9	59.7	63.0
15	Goods	27.8	30.7	32.2	35.3	38.3	44.5	45.6
16	Services	9.4	10.2	11.3	12.6	13.7	15.2	17.4
17	Imports	31.5	37.1	39.9	46.6	50.5	55.8	62.3
18	Goods	22.2	26.3	27.8	33.9	36.8	40.9	46.6
19	Services	9.3	10.7	12.2	12.6	13.7	14.9	15.8
20	**Government consumption expenditures and gross investment**	**151.5**	**171.8**	**192.7**	**209.4**	**221.5**	**233.8**	**246.5**
21	Federal	80.4	92.5	104.8	111.4	113.4	113.5	113.7
22	National defense	60.6	71.7	83.5	89.3	89.5	87.6	84.6
23	Nondefense	19.8	20.8	21.3	22.1	23.8	25.8	29.1
24	State and local	71.0	79.2	87.9	98.0	108.2	120.3	132.8

Source: Bureau of Economic Analysis, October 29, 2004

Table 1.1.5 Gross Domestic Product
Page 1 of 6

Table 1.1.5. Gross Domestic Product
Annual data from 1965 To 2003
[Billions of dollars]

Line		1972	1973	1974	1975	1976	1977	1978
1	Gross domestic product	1,238.3	1,382.7	1,500.0	1,638.3	1,825.3	2,030.9	2,294.7
2	Personal consumption expenditures	770.6	852.4	933.4	1,034.4	1,151.9	1,278.6	1,428.5
3	Durable goods	110.4	123.5	122.3	133.5	158.9	181.2	201.7
4	Nondurable goods	308.0	343.1	384.5	420.7	458.3	497.1	550.2
5	Services	352.2	385.8	426.6	480.2	534.7	600.2	676.6
6	Gross private domestic investment	207.6	244.5	249.4	230.2	292.0	361.3	438.0
7	Fixed investment	198.5	228.6	235.4	236.5	274.8	339.0	412.2
8	Nonresidential	128.8	153.3	169.5	173.7	192.4	228.7	280.6
9	Structures	47.2	55.0	61.2	61.4	65.9	74.6	93.6
10	Equipment and software	81.7	98.3	108.2	112.4	126.4	154.1	187.0
11	Residential	69.7	75.3	66.0	62.7	82.5	110.3	131.6
12	Change in private inventories	9.1	15.9	14.0	-6.3	17.1	22.3	25.8
13	Net exports of goods and services	-3.4	4.1	-0.8	16.0	-1.6	-23.1	-25.4
14	Exports	70.8	95.3	126.7	138.7	149.5	159.4	186.9
15	Goods	51.8	73.9	101.0	109.6	117.8	123.7	145.4
16	Services	19.0	21.3	25.7	29.1	31.7	35.7	41.5
17	Imports	74.2	91.2	127.5	122.7	151.1	182.4	212.3
18	Goods	56.9	71.8	104.5	99.0	124.6	152.6	177.4
19	Services	17.3	19.3	22.9	23.7	26.5	29.8	34.8
20	Government consumption expenditures and gross investment	263.5	281.7	317.9	357.7	383.0	414.1	453.6
21	Federal	119.7	122.5	134.6	149.1	159.7	175.4	190.9
22	National defense	87.0	88.2	95.6	103.9	111.1	120.9	130.5
23	Nondefense	32.7	34.3	39.0	45.1	48.6	54.5	60.4
24	State and local	143.8	159.2	183.4	208.7	223.3	238.7	262.6

Table 1.1.5 Gross Domestic Product

Table 1.1.5. Gross Domestic Product
Annual data from 1965 To 2003
[Billions of dollars]

Line		1979	1980	1981	1982	1983	1984	1985
1	**Gross domestic product**	**2,563.3**	**2,789.5**	**3,128.4**	**3,255.0**	**3,536.7**	**3,933.2**	**4,220.3**
2	**Personal consumption expenditures**	**1,592.2**	**1,757.1**	**1,941.1**	**2,077.3**	**2,290.6**	**2,503.3**	**2,720.3**
3	Durable goods	214.4	214.2	231.3	240.2	280.8	326.5	363.5
4	Nondurable goods	624.5	696.1	758.9	787.6	831.2	884.6	928.7
5	Services	753.3	846.9	950.8	1,049.4	1,178.6	1,292.2	1,428.1
6	**Gross private domestic investment**	**492.9**	**479.3**	**572.4**	**517.2**	**564.3**	**735.6**	**736.2**
7	Fixed investment	474.9	485.6	542.6	532.1	570.1	670.2	714.4
8	Nonresidential	333.9	362.4	420.0	426.5	417.2	489.6	526.2
9	Structures	117.7	136.2	167.3	177.6	154.3	177.4	194.5
10	Equipment and software	216.2	226.2	252.7	248.9	262.9	312.2	331.7
11	Residential	141.0	123.2	122.6	105.7	152.9	180.6	188.2
12	Change in private inventories	18.0	-6.3	29.8	-14.9	-5.8	65.4	21.8
13	**Net exports of goods and services**	**-22.5**	**-13.1**	**-12.5**	**-20.0**	**-51.7**	**-102.7**	**-115.2**
14	Exports	230.1	280.8	305.2	283.2	277.0	302.4	302.0
15	Goods	184.0	225.8	239.1	215.0	207.3	225.6	222.2
16	Services	46.1	55.0	66.1	68.2	69.7	76.7	79.8
17	Imports	252.7	293.8	317.8	303.2	328.6	405.1	417.2
18	Goods	212.8	248.6	267.8	250.5	272.7	336.3	343.3
19	Services	39.9	45.3	49.9	52.6	56.0	68.8	73.9
20	**Government consumption expenditures and gross investment**	**500.8**	**566.2**	**627.5**	**680.5**	**733.5**	**797.0**	**879.0**
21	Federal	210.6	243.8	280.2	310.8	342.9	374.4	412.8
22	National defense	145.2	168.0	196.3	225.9	250.7	281.6	311.2
23	Nondefense	65.4	75.8	84.0	84.9	92.3	92.8	101.6
24	State and local	290.2	322.4	347.3	369.7	390.5	422.6	466.2

Source: Bureau of Economic Analysis, October 29, 2004

Table 1.1.5 Gross Domestic Product
Page 3 of 6

Table 1.1.5. Gross Domestic Product
Annual data from 1965 To 2003
[Billions of dollars]

Line		1986	1987	1988	1989	1990	1991	1992
1	**Gross domestic product**	**4,462.8**	**4,739.5**	**5,103.8**	**5,484.4**	**5,803.1**	**5,995.9**	**6,337.7**
2	**Personal consumption expenditures**	**2,899.7**	**3,100.2**	**3,353.6**	**3,598.5**	**3,839.9**	**3,986.1**	**4,235.3**
3	Durable goods	403.0	421.7	453.6	471.8	474.2	453.9	483.6
4	Nondurable goods	958.4	1,015.3	1,083.5	1,166.7	1,249.9	1,284.8	1,330.5
5	Services	1,538.3	1,663.3	1,816.5	1,960.0	2,115.9	2,247.4	2,421.2
6	**Gross private domestic investment**	**746.5**	**785.0**	**821.6**	**874.9**	**861.0**	**802.9**	**864.8**
7	Fixed investment	739.9	757.8	803.1	847.3	846.4	803.3	848.5
8	Nonresidential	519.8	524.1	563.8	607.7	622.4	598.2	612.1
9	Structures	176.5	174.2	182.8	193.7	202.9	183.6	172.6
10	Equipment and software	343.3	349.9	381.0	414.0	419.5	414.6	439.6
11	Residential	220.1	233.7	239.3	239.5	224.0	205.1	236.3
12	Change in private inventories	6.6	27.1	18.5	27.7	14.5	-0.4	16.3
13	**Net exports of goods and services**	**-132.7**	**-145.2**	**-110.4**	**-88.2**	**-78.0**	**-27.5**	**-33.2**
14	Exports	320.5	363.9	444.1	503.3	552.4	596.8	635.3
15	Goods	226.0	257.5	325.8	369.4	396.6	423.5	448.0
16	Services	94.5	106.4	118.3	134.0	155.7	173.3	187.4
17	Imports	453.3	509.1	554.5	591.5	630.3	624.3	668.6
18	Goods	370.0	414.8	452.1	484.8	508.1	500.7	544.9
19	Services	83.3	94.3	102.4	106.7	122.3	123.6	123.6
20	**Government consumption expenditures and gross investment**	**949.3**	**999.5**	**1,039.0**	**1,099.1**	**1,180.2**	**1,234.4**	**1,271.0**
21	Federal	438.6	460.1	462.3	482.2	508.3	527.7	533.9
22	National defense	330.9	350.0	354.9	362.2	374.0	383.2	376.9
23	Nondefense	107.8	110.0	107.4	120.0	134.3	144.5	157.0
24	State and local	510.7	539.4	576.7	616.9	671.9	706.7	737.0

Source: Bureau of Economic Analysis, October 29, 2004

Table 1.1.5 Gross Domestic Product

Table 1.1.5. Gross Domestic Product
Annual data from 1965 To 2003
[Billions of dollars]

Line		1993	1994	1995	1996	1997	1998	1999
1	**Gross domestic product**	**6,657.4**	**7,072.2**	**7,397.7**	**7,816.9**	**8,304.3**	**8,747.0**	**9,268.4**
2	**Personal consumption expenditures**	**4,477.9**	**4,743.3**	**4,975.8**	**5,256.8**	**5,547.4**	**5,879.5**	**6,282.5**
3	Durable goods	526.7	582.2	611.6	652.6	692.7	750.2	817.6
4	Nondurable goods	1,379.4	1,437.2	1,485.1	1,555.5	1,619.0	1,683.6	1,804.8
5	Services	2,571.8	2,723.9	2,879.1	3,048.7	3,235.8	3,445.7	3,660.0
6	**Gross private domestic investment**	**953.4**	**1,097.1**	**1,144.0**	**1,240.3**	**1,389.8**	**1,509.1**	**1,625.7**
7	Fixed investment	932.5	1,033.3	1,112.9	1,209.5	1,317.8	1,438.4	1,558.8
8	Nonresidential	666.6	731.4	810.0	875.4	968.7	1,052.6	1,133.9
9	Structures	177.2	186.8	207.3	224.6	250.3	275.2	282.2
10	Equipment and software	489.4	544.6	602.8	650.8	718.3	777.3	851.7
11	Residential	266.0	301.9	302.8	334.1	349.1	385.8	424.9
12	Change in private inventories	20.8	63.8	31.1	30.8	72.0	70.8	66.9
13	**Net exports of goods and services**	**-65.0**	**-93.6**	**-91.4**	**-96.2**	**-101.6**	**-159.9**	**-260.5**
14	Exports	655.8	720.9	812.2	868.6	955.3	955.9	991.2
15	Goods	459.9	510.1	583.3	618.3	687.7	680.9	697.2
16	Services	195.9	210.8	228.9	250.2	267.6	275.1	294.0
17	Imports	720.9	814.5	903.6	964.8	1,056.9	1,115.9	1,251.7
18	Goods	592.8	676.8	757.4	807.4	885.3	929.0	1,045.5
19	Services	128.1	137.7	146.1	157.4	171.5	186.9	206.3
20	**Government consumption expenditures and gross investment**	**1,291.2**	**1,325.5**	**1,369.2**	**1,416.0**	**1,468.7**	**1,518.3**	**1,620.8**
21	Federal	525.2	519.1	519.2	527.4	530.9	530.4	555.8
22	National defense	362.9	353.7	348.7	354.6	349.6	345.7	360.6
23	Nondefense	162.4	165.5	170.5	172.8	181.3	184.7	195.2
24	State and local	766.0	806.3	850.0	888.6	937.8	987.9	1,065.0

Source: Bureau of Economic Analysis, October 29, 2004

Table 1.1.5 Gross Domestic Product
Page 5 of 6

Table 1.1.5. Gross Domestic Product
Annual data from 1965 To 2003
[Billions of dollars]

Line		2000	2001	2002	2003
1	**Gross domestic product**	**9,817.0**	**10,128.0**	**10,487.0**	**11,004.0**
2	**Personal consumption expenditures**	**6,739.4**	**7,055.0**	**7,376.1**	**7,760.9**
3	Durable goods	863.3	883.7	916.2	950.7
4	Nondurable goods	1,947.2	2,017.1	2,080.1	2,200.1
5	Services	3,928.8	4,154.3	4,379.8	4,610.1
6	**Gross private domestic investment**	**1,735.5**	**1,614.3**	**1,579.2**	**1,665.8**
7	Fixed investment	1,679.0	1,646.1	1,568.0	1,667.0
8	Nonresidential	1,232.1	1,176.8	1,063.9	1,094.7
9	Structures	313.2	322.6	271.6	261.6
10	Equipment and software	918.9	854.2	792.4	833.1
11	Residential	446.9	469.3	504.1	572.3
12	Change in private inventories	56.5	-31.7	11.2	-1.2
13	**Net exports of goods and services**	**-379.5**	**-367.0**	**-424.9**	**-498.1**
14	Exports	1,096.3	1,032.8	1,005.0	1,046.2
15	Goods	784.3	731.2	697.0	726.4
16	Services	311.9	301.6	308.0	319.8
17	Imports	1,475.8	1,399.8	1,429.9	1,544.3
18	Goods	1,243.5	1,167.9	1,189.6	1,282.0
19	Services	232.3	231.9	240.2	262.3
20	**Government consumption expenditures and gross investment**	**1,721.6**	**1,825.6**	**1,956.6**	**2,075.5**
21	Federal	578.8	612.9	680.8	752.2
22	National defense	370.3	392.6	437.4	496.4
23	Nondefense	208.5	220.3	243.4	255.7
24	State and local	1,142.8	1,212.8	1,275.8	1,323.3

Source: Bureau of Economic Analysis, October 29, 2004

Table 1.1.5 Gross Domestic Product

Table 1.1.6. Real Gross Domestic Product, Chained Dollars

Annual data from 1929 To 2003

[Billions of chained (2000) dollars]

Line		1965	1966	1967	1968	1969	1970	1971	1972
1	Gross domestic product	3,191.1	3,399.1	3,484.6	3,652.7	3,765.4	3,771.9	3,898.6	4,105.0
2	Personal consumption expenditures	2,007.7	2,121.8	2,185.0	2,310.5	2,396.4	2,451.9	2,545.5	2,701.3
3	Durable goods	.....	.....	.....	.....	.....	.....	.....	.....
4	Nondurable goods	.....	.....	.....	.....	.....	.....	.....	.....
5	Services	.....	.....	.....	.....	.....	.....	.....	.....
6	Gross private domestic investment	393.1	427.7	408.1	431.9	457.1	427.1	475.7	532.1
7	Fixed investment	.....	.....	.....	.....	.....	.....	.....	.....
8	Nonresidential	.....	.....	.....	.....	.....	.....	.....	.....
9	Structures	.....	.....	.....	.....	.....	.....	.....	.....
10	Equipment and software	.....	.....	.....	.....	.....	.....	.....	.....
11	Residential	.....	.....	.....	.....	.....	.....	.....	.....
12	Change in private inventories								
13	Net exports of goods and services	.....	.....	.....	.....	.....	.....	.....	.....
14	Exports	117.8	126.0	128.9	139.0	145.7	161.4	164.1	176.5
15	Goods	.....	.....	.....	.....	.....	.....	.....	.....
16	Services	.....	.....	.....	.....	.....	.....	.....	.....
17	Imports	136.7	157.1	168.5	193.6	204.6	213.4	224.7	250.0
18	Goods	.....	.....	.....	.....	.....	.....	.....	.....
19	Services	.....	.....	.....	.....	.....	.....	.....	.....
20	Government consumption expenditures and gross investment	861.3	937.1	1,008.9	1,040.5	1,038.0	1,012.9	990.8	983.5
21	Federal	.....	.....	.....	.....	.....	.....	.....	.....
22	National defense	.....	.....	.....	.....	.....	.....	.....	.....
23	Nondefense	.....	.....	.....	.....	.....	.....	.....	.....
24	State and local	.....	.....	.....	.....	.....	.....	.....	.....
25	Residual	-52.1	-56.4	-77.8	-75.6	-67.2	-68.0	-52.8	-38.4

Source: Bureau of Economic Analysis, October 29, 2004

Note. Chained (2000) dollar series are calculated as the product of the chain-type quantity index and the 2000 current-dollar value of the corresponding series, divided by 100. Because the formula for the chain-type quantity indexes uses weights of more than one period, the corresponding chained-dollar estimates are usually not additive. The residual line is the difference between the first line and the sum of the most detailed lines.

Table 1.1.6. Real Gross Domestic Product, Chained Dollars
Page 1 of 5

Table 1.1.6. Real Gross Domestic Product, Chained Dollars

Annual data from 1929 To 2003

[Billions of chained (2000) dollars]

Line		1973	1974	1975	1976	1977	1978	1979	1980
1	Gross domestic product	4,341.5	4,319.6	4,311.2	4,540.9	4,750.5	5,015.0	5,173.4	5,161.7
2	Personal consumption expenditures	2,833.8	2,812.3	2,876.9	3,035.5	3,164.1	3,303.1	3,383.4	3,374.1
3	Durable goods	.....	.....	.....	.....	.....	.....	.....	.....
4	Nondurable goods	.....	.....	.....	.....	.....	.....	.....	.....
5	Services	.....	.....	.....	.....	.....	.....	.....	.....
6	Gross private domestic investment	594.4	550.6	453.1	544.7	627.0	702.6	725.0	645.3
7	Fixed investment	.....	.....	.....	.....	.....	.....	.....	.....
8	Nonresidential	.....	.....	.....	.....	.....	.....	.....	.....
9	Structures	.....	.....	.....	.....	.....	.....	.....	.....
10	Equipment and software	.....	.....	.....	.....	.....	.....	.....	.....
11	Residential	.....	.....	.....	.....	.....	.....	.....	.....
12	Change in private inventories	.....	.....	.....	.....	.....	.....	.....	.....
13	Net exports of goods and services	.....	.....	.....	.....	.....	.....	.....	.....
14	Exports	209.7	226.3	224.9	234.7	240.3	265.7	292.0	323.5
15	Goods	.....	.....	.....	.....	.....	.....	.....	.....
16	Services	.....	.....	.....	.....	.....	.....	.....	.....
17	Imports	261.6	255.7	227.3	271.7	301.4	327.6	333.0	310.9
18	Goods	.....	.....	.....	.....	.....	.....	.....	.....
19	Services	.....	.....	.....	.....	.....	.....	.....	.....
20	Government consumption expenditures and gross investment	980.0	1,004.7	1,027.4	1,031.9	1,043.3	1,074.0	1,094.1	1,115.4
21	Federal	.....	.....	.....	.....	.....	.....	.....	.....
22	National defense	.....	.....	.....	.....	.....	.....	.....	.....
23	Nondefense	.....	.....	.....	.....	.....	.....	.....	.....
24	State and local	.....	.....	.....	.....	.....	.....	.....	.....
25	Residual	-14.8	-18.6	-43.8	-34.2	-22.8	-2.8	11.9	14.3

Source: Bureau of Economic Analysis, October 29, 2004

Note. Chained (2000) dollar series are calculated as the product of the chain-type quantity index and the 2000 current-dollar value of the corresponding series, divided by 100. Because the formula for the chain-type quantity indexes uses weights of more than one period, the corresponding chained-dollar estimates are usually not additive. The residual line is the difference between the first line and the sum of the most detailed lines.

Table 1.1.6. Real Gross Domestic Product, Chained Dollars

Table 1.1.6. Real Gross Domestic Product, Chained Dollars

Annual data from 1929 To 2003

[Billions of chained (2000) dollars]

Line		1981	1982	1983	1984	1985	1986	1987	1988
1	**Gross domestic product**	**5,291.7**	**5,189.3**	**5,423.8**	**5,813.6**	**6,053.7**	**6,263.6**	**6,475.1**	**6,742.7**
2	**Personal consumption expenditures**	**3,422.2**	**3,470.3**	**3,668.6**	**3,863.3**	**4,064.0**	**4,228.9**	**4,369.8**	**4,546.9**
3	Durable goods	.....	.....	.....	.....	.....	.....	.....	.....
4	Nondurable goods	.....	.....	.....	.....	.....	.....	.....	.....
5	Services	.....	.....	.....	.....	.....	.....	.....	.....
6	**Gross private domestic investment**	**704.9**	**606.0**	**662.5**	**857.7**	**849.7**	**843.9**	**870.0**	**890.5**
7	Fixed investment	.....	.....	.....	.....	.....	.....	.....	.....
8	Nonresidential	.....	.....	.....	.....	.....	.....	.....	.....
9	Structures	.....	.....	.....	.....	.....	.....	.....	.....
10	Equipment and software	.....	.....	.....	.....	.....	.....	.....	.....
11	Residential	.....	.....	.....	.....	.....	.....	.....	.....
12	Change in private inventories	.....	.....	.....	.....	.....	.....	.....	.....
13	**Net exports of goods and services**	.....	.....	.....	.....	.....	.....	.....	.....
14	Exports	327.4	302.4	294.6	318.7	328.3	353.7	391.8	454.6
15	Goods	.....	.....	.....	.....	.....	.....	.....	.....
16	Services	.....	.....	.....	.....	.....	.....	.....	.....
17	Imports	319.1	315.0	354.8	441.1	469.8	510.0	540.2	561.4
18	Goods	.....	.....	.....	.....	.....	.....	.....	.....
19	Services	.....	.....	.....	.....	.....	.....	.....	.....
20	**Government consumption expenditures and gross investment**	**1,125.6**	**1,145.4**	**1,187.3**	**1,227.0**	**1,312.5**	**1,392.5**	**1,426.7**	**1,445.1**
21	Federal	.....	.....	.....	.....	.....	.....	.....	.....
22	National defense	.....	.....	.....	.....	.....	.....	.....	.....
23	Nondefense	.....	.....	.....	.....	.....	.....	.....	.....
24	State and local	.....	.....	.....	.....	.....	.....	.....	.....
25	Residual	30.7	-19.8	-34.4	-12.0	-31.0	-45.4	-43.0	-33.0

Source: Bureau of Economic Analysis, October 29, 2004

Note. Chained (2000) dollar series are calculated as the product of the chain-type quantity index and the 2000 current-dollar value of the corresponding series, divided by 100. Because the formula for the chain-type quantity indexes uses weights of more than one period, the corresponding chained-dollar estimates are usually not additive. The residual line is the difference between the first line and the sum of the most detailed lines.

Table 1.1.6. Real Gross Domestic Product, Chained Dollars
Page 3 of 5

Table 1.1.6. Real Gross Domestic Product, Chained Dollars

Annual data from 1929 To 2003

[Billions of chained (2000) dollars]

Line		1989	1990	1991	1992	1993	1994	1995	1996
1	Gross domestic product	6,981.4	7,112.5	7,100.5	7,336.6	7,532.7	7,835.5	8,031.7	8,328.9
2	Personal consumption expenditures	4,675.0	4,770.3	4,778.4	4,934.8	5,099.8	5,290.7	5,433.5	5,619.4
3	Durable goods	.....	453.5	427.9	453.0	488.4	529.4	552.6	595.9
4	Nondurable goods	.....	1,484.0	1,480.5	1,510.1	1,550.4	1,603.9	1,638.6	1,680.4
5	Services	.....	2,851.7	2,900.0	3,000.8	3,085.7	3,176.6	3,259.9	3,356.0
6	Gross private domestic investment	926.2	895.1	822.2	889.0	968.3	1,099.6	1,134.0	1,234.3
7	Fixed investment	.....	886.6	829.1	878.3	953.5	1,042.3	1,109.6	1,209.2
8	Nonresidential	.....	595.1	563.2	581.3	631.9	689.9	762.5	833.6
9	Structures	.....	275.2	244.6	229.9	228.3	232.3	247.1	261.1
10	Equipment and software	.....	355.0	345.9	371.1	417.4	467.2	523.1	578.7
11	Residential	.....	298.9	270.2	307.6	332.7	364.8	353.1	381.3
12	Change in private inventories	.....	15.4	-0.5	16.5	20.6	63.6	29.9	28.7
13	Net exports of goods and services	.....	-54.7	-14.6	-15.9	-52.1	-79.4	-71.0	-79.6
14	Exports	506.8	552.5	589.1	629.7	650.0	706.5	778.2	843.4
15	Goods	.....	367.2	392.5	421.9	435.6	478.0	533.9	581.1
16	Services	.....	188.7	199.9	210.8	217.5	231.1	245.8	263.5
17	Imports	586.0	607.1	603.7	645.6	702.1	785.9	849.1	923.0
18	Goods	.....	469.7	469.3	513.1	564.8	640.0	697.6	762.7
19	Services	.....	142.7	139.0	135.5	139.4	147.3	152.1	160.5
20	Government consumption expenditures and gross investment	1,482.5	1,530.0	1,547.2	1,555.3	1,541.1	1,541.3	1,549.7	1,564.9
21	Federal	.....	659.1	658.0	646.6	619.6	596.4	580.3	573.5
22	National defense	.....	479.4	474.2	450.7	425.3	404.6	389.2	383.8
23	Nondefense	.....	178.6	182.8	195.4	194.1	191.7	191.0	189.6
24	State and local	.....	868.4	886.8	906.5	919.5	943.3	968.3	990.5
25	Residual	-23.1	-91.1	-96.0	-89.1	-78.6	-63.7	-51.1	-38.5

Source: Bureau of Economic Analysis, October 29, 2004

Note. Chained (2000) dollar series are calculated as the product of the chain-type quantity index and the 2000 current-dollar value of the corresponding series, divided by 100. Because the formula for the chain-type quantity indexes uses weights of more than one period, the corresponding chained-dollar estimates are usually not additive. The residual line is the difference between the first line and the sum of the most detailed lines.

Table 1.1.6. Real Gross Domestic Product, Chained Dollars

Table 1.1.6. Real Gross Domestic Product, Chained Dollars

Annual data from 1929 To 2003

[Billions of chained (2000) dollars]

Line		1997	1998	1999	2000	2001	2002	2003
1	Gross domestic product	8,703.5	9,066.9	9,470.3	9,817.0	9,890.7	10,074.8	10,381.3
2	Personal consumption expenditures	5,831.8	6,125.8	6,438.6	6,739.4	6,910.4	7,123.4	7,355.6
3	Durable goods	646.9	720.3	804.6	863.3	900.7	959.6	1,030.6
4	Nondurable goods	1,725.3	1,794.4	1,876.6	1,947.2	1,986.7	2,037.4	2,112.4
5	Services	3,468.0	3,615.0	3,758.0	3,928.8	4,023.2	4,128.6	4,220.3
6	Gross private domestic investment	1,387.7	1,524.1	1,642.6	1,735.5	1,598.4	1,560.7	1,628.8
7	Fixed investment	1,320.6	1,455.0	1,576.3	1,679.0	1,629.4	1,548.9	1,627.3
8	Nonresidential	934.2	1,037.8	1,133.3	1,232.1	1,180.5	1,075.6	1,110.8
9	Structures	280.1	294.5	293.2	313.2	306.1	251.6	237.4
10	Equipment and software	658.3	745.6	840.2	918.9	874.2	826.5	879.2
11	Residential	388.6	418.3	443.6	446.9	448.5	470.0	511.2
12	Change in private inventories	71.2	72.6	68.9	56.5	-31.7	11.7	-0.8
13	Net exports of goods and services	-104.6	-203.7	-296.2	-379.5	-399.1	-472.1	-518.5
14	Exports	943.7	966.5	1,008.2	1,096.3	1,036.7	1,012.3	1,031.8
15	Goods	664.5	679.4	705.2	784.3	736.3	706.4	721.7
16	Services	279.2	287.2	303.2	311.9	300.4	305.7	309.9
17	Imports	1,048.3	1,170.3	1,304.4	1,475.8	1,435.8	1,484.4	1,550.3
18	Goods	872.6	974.4	1,095.2	1,243.5	1,204.1	1,248.5	1,307.3
19	Services	175.6	195.6	209.1	232.3	231.6	235.9	243.3
20	Government consumption expenditures and gross investment	1,594.0	1,624.4	1,686.9	1,721.6	1,780.3	1,857.9	1,909.4
21	Federal	567.6	561.2	573.7	578.8	601.4	646.6	689.6
22	National defense	373.0	365.3	372.2	370.3	384.9	414.6	451.8
23	Nondefense	194.5	195.9	201.5	208.5	216.5	232.0	237.6
24	State and local	1,025.9	1,063.0	1,113.2	1,142.8	1,179.0	1,211.4	1,219.8
25	Residual	-23.8	-14.6	-5.8	0.2	1.6	3.7	0.8

Source: Bureau of Economic Analysis, October 29, 2004

Note. Chained (2000) dollar series are calculated as the product of the chain-type quantity index and the 2000 current-dollar value of the corresponding series, divided by 100. Because the formula for the chain-type quantity indexes uses weights of more than one period, the corresponding chained-dollar estimates are usually not additive. The residual line is the difference between the first line and the sum of the most detailed lines.

Table 1.1.6. Real Gross Domestic Product, Chained Dollars
Page 5 of 5

Table 5.1. Saving and Investment

Annual data from 1965 To 2003

[Billions of dollars]

Line		1965	1966	1967	1968	1969	1970	1971
1	**Gross saving**	**158.5**	**168.7**	**170.5**	**182.0**	**198.3**	**192.7**	**208.9**
2	**Net saving**	**89.1**	**93.1**	**89.0**	**93.6**	**100.4**	**86.0**	**93.9**
3	Net private saving	79.2	83.1	91.4	88.4	83.7	94.0	115.8
4	Personal saving	43.0	44.4	54.4	52.8	52.5	69.5	80.6
5	Undistributed corporate profits with inventory valuation and capital consumption adjustments	36.2	38.7	36.9	35.6	31.2	24.6	34.8
6	**Undistributed profits**	**28.9**	**32.1**	**29.1**	**29.3**	**27.2**	**21.9**	**29.7**
7	Inventory valuation adjustment	-1.2	-2.1	-1.6	-3.7	-5.9	-6.6	-4.6
8	Capital consumption adjustment	8.6	8.6	9.3	10.0	9.9	9.2	9.7
9	Wage accruals less disbursements	0.0	0.0	0.0	0.0	0.0	0.0	0.4
10	Net government saving	9.9	10.0	-2.4	5.2	16.7	-8.1	-21.9
11	Federal	3.3	2.3	-9.4	-2.3	8.7	-15.2	-28.4
12	State and local	6.5	7.8	7.0	7.5	8.0	7.1	6.5
13	**Consumption of fixed capital**	**69.4**	**75.6**	**81.5**	**88.4**	**97.9**	**106.7**	**115.0**
14	Private	50.5	55.5	59.9	65.2	73.1	80.0	86.7
15	Domestic business	41.9	46.3	50.0	54.4	61.2	67.2	72.5
16	Households and institutions	8.5	9.2	9.9	10.8	12.0	12.9	14.2
17	Government	18.9	20.1	21.6	23.1	24.8	26.7	28.3
18	Federal	12.7	13.2	14.0	14.8	15.5	16.1	16.5
19	State and local	6.2	6.9	7.5	8.3	9.3	10.6	11.8
20	**Gross domestic investment, capital account transactions, and net lending, NIPAs**	**160.0**	**175.0**	**175.1**	**186.6**	**201.5**	**200.0**	**220.5**
21	Gross domestic investment	153.8	171.1	171.6	184.8	199.7	196.0	219.9
22	Gross private domestic investment	118.2	131.3	128.6	141.2	156.4	152.4	178.2
23	Gross government investment	35.6	39.8	43.0	43.6	43.3	43.6	41.8
24	Capital account transactions (net)[1]	.....	.....	.....	.....	.....	.....	.....
25	Net lending or net borrowing (-), NIPAs[2]	6.2	3.9	3.6	1.7	1.8	4.0	0.6
26	**Statistical discrepancy**	**1.6**	**6.3**	**4.6**	**4.6**	**3.2**	**7.3**	**11.6**
	Addenda:							
27	Gross private saving	129.7	138.6	151.3	153.7	156.8	174.1	202.5
28	Gross government saving	28.8	30.1	19.2	28.3	41.5	18.6	6.4
29	Federal	16.0	15.5	4.7	12.5	24.2	0.9	-11.9
30	State and local	12.8	14.6	14.5	15.8	17.3	17.7	18.3
31	Net domestic investment	84.4	95.5	90.1	96.5	101.8	89.3	104.9
32	**Gross saving as a percentage of gross national income**	**21.9**	**21.4**	**20.5**	**20.0**	**20.1**	**18.6**	**18.6**
33	**Net saving as a percentage of gross national income**	**12.3**	**11.8**	**10.7**	**10.3**	**10.2**	**8.3**	**8.4**

Source: Bureau of Economic Analysis, October 29, 2004

1. Consists of capital transfers and the acquisition and disposal of nonproduced nonfinancial assets.

2. Prior to 1982, equals the balance on current account, NIPAs as shown in table 4.1; estimates of capital account transactions (line 24) are not available.

Table 5.1 Saving and Investment

Table 5.1. Saving and Investment

Annual data from 1965 To 2003

[Billions of dollars]

Line		1972	1973	1974	1975	1976	1977	1978
1	**Gross saving**	**237.5**	**292.0**	**301.5**	**297.0**	**342.1**	**397.5**	**478.0**
2	**Net saving**	**111.0**	**152.7**	**139.0**	**109.2**	**137.0**	**167.5**	**215.7**
3	Net private saving	119.8	148.3	143.4	175.8	181.3	198.5	223.5
4	Personal saving	77.2	102.7	113.6	125.6	122.3	125.3	142.5
5	Undistributed corporate profits with inventory valuation and capital consumption adjustments	42.9	45.6	29.8	50.2	59.0	73.2	81.0
6	**Undistributed profits**	**38.6**	**55.0**	**61.8**	**60.9**	**75.4**	**91.2**	**110.5**
7	Inventory valuation adjustment	-6.6	-19.6	-38.2	-10.5	-14.1	-15.7	-23.7
8	Capital consumption adjustment	10.9	10.2	6.2	-0.2	-2.3	-2.3	-5.8
9	Wage accruals less disbursements	-0.3	0.0	0.0	0.0	0.0	0.0	0.0
10	Net government saving	-8.8	4.4	-4.4	-66.6	-44.4	-31.0	-7.8
11	Federal	-24.4	-11.3	-13.8	-69.0	-51.7	-44.1	-26.5
12	State and local	15.6	15.7	9.3	2.5	7.4	13.1	18.7
13	**Consumption of fixed capital**	**126.5**	**139.3**	**162.5**	**187.7**	**205.2**	**230.0**	**262.3**
14	Private	97.1	107.9	126.6	147.8	162.5	184.3	212.8
15	Domestic business	80.9	89.9	105.9	124.4	136.9	155.3	179.3
16	Households and institutions	16.2	18.0	20.7	23.4	25.6	29.0	33.6
17	Government	29.5	31.4	35.9	40.0	42.6	45.7	49.5
18	Federal	16.6	17.1	18.2	19.7	21.4	23.1	25.0
19	State and local	12.8	14.3	17.7	20.2	21.3	22.6	24.5
20	**Gross domestic investment, capital account transactions, and net lending, NIPAs**	**246.6**	**300.7**	**312.3**	**314.7**	**367.2**	**419.8**	**504.6**
21	Gross domestic investment	250.2	291.3	305.7	293.3	358.4	428.8	515.0
22	Gross private domestic investment	207.6	244.5	249.4	230.2	292.0	361.3	438.0
23	Gross government investment	42.6	46.8	56.3	63.1	66.4	67.5	77.1
24	Capital account transactions (net)[1]	.....	.....	.....	.....	.....	.....	.....
25	Net lending or net borrowing (-), NIPAs[2]	-3.6	9.3	6.6	21.4	8.9	-9.0	-10.4
26	**Statistical discrepancy**	**9.1**	**8.6**	**10.9**	**17.7**	**25.1**	**22.3**	**26.6**
	Addenda:							
27	Gross private saving	216.8	256.3	270.0	323.6	343.8	382.8	436.3
28	Gross government saving	20.7	35.8	31.5	-26.6	-1.7	14.7	41.7
29	Federal	-7.7	5.8	4.5	-49.3	-30.3	-21.0	-1.5
30	State and local	28.5	30.0	27.0	22.7	28.6	35.7	43.2
31	Net domestic investment	123.7	152.1	143.2	105.6	153.2	198.8	252.7
32	**Gross saving as a percentage of gross national income**	**19.2**	**21.1**	**20.0**	**18.2**	**18.8**	**19.6**	**20.9**
33	**Net saving as a percentage of gross national income**	**9.0**	**11.0**	**9.2**	**6.7**	**7.5**	**8.3**	**9.4**

Source: Bureau of Economic Analysis, October 29, 2004

1. Consists of capital transfers and the acquisition and disposal of nonproduced nonfinancial assets.

2. Prior to 1982, equals the balance on current account, NIPAs as shown in table 4.1; estimates of capital account transactions (line 24) are not available.

Table 5.1 Saving and Investment
Page 2 of 7

Table 5.1. Saving and Investment
Annual data from 1965 To 2003
[Billions of dollars]

Line		1979	1980	1981	1982	1983	1984	1985
1	**Gross saving**	**536.7**	**549.4**	**654.7**	**629.1**	**609.4**	**773.4**	**767.5**
2	**Net saving**	**236.6**	**206.5**	**266.6**	**202.2**	**165.6**	**300.9**	**260.7**
3	Net private saving	234.9	251.3	312.3	336.2	333.7	445.0	413.4
4	Personal saving	159.1	201.4	244.3	270.8	233.6	314.8	280.0
5	Undistributed corporate profits with inventory valuation and capital consumption adjustments	75.7	49.9	68.0	65.4	100.1	130.3	133.4
6	**Undistributed profits**	**124.4**	**102.2**	**85.6**	**54.3**	**69.8**	**80.3**	**60.5**
7	Inventory valuation adjustment	-40.1	-42.1	-24.6	-7.5	-7.4	-4.0	0.0
8	Capital consumption adjustment	-8.5	-10.2	7.0	18.6	37.8	54.0	72.9
9	Wage accruals less disbursements	0.0	0.0	0.0	0.0	0.0	0.0	0.0
10	Net government saving	1.7	-44.8	-45.7	-134.1	-168.1	-144.1	-152.6
11	Federal	-11.3	-53.6	-53.3	-131.9	-173.0	-168.1	-175.0
12	State and local	13.0	8.8	7.6	-2.2	4.9	23.9	22.3
13	**Consumption of fixed capital**	**300.1**	**343.0**	**388.1**	**426.9**	**443.8**	**472.6**	**506.7**
14	Private	245.7	281.1	317.9	349.8	362.1	385.6	414.0
15	Domestic business	206.9	236.8	268.9	297.3	307.4	328.0	353.0
16	Households and institutions	38.8	44.3	49.0	52.5	54.7	57.6	61.0
17	Government	54.5	61.8	70.1	77.1	81.7	87.0	92.7
18	Federal	27.0	30.1	33.8	37.6	40.8	44.6	48.1
19	State and local	27.5	31.8	36.3	39.5	40.9	42.3	44.6
20	**Gross domestic investment, capital account transactions, and net lending, NIPAs**	**582.8**	**590.9**	**685.6**	**629.4**	**655.1**	**788.0**	**784.1**
21	Gross domestic investment	581.4	579.5	679.3	629.5	687.2	875.0	895.0
22	Gross private domestic investment	492.9	479.3	572.4	517.2	564.3	735.6	736.2
23	Gross government investment	88.5	100.3	106.9	112.3	122.9	139.4	158.8
24	Capital account transactions (net)[1]	.....	.....	.....	-0.2	-0.2	-0.2	-0.3
25	Net lending or net borrowing (-), NIPAs[2]	1.4	11.4	6.3	0.0	-31.8	-86.7	-110.5
26	**Statistical discrepancy**	**46.0**	**41.4**	**30.9**	**0.3**	**45.7**	**14.6**	**16.7**
	Addenda:							
27	Gross private saving	480.5	532.4	630.3	686.0	695.8	830.6	827.3
28	Gross government saving	56.2	17.0	24.4	-56.9	-86.5	-57.2	-59.9
29	Federal	15.7	-23.6	-19.4	-94.2	-132.3	-123.5	-126.9
30	State and local	40.5	40.6	43.9	37.3	45.8	66.3	67.0
31	Net domestic investment	281.2	236.6	291.2	202.6	243.4	402.4	388.3
32	**Gross saving as a percentage of gross national income**	**21.1**	**19.7**	**20.9**	**19.1**	**17.3**	**19.6**	**18.1**
33	**Net saving as a percentage of gross national income**	**9.3**	**7.4**	**8.5**	**6.1**	**4.7**	**7.6**	**6.2**

Source: Bureau of Economic Analysis, October 29, 2004

1. Consists of capital transfers and the acquisition and disposal of nonproduced nonfinancial assets.

2. Prior to 1982, equals the balance on current account, NIPAs as shown in table 4.1; estimates of capital account transactions (line 24) are not available.

Table 5.1 Saving and Investment

Table 5.1. Saving and Investment

Annual data from 1965 To 2003

[Billions of dollars]

Line		1986	1987	1988	1989	1990	1991	1992
1	**Gross saving**	733.5	796.8	915.0	944.7	940.4	964.1	948.2
2	**Net saving**	202.2	234.9	317.4	300.4	258.0	238.2	196.3
3	Net private saving	372.0	367.4	434.0	409.7	422.7	456.1	493.0
4	Personal saving	268.4	241.4	272.9	287.1	299.4	324.2	366.0
5	Undistributed corporate profits with inventory valuation and capital consumption adjustments	103.7	126.1	161.1	122.6	123.3	131.9	142.7
6	**Undistributed profits**	30.1	74.9	114.5	79.7	95.0	103.7	124.5
7	Inventory valuation adjustment	7.1	-16.2	-22.2	-16.3	-12.9	4.9	-2.8
8	Capital consumption adjustment	66.5	67.5	68.7	59.2	41.2	23.3	21.1
9	Wage accruals less disbursements	0.0	0.0	0.0	0.0	0.0	0.0	-15.8
10	Net government saving	-169.9	-132.6	-116.6	-109.3	-164.8	-217.9	-296.7
11	Federal	-190.8	-145.0	-134.5	-130.1	-172.0	-213.7	-297.4
12	State and local	21.0	12.4	17.9	20.8	7.2	-4.2	0.7
13	**Consumption of fixed capital**	531.3	561.9	597.6	644.3	682.5	725.9	751.9
14	Private	431.8	455.3	483.5	522.1	551.6	586.9	607.3
15	Domestic business	366.9	385.7	408.9	440.6	466.4	497.4	510.5
16	Households and institutions	64.9	69.5	74.6	81.5	85.1	89.5	96.8
17	Government	99.5	106.7	114.1	122.2	130.9	139.1	144.6
18	Federal	51.6	55.2	59.3	63.5	67.9	72.2	74.7
19	State and local	47.9	51.4	54.8	58.7	63.0	66.9	69.9
20	**Gross domestic investment, capital account transactions, and net lending, NIPAs**	780.5	818.5	895.5	984.3	1,006.7	1,036.6	1,051.0
21	Gross domestic investment	919.7	969.2	1,007.7	1,072.6	1,076.7	1,023.2	1,087.9
22	Gross private domestic investment	746.5	785.0	821.6	874.9	861.0	802.9	864.8
23	Gross government investment	173.2	184.3	186.1	197.7	215.7	220.3	223.1
24	Capital account transactions (net)[1]	-0.3	-0.4	-0.5	-0.3	6.6	4.5	0.6
25	Net lending or net borrowing (-), NIPAs[2]	-138.9	-150.4	-111.7	-88.0	-76.6	9.0	-37.5
26	**Statistical discrepancy**	47.0	21.7	-19.5	39.7	66.2	72.5	102.7
	Addenda:							
27	Gross private saving	803.9	822.7	917.5	931.8	974.3	1,042.9	1,100.4
28	Gross government saving	-70.4	-25.9	-2.5	12.9	-33.8	-78.8	-152.1
29	Federal	-139.2	-89.8	-75.2	-66.7	-104.1	-141.5	-222.7
30	State and local	68.8	63.9	72.7	79.6	70.3	62.7	70.6
31	Net domestic investment	388.4	407.3	410.1	428.4	394.2	297.3	336.0
32	**Gross saving as a percentage of gross national income**	16.5	16.8	17.8	17.3	16.3	16.2	15.1
33	**Net saving as a percentage of gross national income**	4.6	5.0	6.2	5.5	4.5	4.0	3.1

Source: Bureau of Economic Analysis, October 29, 2004

1. Consists of capital transfers and the acquisition and disposal of nonproduced nonfinancial assets.

2. Prior to 1982, equals the balance on current account, NIPAs as shown in table 4.1; estimates of capital account transactions (line 24) are not available.

Table 5.1 Saving and Investment
Page 4 of 7

Table 5.1. Saving and Investment

Annual data from 1965 To 2003

[Billions of dollars]

Line		1993	1994	1995	1996	1997	1998	1999
1	**Gross saving**	**962.4**	**1,070.7**	**1,184.5**	**1,291.1**	**1,461.1**	**1,598.7**	**1,674.3**
2	**Net saving**	**186.0**	**237.1**	**306.2**	**373.0**	**486.6**	**568.6**	**573.0**
3	Net private saving	458.6	438.9	491.1	489.0	503.3	477.8	419.0
4	Personal saving	284.0	249.5	250.9	228.4	218.3	276.8	158.6
5	Undistributed corporate profits with inventory valuation and capital consumption adjustments	168.1	171.8	223.8	256.9	287.9	201.7	255.3
6	**Undistributed profits**	**143.3**	**148.6**	**201.4**	**203.8**	**217.6**	**118.3**	**179.9**
7	Inventory valuation adjustment	-4.0	-12.4	-18.3	3.1	14.1	20.2	1.0
8	Capital consumption adjustment	28.8	35.7	40.7	50.1	56.2	63.1	74.5
9	Wage accruals less disbursements	6.4	17.6	16.4	3.6	-2.9	-0.7	5.2
10	Net government saving	-272.6	-201.9	-184.9	-116.0	-16.7	90.8	154.0
11	Federal	-273.5	-212.3	-197.0	-141.8	-55.8	38.8	103.6
12	State and local	0.9	10.5	12.0	25.8	39.1	52.0	50.4
13	**Consumption of fixed capital**	**776.4**	**833.7**	**878.4**	**918.1**	**974.4**	**1,030.2**	**1,101.3**
14	Private	624.7	675.1	713.4	748.8	800.3	851.2	914.3
15	Domestic business	524.6	568.0	600.2	630.7	675.2	718.3	769.8
16	Households and institutions	100.1	107.1	113.2	118.2	125.1	132.9	144.5
17	Government	151.8	158.6	165.0	169.3	174.1	179.0	187.0
18	Federal	77.9	80.2	81.9	82.0	82.5	82.8	84.8
19	State and local	73.8	78.5	83.1	87.2	91.6	96.2	102.1
20	**Gross domestic investment, capital account transactions, and net lending, NIPAs**	**1,102.0**	**1,213.2**	**1,285.7**	**1,384.8**	**1,531.7**	**1,584.1**	**1,638.5**
21	Gross domestic investment	1,172.4	1,318.4	1,376.7	1,485.2	1,641.9	1,771.5	1,912.4
22	Gross private domestic investment	953.4	1,097.1	1,144.0	1,240.3	1,389.8	1,509.1	1,625.7
23	Gross government investment	219.0	221.4	232.7	244.9	252.2	262.4	286.8
24	Capital account transactions (net)[1]	1.3	1.7	0.9	0.7	1.0	0.7	4.8
25	Net lending or net borrowing (-), NIPAs[2]	-71.7	-106.9	-91.9	-101.0	-111.3	-188.1	-278.7
26	**Statistical discrepancy**	**139.5**	**142.5**	**101.2**	**93.7**	**70.7**	**-14.6**	**-35.7**
	Addenda:							
27	Gross private saving	1,083.3	1,114.0	1,204.5	1,237.8	1,303.6	1,328.9	1,333.3
28	Gross government saving	-120.8	-43.2	-19.9	53.3	157.5	269.8	341.0
29	Federal	-195.5	-132.2	-115.1	-59.7	26.7	121.6	188.5
30	State and local	74.7	88.9	95.2	113.0	130.7	148.2	152.5
31	Net domestic investment	395.9	484.7	498.4	567.1	667.5	741.3	811.2
32	**Gross saving as a percentage of gross national income**	**14.7**	**15.4**	**16.2**	**16.6**	**17.7**	**18.2**	**17.9**
33	**Net saving as a percentage of gross national income**	**2.8**	**3.4**	**4.2**	**4.8**	**5.9**	**6.5**	**6.1**

Source: Bureau of Economic Analysis, October 29, 2004

1. Consists of capital transfers and the acquisition and disposal of nonproduced nonfinancial assets.

2. Prior to 1982, equals the balance on current account; NIPAs as shown in table 4.1; estimates of capital account transactions (line 24) are not available.

Table 5.1 Saving and Investment

Table 5.1. Saving and Investment
Annual data from 1965 To 2003

[Billions of dollars]

Line		2000	2001	2002	2003
1	**Gross saving**	**1,770.5**	**1,657.6**	**1,484.3**	**1,487.7**
2	**Net saving**	**582.7**	**376.1**	**180.3**	**133.8**
3	Net private saving	343.3	324.6	459.8	501.5
4	Personal saving	168.5	132.3	159.2	110.6
5	Undistributed corporate profits with inventory valuation and capital consumption adjustments	174.8	192.3	300.7	390.9
6	**Undistributed profits**	**130.3**	**132.9**	**184.1**	**244.2**
7	Inventory valuation adjustment	-14.1	11.3	-1.2	-14.1
8	Capital consumption adjustment	58.6	48.1	117.8	160.8
9	Wage accruals less disbursements	0.0	0.0	0.0	0.0
10	Net government saving	239.4	51.5	-279.5	-367.8
11	Federal	189.5	46.7	-254.5	-364.5
12	State and local	50.0	4.8	-25.0	-3.2
13	**Consumption of fixed capital**	**1,187.8**	**1,281.5**	**1,303.9**	**1,353.9**
14	Private	990.8	1,075.5	1,092.8	1,135.9
15	Domestic business	836.1	903.7	912.6	942.6
16	Households and institutions	154.8	171.7	180.2	193.3
17	Government	197.0	206.0	211.2	218.1
18	Federal	87.2	88.2	89.0	90.2
19	State and local	109.8	117.8	122.1	127.9
20	**Gross domestic investment, capital account transactions, and net lending, NIPAs**	**1,643.3**	**1,567.9**	**1,468.9**	**1,513.3**
21	Gross domestic investment	2,040.0	1,938.3	1,926.6	2,024.2
22	Gross private domestic investment	1,735.5	1,614.3	1,579.2	1,665.8
23	Gross government investment	304.5	324.0	347.4	358.5
24	Capital account transactions (net)[1]	0.8	1.1	1.3	3.1
25	Net lending or net borrowing (-), NIPAs[2]	-397.4	-371.5	-458.9	-514.0
26	**Statistical discrepancy**	**-127.2**	**-89.6**	**-15.3**	**25.6**
	Addenda:				
27	Gross private saving	1,334.1	1,400.1	1,552.6	1,637.4
28	Gross government saving	436.4	257.5	-68.4	-149.7
29	Federal	276.6	134.9	-165.5	-274.3
30	State and local	159.8	122.6	97.1	124.7
31	Net domestic investment	852.1	656.9	622.7	670.3
32	**Gross saving as a percentage of gross national income**	**17.7**	**16.2**	**14.1**	**13.5**
33	**Net saving as a percentage of gross national income**	**5.8**	**3.7**	**1.7**	**1.2**

Source: Bureau of Economic Analysis, October 29, 2004

1. Consists of capital transfers and the acquisition and disposal of nonproduced nonfinancial assets.

2. Prior to 1982, equals the balance on current account, NIPAs as shown in table 4.1; estimates of capital account transactions (line 24) are not available.

Table 5.1 Saving and Investment
Page 6 of 7